Betty Crocker's

BEST OF
Healthy and
Hearty
COOKING

More Than
400 Recipes
Your Family
Will Love

MACMILLAN • USA

MACMILLAN
A Simon & Schuster Macmillan Company
1633 Broadway
New York, NY 10019-6785

Macmillan Publishing books may be purchased for business or sales promotional use. For information please write: Special Markets Department, Macmillan Publishing USA, 1633 Broadway, New York, NY 10019.

MACMILLAN is a registered trademark of Macmillan, Inc.

BETTY CROCKER, Cheerios, Apple-Cinnamon Cheerios, Sweet Rewards, Wheaties, Hamburger Helper and Bisquick are registered trademarks of General Mills, Inc.

The Marvelous Marinade Recipe Contest and Zip-Loc® Bags are registered trademarks of Dow Brands.

Library of Congress Cataloging-in-Publication Data available

ISBN: 0-02-8624521

General Mills, Inc.

Betty Crocker Kitchens Director: Marcia Copeland
Managing Editor: Lois Tlusty
Nutritionist: Elyse Cohen, M.S., L.N.
Recipe Development: Betty Crocker Kitchens Home Economists
Food Styling: Betty Crocker Kitchens Food Stylists
Photography: Photographic Services Department

For consistent baking results, the Betty Crocker Kitchens recommend Gold Medal Flour.

Manufactured in the United States of America

10 9 8 7 6 5 4 3 2 1

Cover design by Iris Jeromnimon
Cover photo by David Bishop
Book design by George McKeon

Cover photos: Zucchini Lasagna (page 311), Chicken Vegetable Kabobs (page 254), Carrot Zucchini Muffins (page 344), Sweet and Spicy Carrot Salad (page 383), Hearty Multigrain Biscuits (page 352), Guacamole (page 31), Spicy Tortilla Chips (page 40), Cheesecake with Strawberry Topping (page 408), Glazed Lemon Bars (page 413), Chocolate Glazed Brownies (page 412), Morning Parfaits (page 70).

Introduction

Most of us know that a large part of today's healthy living is about our food choices. We want the flavors of tried-and-true recipes with a reasonable calorie and fat content to fit our family's everyday good eating habits. Thankfully, there's *Betty Crocker's Best of Healthy and Hearty Cooking*.

It's never too early to start eating right, and it's a habit you can keep throughout your life. Throughout this book you'll find helpful information about the food pyramid, nutrition facts and labels. You'll even find guidelines to cut calories and fat from your favorite recipes, tips on meal planning and helpful cooking advice. And don't forget exercise! Get the right start with helpful advice about choosing the right fitness plan for you.

Every main-dish recipe is under 400 calories with 12 or fewer grams of fat; side dishes, desserts, appetizers and snacks are all under 200 calories with 6 or fewer grams of fat. Get started with two weeks of menus with the fat, calories and fiber content already calculated, covering breakfast through dinner—and even snacks!

With over 400 delicious recipes to choose from, it's easy to get a variety of nutritious foods into a sensible diet. First, snack on Spicy Tortilla Chips and Guacamole, yummy White Bean Pita Pizzas or kid-friendly Jungle Fun Toss. You'll never run out of ideas with all the main-dish meat, poultry, fish and seafood, meatless and grilling entrées to choose from. Serve up Snappy Meat and Potato Skillet, Garlicky Meatballs over Rice, Spicy Mexican Torte or flavorful Pork Fajitas. Fire up the grill and enjoy Italian Flank Steak, juicy Honey-Glazed Chicken or Grilled Halibut with Tomato-Avocado Salsa, knowing that everything you make is good for you and great tasting, too.

Studies show that eating more vegetables, grains and breads is part of a good eating plan. Sound boring? Not when you can dig into Fluffy Corn Bread, Broccoli and Pasta in Dijon Sauce, Creamy Coleslaw or Crunchy Lemon Rice to complement your meal.

Don't forget dessert! You'll flip for Upside-Down Apple Cake, Raspberry Marbled Brownies or Peanut Butter–Marshmallow Treats. Yes, even these tasty goodies are part of good eating habits.

Trust Betty Crocker to help you enjoy the benefits of a sensible, balanced diet. With *Betty Crocker's Best of Healthy and Hearty Cooking*, give your family what they love, knowing that it's an eating plan for better living!

Betty Crocker

Recipe Nutrition Criteria

We have provided nutrition information with each recipe to help you put together a healthy eating plan for yourself and your family. All the delicious recipes in this cookbook meet the following nutrition criteria:

- Main dish recipes are under 400 calories with 12 or fewer grams of fat per serving.

- Appetizer, snack, side dish and dessert recipes contain no more than 200 calories with 6 or fewer grams of fat per serving.

Contents

All About Healthy Eating

NUTRITION THROUGH THE LIFE CYCLE

Throughout our life, we have changing nutritional needs. We've divided the life cycle into several age categories to highlight the needs and concerns found in each time of life: pregnancy and lactation; infancy (birth to 1 year); toddlers (1 to 2 years); children of preschool and school age (3 to 12 years); teenagers (13 to 18 years); adults (19 to 50 years); and older adults (over 51 years).

Pregnancy and Lactation

The best time to begin thinking about eating healthy for pregnancy is before becoming pregnant. And since a pregnant mother is supporting the growth and development of a fetus, increased nutrient needs are important.

To ensure adequate size of the fetus, experts recommend a weight gain averaging 25 to 35 pounds for a mother of normal body weight. This recommendation may be different if a woman is underweight or overweight at the start of the pregnancy. Cigarette, drug or alcohol use can put the infant at increased risk for low birth weight, making the baby more susceptible to both short-term and long-term illness or disability.

In addition to normal caloric intake, an average of 200 calories per day is recommended during the first trimester to ensure a gradual weight gain of 1 to 1 1/2 pounds per month. In the second and third trimesters, an extra 300 to 500 calories per day above normal intake is recommended. During lactation, about 300 to 500 extra calories are needed to aid in milk production.

Supplements recommended for pregnancy—and also if you are planning to become pregnant—include iron and folic acid, two key nutrients often lacking in women's diets during child-bearing years. A daily dose of 400 micrograms of folic acid has been shown to greatly reduce risk of neural tube defects, such as those seen with spina bifida. Iron intake is recommended at 30 milligrams daily. Calcium (1000 to 1300 milligrams daily) and prenatal supplements are often recommended as well. During lactation, daily intake of calcium (1000 to 1300 milligrams) plus iron (15 milligrams) and folic acid (260 to 280 micrograms) is usually recommended. Your physician may suggest you continue taking prenatal vitamins.

Expectant mothers should try to eat balanced meals, including foods from all parts of the Food Guide Pyramid each day. An additional serving each of dairy and meat is suggested for pregnant women. (See the Food Guide Pyramid Servings chart on page 20.)

Active women may continue exercising throughout their pregnancy with the approval of their physician. Exercise has been shown to reduce certain complications with delivery due to better muscle tone. Women with more sedentary lifestyles who wish to begin exercising during pregnancy are advised to start under the direction of their physician at low intensity levels for short duration. Exercise does not seem to affect milk production during lactation but may increase fluid needs by up to 3 glasses daily.

Infancy

Infancy is the period of time from birth to one year of age. The birth weight of an infant generally triples in the first year of life.

To ensure adequate growth and development, particularly of newborns, experts recommend breast-feeding over formula feeding. Breast milk promotes optimal health for infants. Infants grow better and receive the added bonus of immunologic benefits with breast milk. If you are feeding a formula instead of breast milk, experts recommend one that is fortified with iron.

Newborns know when it's time to eat. They seem to be able to regulate their feeding pattern themselves. And breast milk is utilized very efficiently by newborns. You may have to breast feed newborns more often than if you formula feed them. Expect 8 to 10 breast feedings per day in the first few months, and fewer feedings later on. With formula-feeding, anticipate 6 to 9 feedings per day. A weight gain of 2 pounds per month for the first 3 months of life is an indicator that your newborn is feeding and growing properly.

The need for iron is increased during the first year of life, making the risk for iron deficiency quite high. Breast milk provides adequate iron for the first few months of life. Later on, iron deficiency is preventable through the use of iron supplements and iron-fortified foods, such as formulas and cereals. The iron available from these foods is better absorbed in infants than in adults.

You can start introducing solid foods to infants' diets around 6 months of age. Typical first foods include rice cereals, vegetable and fruit purees, pureed meats, and cooked egg yolk. It's best to introduce new foods one at a time to monitor for possible allergic reactions. Be aware that some infants can be allergic to milk and dairy foods, too.

By 8 months, primary teeth are present and you can begin to give your child foods that require some chewing. Developmentally, infants start to feed themselves with their fingers while still taking food from you by the spoon. Finger foods and playing with their foods both serve as part of their developmental process, aiding in dexterity and early hand-eye coordination.

During the first year of life, there is no need to restrict fat intake. Feed your infant regular foods, as they need fat for growth, to provide protection and insulation of their organs, to help regulate body temperature and to aid in the absorption of certain vitamins that are fat soluble, such as vitamins A, D, E and K.

Besides fat, infants need adequate protein for growth and cell repair. Estimates for protein intake range from about 9 to 15 percent of calories. Carbohydrate is used for energy too, at 45 to 55 percent of calories. The other 30 to 46 percent of calories come from fat.

Toddlers

The age range for toddlers is 1 to 2 years. This is an active time that includes walking, climbing, exploring and picking things up. Growth slows down and toddlers begin to look leaner than they did as infants. They lose body fat as they begin walking and become better coordinated and able to move around easily.

Toddlers need to eat a variety of foods from the Food Guide Pyramid—three meals per day plus at least two snacks. (See the Food Guide Pyramid on page 20.) But beware—they may be quite finicky about food choices. For weeks your toddler may only eat one food and then one day decide they prefer another food, rejecting the first. Unfortunately, these food jags are real for toddlers. And experts advise not forcing them to eat unwanted foods, as it may impact food choices later in life.

Avoid adding salt and sugar to toddlers' foods. Toddler palates are simpler than those in adults, and what tastes good to you may not taste good to them. Introduce new foods as tolerated, one at a time, again keeping an eye out for potential allergic reactions to new foods. Do not feed toddlers foods they could easily choke on, such as hot dogs, grapes, nuts, raisins, popcorn or raw carrots.

As during the first year of life, there is no need to restrict fat or cholesterol intake for toddlers. Experts agree that fat should not be limited in any way until after age 2, even if the toddler is above average in weight for height. Fat and cholesterol are important for growth and development, protection and insulation of body organs, and absorption of certain vitamins. And limiting fats too early can be detrimental to the child's development.

And don't forget about water. Since toddlers cry so much and can quickly run a high fever, they are continually losing fluid. Their bodies are so small that just a slight fluid imbalance can be serious. So be sure they receive adequate water.

If obesity runs in the family, it's best to encourage active lifestyles early—even this early. The combination of healthy eating patterns and the importance of physical activity may help to offset risk for obesity later in life. Little ones learn by example, so if you can create family activities that include physical activity, your child will benefit.

Children

Preschool and school age children are between 3 and 12 years old. In the preschool years, children are still developing their eating patterns and habits. By the time they are a little older, their lifelong eating and mealtime behavior patterns are well established.

Parents serve as role models, and experts advise it's best to start promoting healthy eating and physical activity patterns when your children are at a young age. Outside influences—friends, media, school lunch programs—all factor into children's choices as well.

Children need to eat a variety of foods from all parts of the Food Guide Pyramid. Help your children choose foods lower in fat, higher in complex carbohydrates and packed with fiber. Experts suggest low-fat milk and dairy products plus fruits, vegetables, grains and meats. Lower-fat foods are okay for children, and experts recommend switching to low-fat dairy items such as milk and yogurt.

Children need three meals per day plus snacks. Snacks are important as children may not get enough calories from meals alone. Breakfast is also key—skipping breakfast can affect a child's intellectual performance in school. And chronically undernourished children are more likely to become sick, miss class and score lower on tests at school.

Children have fewer nutritional deficiencies than any other age group—probably because someone else is planning and preparing meals for them. Problem nutrients for children include calcium, and, for some socioeconomic groups, iron can be a potential problem. Dietitians recommend children drink plenty of milk and eat dairy foods like yogurt, plus ready-to-eat breakfast cereals and meats to ensure they're getting adequate nutrition.

Allow kids to help in food selection and preparation. Children are often more willing to eat what they pick out or help to prepare. Experts suggest not using food as a means of controlling your child's behavior, as a form of discipline, as a reward or as a primary form of affection. These actions can set up some undesirable eating and behavior patterns for children.

Children use more energy than adults in similar activities. Even so, obesity is increasingly becoming a bigger problem for children in the United States. According to the Centers for Disease Control and Prevention, the percentage of overweight children has more than doubled in the past 30 years. We know that obesity, even in younger years, has been linked with an increased risk for diabetes, high blood pressure, and increased blood cholesterol later in life. Obesity in children can also cause increased stress from peer teasing.

Experts recommend not putting children on diets without consulting a physician or dietitian, as any diet must meet the child's nutritional needs. Experts advise feeding obese children less food than they would normally eat, but not less than what a normal weight child would eat. Achieving healthy weight takes time. Sometimes it is suggested to try to slow weight gain until the child's normal growth catches them up to his or her weight.

Some experts have recommended a positive message, such as "be more active," instead of a negative one, such as "eat less food." Regular physical activity is good for kids, especially if it's fun. Creating a lifestyle pattern of regular physical activity that will carry over to adult years is beneficial. By doing "active" things as a family and advocating regular physical activity, you can help a child achieve and maintain a normal weight later in life.

Teenagers

Teenagers—13- to 18-year olds—are independent in their decision making. They spend more time away from home, have more say over what they eat and make more independent food choices. This is a time of altering and redefining lifestyle and self-concept. Complicating the teenage picture is rapid physical and hormonal growth and development, with notable nutritional implications.

Requirements for energy and all nutrients are increased during the teen years. Calorie needs depend on height, weight, age, gender and level of activity and may change as a teen progresses to adulthood.

Even in this volatile stage, parents can set good examples. Serving balanced family meals with foods from all parts of the Food Guide Pyramid is an important reminder of good nutrition. Keep the kitchen stocked with healthy choices that are convenient.

Foods such as fruits, vegetables, low-fat milk and yogurt, ready-to-eat cereal, whole grain breads, popcorn and pretzels make great grab-and-go snacks or mini-meals that fit with busy teens' lifestyles.

Remember that all foods, even fast foods, provide nutritional benefits as long as a variety of foods are eaten throughout the day. Try to discourage your teens from skipping meals. A missed meal often means overindulgence when overly hungry and a greater tendency to make poor food choices out of haste.

With the teenage years comes an altered body image, which increases stress—making teens, particularly girls, more vulnerable to eating disorders, such as anorexia and bulimia. These eating disorders involve excessive weight loss, sometimes to the point of starvation (anorexia nervosa) or binge-eating excessive quantities of food in a short time period and then vomiting or using laxatives (bulimia). Such disorders are increasing and can cause severe health problems, even death, among young people. Scientists are trying to determine the causes of eating disorders but believe both mind and body play a role and are important in treatment. If a member of your household has an eating disorder, seek medical help at once. To help keep things in perspective, encourage high self-esteem, healthful eating habits and regular exercise.

Teens are often already involved in sports or physical activities. And if they're not, it's not too late to encourage their participation. Studies show there is value in physical activity throughout life—to maintain a healthy body weight and to reduce risk of diseases later in life. Physical activity should be a key component of school health and physical education programs—but it must be fun. If your child's school does not have an athletic program, you may wish to seek out some community activities or leagues.

Problem nutrients for teens include calcium, iron and magnesium, particularly for females, and calcium for males. Dietitians recommend that teens eat plenty of dark green leafy vegetables, low-fat milk and other dairy foods, ready-to-eat breakfast cereals and meats (or alternatives like dried beans and peanut butter) to ensure they're getting adequate nutrition. A supplement may be taken as an insurance measure.

We have already discussed that obesity has been linked with an increased risk for diabetes, high blood pressure and increased blood cholesterol later in life. And in teens, in addition to heredity, sometimes growth and sexual maturation patterns, peer influence and psycho-social development may play a role in increasing risk, as teens experiment with activities that may become habits, such as smoking and drinking alcohol.

Adults

By the time we become adults, ages 19 to 50 years, our eating and behavior patterns are well established. If exercise is important to us, sports and activities that we enjoy have already been incorporated into our lifestyle.

Energy requirements drop as we move from teens to adults. Calorie needs are dependent on height, weight, age, gender and level of activity and may change throughout adult life. Balance, variety and moderation and the use of the Food Guide Pyramid are keys to healthy eating. Experts recommend a diet low in fat and high in complex carbohydrates, including fiber-rich sources. Preventive dietary measures and the inclusion of physical activity may delay the onset of chronic disease, such as coronary heart disease, hypertension, diabetes, obesity and cancer.

As aging increases, nutrition for longevity becomes a greater concern. Hereditary tendencies toward high blood cholesterol, coronary heart disease, and chronic disease may begin to set in with increasing age. The importance of bone health may be emphasized and requirements for calcium and vitamin D are increased to help offset osteoporosis. Preventive measures, such as a reduced-fat diet with plenty of fiber-rich foods such as fruits, vegetables and whole grains are important.

Studies show the inclusion of antioxidants in the diet, such as vitamins A, C, E and the mineral selenium, may help to slow the aging process by reducing oxidation, a naturally occurring process during aging.

Problem nutrients for all adults include calcium, iron, folic acid, magnesium and, particularly for females, zinc. Calcium, magnesium and zinc are nutrients where males may have a shortage. Dietitians recommend that adults eat plenty of dark green leafy vegetables, low-fat milk and other dairy foods, ready-to-eat breakfast cereals and meats (or alternatives like dried beans and peanut butter) to ensure they're getting adequate nutrition. Supplements, particularly calcium and iron for women, may be advised to ensure meeting nutrient needs.

The importance of exercise may increase as obesity becomes a real issue and lifestyles become more sedentary for adults. Adults need to make a concerted effort to include individual or group exercise in their lifestyle, which may become difficult as career and family become focal points. Studies show adults who exercise tend to eat more and weigh less and are better able to maintain their body weight. Exercise also helps to keep HDL (good) cholesterol elevated and reduce total blood cholesterol. Exercise, particularly if it is weight-bearing, such as running or walking, can improve or maintain bone density.

Adults over age 35 who are beginning an exercise program after years of being sedentary should undergo a medical evaluation including a stress test before starting an exercise program. Experts recommend starting slowly and keeping the intensity and duration of the exercise down until you've become more accustomed to more physical activity.

For adults who follow a vegetarian regime, studies indicate that there may be a decreased risk for obesity, coronary heart disease, some cancers, constipation, hypertension and diabetes.

Older Adults

Older adults include those adults who are age 51 years and above. By the end of the century, Americans older than 50 will number over 40 million. As many as 80 percent of adults over age 65 are estimated to have at least one diagnosed disease. The quantity of drugs taken by older adults may be more than double that of the general population. Drug interactions with foods may greatly impact the absorption of certain nutrients and place older Americans at risk.

With aging there is a decrease in energy requirements as lean body tissue turns to fat. If calories aren't decreased, weight gain is the result. Variety and moderation are keys to a healthful diet for older adults as well as for the rest of the population. Foods from all parts of the Food Guide Pyramid are recommended for a balanced meal plan.

With aging, there is an increased need for fluids to offset an increased risk of dehydration. Decreased kidney function and a decreased ability to regulate body temperature during exercise and in extreme climates make older adults more vulnerable to fluid imbalance.

Older adults are at risk for deficiency of several nutrients, including vitamin D due to less exposure to sunlight, particularly for home-bound individuals. Other deficiency risks include calcium, magnesium and zinc. Dietitians recommend older adults eat plenty of dark green leafy vegetables, low-fat milk and other dairy foods, ready-to-eat breakfast cereals and meats (or foods like peanut butter) to ensure they're getting adequate nutrition.

Aging can cause loss of taste and smell. And since zinc plays a part in taste acuity, low zinc levels among aging populations may cause the loss of taste. Because stomach acid decreases with age, older adults don't break down foods and absorb nutrients as well. A declining immune function places older adults at greater risk for illness.

With aging, the ability of the skin to convert vitamin D to its active form via sunlight exposure is less efficient. There is a decreased ability to digest lactose with aging, which must be offset with increased calcium and vitamin D supplementation. Studies show osteoporotic changes can be slowed with calcium supplementation and estrogen replacement therapies.

Studies also show that antioxidants in the diet, such as vitamins A, C, E and the mineral selenium, may help to slow the aging process by reducing oxidation, a naturally occurring process that happens during aging. These antioxidants may aid in decreasing risk for cancer, cataracts and coronary heart disease.

For those older adults who are less mobile or home-bound, home-delivered meal programs, groceries and convenience foods are key, particularly if the foods are nutrient dense—offering a lot of nutrients in a small portion. Without these services, food intake might greatly decrease for the aging adult.

There is a large difference in health and activity levels among older adults. Exercise continues to be important with increasing age to improve muscle tone, maintain flexibility and increase muscle strength, endurance and a heightened sense of well-being. Exercise cannot slow chronologic aging but can slow functional aging by improving physical capacities in older adults. Physical activity is a way to stay fit and is part of a healthier lifestyle following an illness or rehabilitation program. Exercise may also delay the onset of osteoporosis changes.

The importance of exercise increases for obese older adults. As we've discussed, obesity puts us at risk for other diseases. Exercise helps to keep HDL (good) cholesterol elevated and to reduce total blood cholesterol. Exercise, particularly if it is weight-bearing, such as running or walking, can improve or maintain bone density and improve circulation that may help with arthritis. Regular exercise is helpful in diabetes maintenance and may alter meal and insulin needs.

Summary

Our nutritional needs change and must be reassessed as we move through the life cycle. But it is clear that the combination of proper diet and ample physical activity or exercise can improve the quality of life for all ages, from infants to older adults.

MEAL PLANNING

When searching for delicious, satisfying meals, many of us become confused trying to reconcile our desire for good health with our love of food. It can be difficult to plan healthy meals, especially for family members who don't want to give up their favorite foods. (See pages 420–426 for two weeks of delicious menus to help with planning.) It may also seem impossible to eat healthy meals away from home. In this section, you'll find many "secrets" to help you plan healthy, good-tasting meals you and your family will enjoy—whether eating at home or dining out.

Healthy Eating at Home

Few people would disagree with the old saying that variety is the spice of life. Eating many different foods with contrasting flavors and textures helps to ensure we're getting the many nutrients that are vital to feeling and looking good.

The Food Guide Pyramid (page 20) illustrates a variety of different foods along with the amounts of each food you need to eat daily in order to maintain good health. To create meals that are appealing both in taste and appearance, incorporate different foods from each group and try unfamiliar foods. For instance, you could plan at least one meatless meal a week as a way to become more acquainted with the wonderful variety of delicious beans and grains. And don't forget the many different forms of your favorite foods, such as canned, juiced, dried or frozen fruit. These can be a treat when fresh produce is out of season or is very expensive.

Anything's Okay in Moderation

Nutrition experts today advise most of us to reduce the amounts of fat, saturated fat, cholesterol and sodium that we eat. They also recommend we boost our intake of fiber and that women and children eat more calcium, folic acid and iron. While that's sound advice, it doesn't mean we must completely omit fat, cholesterol and sodium from our diets, nor should we go overboard on fiber, calcium, folic acid and iron. And it doesn't mean we need to count every calorie, gram of fat or milligram of sodium we eat.

What this advice does encourage is moderation as an overall approach to healthier eating. That means all foods can be part of a healthy diet if we control how much of them we eat; eating reasonable-sized portions of foods—whether high in fat and calories or not—is a key to a healthy diet. When we plan our meals to feature foods high in fiber, calcium and iron, and enjoy small amounts of foods high in fat, cholesterol and/or sodium, healthy eating is simple and enjoyable. (See the Food Guide Pyramid, page 20.)

The Cooking Connection

The way you cook can be just as important as what you choose to cook. Consider investing in nonstick cookware and use a nonstick cooking spray. Many cooking methods enable you to use significantly less fat and still prepare a tasty meal. A brief description of some of these cooking methods follows.

- Grill or roast meat on a rack. This allows the fat to drip off instead of pooling around the meat, where it can be reabsorbed.

- Microwave foods. Minimal amounts of added fat or liquids are needed, thereby reducing calories from added fat and minimizing loss of water-soluble vitamins in cooking liquids.

- Pan-broil foods by starting with a cold ungreased skillet in which meats are cooked slowly. Fat is poured off as it accumulates, before it can be reabsorbed.

- Poach foods by simmering them in a hot liquid just below the boiling point. No added fat is necessary.

- Steam foods in a steamer basket over boiling water. This allows foods such as vegetables to retain their water-soluble vitamins.

● Stir-fry foods in a small amount of oil. Cook small, uniform pieces of food over high heat, stirring constantly. A wok or large skillet is used to stir-fry.

Remember that important vitamins found in vegetables can be destroyed by overcooking or lost entirely by being cooked in too much water; aim for a crisp-tender mixture by cooking for only a short period of time, and cook in as little water as possible. To gain the benefit of vitamins that dissolve into cooking liquids, use the leftover liquid in creative ways; add it to soups, stews and sauces or use it for basting meats.

Please Your Palate with Produce

Each season of the year brings a delightful variety of produce guaranteed to please discriminating palates as well as supply nutrients vital to healthy diets. Experiment with the "exotic" fruits and vegetables, such as golden raspberries, passion fruit, chayote squash and Jerusalem artichokes, that flood today's supermarkets; many stores provide printed materials to help you prepare these new items. Visit local farmers' markets and "pick-your-own" gardens and orchards to purchase produce fresh off the tree or out of the field at the best prices of the season. For great flavor year-round, you can freeze, can or dry some of your favorite fruits and vegetables.

Take Advantage of Whole Grains

Packed with complex carbohydrates, B vitamins and iron, low-fat grain foods form the foundation of a healthy diet. The Food Guide Pyramid (page 20) recommends 6 to 11 servings daily of these satisfying foods and specifies that several servings should be whole grain.

Whole grains add delicious flavor, hearty texture and important dietary fiber to foods. To meet your daily requirement, try whole grain cereals for breakfast, snacks—even dinner! Serve whole grain breads and rolls, brown rice and whole wheat pasta often. Combine brown rice or whole wheat pasta with beans or peas for a low-fat, complete-protein alternative to meats. Add flavor, pleasing texture and extra nutrition to biscuits, muffins, breads and coffee cakes by substituting whole wheat flour for half of the white flour. See the Grains Glossary (pages 428–430) for more information.

Plan for Snacks

Most people can benefit from a snack now and then to boost their energy and help them through the day. Plan ahead to keep your snacks healthy. For instant snacking, keep a large container of plain nonfat yogurt on hand. Eat it plain, stir in fresh fruit or blend in a favorite fruit juice for a refreshing shake. For fast, crunchy satisfaction, keep cut-up vegetables such as carrots, peppers, celery, cucumber, jicama or broccoli ready in the refrigerator. If you choose to dunk your vegetables, stir together nonfat plain yogurt and dill weed for an easy and tasty low-fat dip.

Delicious, high in fiber, low in calories and economical, popcorn is one of the best all-around snacks. Use "light" varieties of microwave popcorn, buy a microwave popper and pop without oil, or rely on a hot-air popper to keep fat and calories low. Add flavor by sprinkling on favorite herbs and spices. Try munching on breakfast cereal for a quick pick-me-up; most varieties are low in fat and packed with vitamins and minerals. Pretzels also rate high as a low-fat healthy snack. If you're concerned about sodium intake, look for low-sodium pretzels.

The Wonders of Water

While it may seem a trivial tip to planning healthy meals, getting enough water is absolutely essential to a healthy diet. We need about 64 fluid ounces of water daily, but that doesn't mean we have to drink eight 8-ounce glasses every day. The fluid in fruits and vegetables, soups, sauces and so forth helps meet our requirements for water. It's a good idea, however, to drink several glasses of water or other fluid each day to ensure you get enough. Because they have a diuretic—ultimately dehydrating—effect, don't include any caffeinated or alcoholic beverages you drink as part of your water quota.

SHAPING UP YOUR FAVORITE RECIPES

Changing favorite recipes to fit your plan for healthy eating often boils down to a few simple steps, such as those listed below. By following these suggestions, you can cut fat, cholesterol and sodium and add significantly to the fiber, vitamin and mineral content of foods.

Don't try to make too many changes in your recipes at once. Pick one or two ingredients to focus on first, then make gradual changes until you achieve your desired results. Baked items, such as breads and cakes, are not as easy to change, so you may have to experiment before you have successful results.

- Cut by one-fourth the amount of fat or oil called for in a recipe. If that yields good results, cut the fat by one-third the next time you prepare that recipe. Keep reducing the fat until you find the minimum that will still produce an appealing dish.

- Choose low-fat or nonfat versions of dairy products. Most dairy items offer reduced-fat options.

- Try substituting applesauce for half or all of the fat in muffins, cookies and other baked goods.

- Sauté chopped vegetables in a small amount of water, chicken broth, apple juice, flavored vinegar or wine instead of butter, margarine or oil.

- Use reduced-fat mayonnaise and salad dressings as alternatives to regular products.

- Use egg whites, homemade egg substitute or purchased cholesterol-free egg product instead of whole eggs.

- Add new and unusual greens and other vegetables or cooked beans to salads. These simple additions add fiber and increase vitamins and minerals.

- Limit portions of cooked meat to 2 to 3 ounces per serving by boosting the amounts of vegetables, pasta and beans in chili, soups, stews, stir-fries and casseroles.

- Substitute whole wheat flour for up to one-half of all-purpose flour in recipes. Foods will be slightly heavier, darker and heartier.

- Decrease or eliminate salt from recipes except for yeast breads, which need salt to prevent excessive rising. Reduce added salt in recipes calling for ingredients that already contain salt, such as chicken broth, tomato sauce or soy sauce. Or choose low- or reduced-sodium versions of those ingredients.

- Do not add salt to the cooking water of rice, pasta or vegetables.

- Use a nonstick cooking spray.

- Baste meats with their own juices, broth or vegetable juices instead of oil, margarine or butter, then make a low-fat sauce or gravy by skimming the fat from the pan juices and reducing the juices by boiling in a skillet. You'll get delicious concentrated flavor.

- Choose herbs and spices, mustard, lemon juice or flavored vinegars instead of butter or oils to "spike" foods that need a splash of flavor.

STOCKING UP

Grocery shopping can be a pleasant experience when you follow these tips for smooth sailing through the supermarket.

Before You Shop

- Plan meals and make a grocery list. Stick to your list.

- Don't shop when you're hungry. Eat something nutritious, such as a banana or slice of whole grain bread, before you go shopping. Extra items have a way of sneaking into your cart when you are feeling hungry.

- Leave the kids at home if possible. Satisfying their demands may distract you from carefully selecting food, and their desires can result in a cart full of foods that aren't on your list.

While You Shop

- Read food labels. Knowledge is power, so becoming familiar with what labels tell you increases your awareness. Be sure you understand the label terminology. For example, "reduced-fat" does not necessarily mean that a product is low in fat; it's just that the food has less fat than the original product. New food labeling regulations are designed to clear up confusion about different terms. (See "Reading a Nutrition Label" on page 22.) For more information, you can call the Consumer Nutrition Hotline of the American Dietetic Association at 1-800-366-1655, or call or write individual food companies.

- Study the ingredient list as you read food package labels. Ingredients are always listed in descending quantity. If the ingredient list on a can of baked beans reads "beans, water, brown sugar and salt," you know the can contains more beans than water, more water than brown sugar and more sugar than salt.

- When buying meat, look for lean cuts such as rounds and tenderloins. Many cuts of meat are now labeled with percentages of fat to help you choose the fat content you want.

- Purchase turkeys that are not self-basting. Select ground turkey breast or ground turkey labeled lean; if not so labeled, it may not be low in fat.

- Buy water-packed canned fish products, such as water-packed tuna or salmon, instead of products packed in oil.

- Select skim, nonfat or low-fat dairy products such as milk, yogurt, cheese and sour cream. Many of the new products on the market taste as good—or better—than the original!

- Opt for low-fat or reduced-calorie salad dressings. If you're watching sodium consumption, be aware that many reduced-fat dressings have added extra salt to compensate for the flavor lost with the removal of fat. Read the label to check the sodium content.

- Choose whole grain versions of breads, cereals, crackers, muffins, English muffins, rice and pasta.

- Select healthy options when a busy schedule demands "convenience" foods. Canned beans are ready to serve and offer the same fiber and low-fat protein as their dried counterparts. If you like, rinse them to remove much of the sodium added in the canning process. Try stir-frying thinly sliced turkey cutlets with ready-cut vegetables to produce a great-tasting meal in minutes. Select tomato products without added salt, or choose reduced-salt versions. Look for canned fruits packed in juice, or rinse fruit packed in heavy syrups.

Healthy Staples to Keep on Hand

Keep a plentiful supply of healthy stapes in the house to be certain you have what you need when preparing meals. The list that follows contains items you will use frequently and that you can stock up on easily.

Herbs and spices. Dried or fresh (chopped and frozen), these are essentials for any healthy-cooking kitchen. Herbs and spices enhance foods and boost flavor without adding extra fat or salt. Stock your cabinets with basil, bay leaves, dill weed, oregano, garlic, ginger, red pepper sauce, ground red pepper, salt, chili powder, curry powder, pepper, cinnamon, nutmeg and cloves. Items such as garlic and oregano can be purchased prechopped or minced but must be refrigerated after opening.

Baking and cooking essentials. Cornstarch, baking powder, baking soda, flour, rolled oats, raisins, vegetable oil(s), vinegar(s) and reduced sodium soy sauce should be mainstays in your kitchen.

Whole grains, dried beans and pasta. These items can be kept as staples because they remain edible indefinitely. For optimum flavor, store tightly sealed in a cool, dry place and use within one year of purchase.

Perishables. Foods that will not last for long periods of time but that you will probably use quite frequently include nonfat or low-fat yogurt, other dairy products, lemons, carrots, celery, onions and potatoes.

HEALTHY EATING OUT OF THE HOUSE AND ON THE ROAD

We all enjoy, and probably need, a break from preparing meals. With virtually 30 percent of calories and 40 percent of every food dollar spent on foods eaten away from home, knowing how to make healthy choices when eating out is vital.

At the Restaurant

Don't just depend on ambiance; select restaurants according to what they offer in terms of dining options.

- Call in advance to find out if healthy menu items are available. Low-fat choices are often noted on the menu.

- Ask about the size of the portions. Ask whether special requests, such as food preparation without extra fat, are honored.

Once you're seated at the table with menu in hand, follow these guidelines to ensure a healthy meal.

- Just as at home, choose lean meats, fish and poultry without skin and ask that they be prepared with a minimum of added fat. Most chefs are more than willing to broil, grill, bake, steam and poach foods at your request.

- Restaurants often serve large portions of meat. Ask if half portions or appetizer sizes are available. If not, order the item and plan to take some home for another meal.

- Vegetables are naturally low in fat, but the way they're prepared can quickly change their calorie content. Request plain vegetables; you can add butter or margarine at the table if you wish. Choose baked potatoes instead of French fried potatoes or chips.

- Salad dressings and sauces may be requested "on the side" so you can decide how much you'd like to use. Just remember that the small dishes in which side items are served often hold much more than the amount a chef would normally add to the food. Beware: In examining plates after a meal, chefs report many diners end up eating more of the dressing or sauce than they would have if it had been served on the food.

- Desserts can be sweet, satisfying and slimmed down as well. Choose fruit desserts (look in the appetizer section of the menu too). Sorbet, sherbet or non-fat frozen yogurt are great choices with less fat and fewer calories than ice cream. If you decide to indulge, split a richer treat with a friend or eat only a few bites.

- There's a world of healthy beverages in restaurants. Nonalcoholic "mocktails" are increasingly common, and many restaurants offer nonalcoholic wines and beers along with juice-based non-alcoholic specials. Try flavored mineral waters or herbal teas for a flavor punch. Tap water is free and a great thirst-quencher! Have it spritzed with your favorite citrus juice or served with a twist of lemon or lime.

- Remember, if a meal is not prepared as you requested, feel free to send it back and have it made correctly.

Full-service restaurants provide the greatest variety and flexibility for the health-conscious diner. Foods are usually prepared to order, so you can request specific preparation with ease. Such orders may take somewhat longer to prepare, leaving you tempted to nibble while waiting. Munch on a whole-grain roll without butter or margarine, or choose a tossed salad, easy on the dressing, to tide you over.

Cafeterias and buffets provide a wide variety of foods, but many items may not be prepared as you prefer. Limit fried foods or those with heavy sauces, gravies and dressings. Some establishments allow you to choose your own portion size, so you can more easily control the amount you eat.

Fast-food restaurants usually offer a limited menu with many high-fat items. Choose lighter fare, such as salads or grilled chicken sandwiches, and low-fat milk or juice as a beverage. If ordering fried chicken, remove the skin before eating. If you crave a burger, order a "junior" size without the cheese and extra sauce. Order a small serving of frozen yogurt if you need to satisfy your sweet tooth.

Salad bars provide lots of options—some offer as many as fifteen or more choices. Concentrate on the plain fresh fruits and vegetables. Though prepared creamy salads, such as coleslaw, pasta and potato salads, and other combinations of higher-fat foods are available, help yourself to only a bite. Marinated vegetable salads can be a better choice if you drain off the oily marinade. Go easy on the cheese, bacon bits, nuts, hard-cooked eggs and croutons. And, of course, choose the lower-fat salad dressings or use a sprinkle of vinegar with a dash of pepper.

On the Road

If you travel by air, call the airline at least 24 hours in advance of your flight to request a special meal. Most airlines graciously accommodate passengers with special needs, such as low-calorie, vegetarian or kosher meals. If you travel by car or bus, pack your own meals and snacks. By carrying your own foods, you can ensure you have healthy, well-balanced meals to enjoy. You can snack as you go or eat a sit-down meal during a rest stop.

A GUIDE TO THE FOOD PYRAMID

- The Food Guide Pyramid is divided into six parts, or food groups. "Grains," the very bottom section of the pyramid, is the foundation. The idea is to eat from the bottom up, with the majority of your food choices coming from the bottom of the pyramid. The top section is "Fats, Oils and Sweets," and most people need to limit their use of these foods. The five lower groups are all important, and you need food from all of them.

- Below the name of each food group are some numbers that tell you how

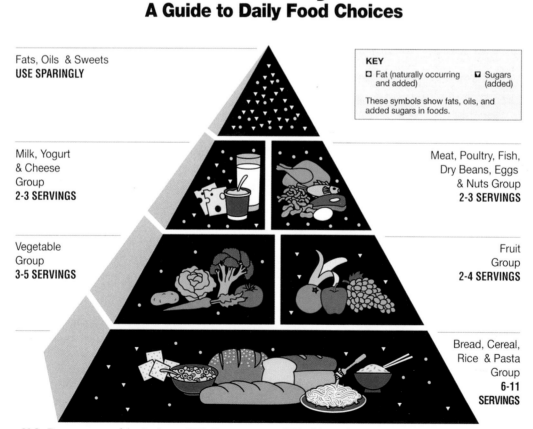

Food Guide Pyramid
A Guide to Daily Food Choices

Fats, Oils & Sweets
USE SPARINGLY

KEY
◻ Fat (naturally occurring and added)
▾ Sugars (added)

These symbols show fats, oils, and added sugars in foods.

Milk, Yogurt & Cheese Group
2-3 SERVINGS

Meat, Poultry, Fish, Dry Beans, Eggs & Nuts Group
2-3 SERVINGS

Vegetable Group
3-5 SERVINGS

Fruit Group
2-4 SERVINGS

Bread, Cereal, Rice & Pasta Group
6-11 SERVINGS

Source: U.S. Department of Agriculture, U.S. Department of Health and Human Services

many servings to eat from that group each day. You need more foods from the groups at the bottom, where it is wider, than you do from the top groups.

- At each meal, serve foods from at least three different food groups. Some foods, such as tacos, combine foods from two or more different groups. Do the best you can to estimate the servings from each food group.

- It's a good idea to plan for snacks just as you plan for meals. Keep a supply of healthful snack foods on hand, such as cut-up vegetables or low-fat crackers and cookies.

LEARNING THE NUTRITION FACTS

Nutrition Facts is the revised nutrition label that food manufacturers are required by law to use in order to tell us the nutritional content of foods. The hope is that this improved label will be more meaningful to everyone and will enable us to make better food choices. This new label made its debut on food packaging in 1994.

Nutrition Facts provides much of the same information as the former label but has a clearer layout and emphasizes certain nutrients we want to know more about, namely, total fat, calories from fat, and total carbohydrate (fiber and sugar). Nutrition Facts provides information for one serving of the food by itself ("as packaged"), as in dry cereal, and may also provide information for the food plus an added ingredient, such as cereal plus skim milk, or for the food "as prepared," since so many packaged foods require us to cook or add other ingredients before we eat them.

Information about specific nutrients is provided in grams or milligrams per serving as packaged; information for the food as prepared may be footnoted only. Percent Daily Value, listed for each nutrient, is a new measure of how a food stacks up when compared to an average diet of 2,000 calories per day and may be listed for the product as packaged and as prepared. Percent Daily Value replaces the former Percent U.S. RDA for vitamins A and C, calcium and iron. The calories per gram for fat, carbohydrate and protein listed at the bottom of the label enable the reader to calculate the number of calories that come from each component. (For information on other nutrition terms, see the Nutrition Glossary on pages 427–428.)

Reading a Nutrition Label

The Nutrition Facts Label can be found on food packages in your supermarket. Reading the label tells you more about the food and the nutrients it supplies. The nutrition and ingredient information you see on the food label is required by the government.

Some food packages have a short or abbreviated nutrition label. These foods contain only a few of the nutrients required on the standard label and can use a short label format. What's on the label depends on what's in the food. Small and medium-sized packages with very little label space also may use a short label format. Here's what the label looks like with an explanation of its new features.

Nutrition Facts Title
The new title "Nutrition Facts" signals the new label.

Serving Size
Serving sizes are standardized based on amounts people actually eat. Now similar food products have similar serving sizes making it easier to compare foods in the same category.

New Label Information
Some label information may not be familiar to you. The nutrient list covers those nutrients most important to your health. You may have seen this information on some old labels, but now it is required by the government and must appear on all food labels.

Vitamins and Minerals
The Percent Daily Value replaces the Percent U.S. RDA for vitamins and minerals. The levels are the same. Only vitamin A, vitamin C, calcium, iron, and fortified nutrients are required on the new label; additional vitamins and minerals can be listed voluntarily.

Label Numbers
Numbers on the nutrition label may be rounded for labeling.

Nutrition Facts

Serving Size 1 cup (30g)
Servings Per Container About 10

Amount Per Serving

Calories 110   Calories from Fat 10

                                                    % Daily Value*

Total Fat 1g   **2%**
    Saturated Fat 0g   **0%**
Cholesterol 0mg   **0%**
Sodium 240mg   **10%**
Total Carbohydrate 24g   **8%**
    Dietary Fiber 3g   **10%**
    Sugars 6g
Protein 3g

Vitamin A 25%   *   Vitamin C 25%
Calcium 4%   *   Iron 45%

* Percent Daily Values are based on a 2,000 calorie diet. Your daily values may be higher or lower depending on your calorie needs:

		Calories:	2,000	2,500
Total Fat	Less than		65g	80g
Sat. Fat	Less than		20g	25g
Cholesterol	Less than		300mg	300mg
Sodium	Less than		2,400mg	2,400mg
Total Carbohydrates			300g	375g
Dietary Fiber			25g	30g

Calories per gram:
Fat 0   *   Carbohydrate 4   *   Protein 4

% Daily Value
The Percent Daily Value shows how a food fits into a 2,000 calorie reference diet. These levels are based on dietary recommendations for most healthy people. Percent Daily Values help you judge whether a food contains "a lot" or "a little" of key nutrients important to health.

Daily Values Footnote
Daily Values are the new label reference numbers. These numbers are set by the government and are based on current nutrition recommendations. Some labels list Daily Values for a diet of 2,000 and 2,500 calories per day. Your own nutrient needs may be less than or more than the Daily Values on the label.

Calories Per Gram Footnote
Some labels tell the appropriate number of calories in a gram of fat, carbohydrate, and protein. (One gram is about the weight of a regular paperclip.) This information helps you calculate the percentage of calories from these nutrients.

Health Claims: What Can Be Said

Can a diet help reduce the risk for disease? Food packages may now carry health claims, a label statement that describes the relationship between a nutrient and a disease or health-related condition.

Seven types of health claims based on nutrient-disease relationships are permitted on food packages and are listed below.

A diet that is:	May help to reduce the risk of:
High in calcium	Osteoporosis (brittle bone disease)
High in fiber-containing grain products, fruits and vegetables	Cancer
High in fruits or vegetables (high in dietary fiber or vitamins A or C)	Cancer
High in fiber from fruits, vegetables and grain products	Heart disease
Low in fat	Cancer
Low in saturated fat and cholesterol	Heart disease
Low in sodium	High blood pressure (hypertension)

Nutrition Claims: What They Mean

The government also set standard definitions for terms used to describe product claims, such as light, low fat and high fiber. Now we can better understand the meaning of these claims and trust what we read on packages and in advertising. These claims can be used only if a food meets strict government definitions. Here are some of the meanings.

Label Claim	Definition (per serving)
Low calorie	40 calories or less
Light or lite	1/3 fewer calories or 50 percent less fat than the original product; if more than half the calories are from fat, fat content must be reduced by 50 percent or more
Light in sodium	50 percent less sodium
Fat free	Less than 0.5 gram of fat
Low fat	3 grams fat or less
Cholesterol free	Less than 2 milligrams cholesterol and 2 grams or less saturated fat
Low cholesterol	20 milligrams or less cholesterol and 2 grams or less saturated fat
Sodium free	Less than 5 milligrams sodium
Very low sodium	35 milligrams or less sodium
Low sodium	140 milligrams or less sodium
High fiber	5 grams or more fiber

ENERGIZE WITH EXERCISE

Paddling a canoe against a strong current can be done, but it will definitely take you longer to get to your destination. So it is with the relationship between weight loss and exercise. You can lose weight without regular exercise, but you won't lose as much, it won't happen as quickly and the weight loss won't be maintained as long.

For overall health benefits and general fitness, experts recommend exercising three to five times per week, with each session lasting 20 to 30 minutes. The 20- to 30-minute portion of the activity should be aerobic or cardiovascular at your target heart rate, preceded by a 5-minute warm-up and followed by a 5-minute cool-down. When trying to lose weight, however, it is more effective to exercise five times per week and increase the time to 45 minutes to one hour.

Exercise that involves the entire body is the most helpful for weight loss, and many forms of exercise meet that objective. Walking, swimming and bicycling are good exercises for beginners or for those who have not exercised for some time.

Whatever exercise you choose, make sure it is one that you really enjoy so it will become a part of a healthful lifestyle. As with starting any regular exercise, check with your doctor first.

Record your daily exercise to keep yourself on track.

36 Key Questions: The Right Start Toward Getting Fit

When Shopping for a Health Club

1. What types of services and facilities are you interested in (aerobics classes, court facilities, pool, exercise machines, personal trainers)? Are the facilities well maintained?

2. If you know a member, get his or her honest, insider's opinion.

3. Is the club in a convenient location?

4. Are the operating hours compatible with your lifestyle?

5. Visit during the time of day you would use the club. Is it overcrowded? Could you use the equipment you want to work out on?

6. Is the fitness staff well qualified? Do they have degrees or certifications in a health/fitness-related field? Are they trained in CPR and first aid?

7. Is the club reputable? How long has it been around? Do the management and personnel change often?

8. Do you have to sign a membership contract? Make sure that you understand the commitment you're making and that all of your questions are answered before signing. Get a copy of your agreement.

9. What membership dues payment options do you have? Who are you actually paying?

10. What is the club's cancellation policy?

11. Try before you buy! Does the club offer a free trial membership?

When Looking for a Personal Trainer

12. Is the trainer certified through a reputable organization such as ACE (American Council on Exercise) or ACSM (American College of Sports Medicine)?

13. Is the trainer certified in CPR and first aid?

14. Does the trainer have his or her own equipment or access to equipment? Can the trainer come to your club to work with you?

15. Can the trainer supply you with references from current and past clients?

When Looking into Exercise Classes

16. Are you familiar with the type of class (step, low impact)? If not, is the instructor willing to spend some time before class to give you a few pointers?

17. Is the format of the class safe? Does it include warm-up, stretching, and cardiovascular portions and a cool-down?

18. Is the class area big enough to safely accommodate the number of participants?

19. Does the floor of the aerobics area provide shock absorption to prevent injury? Athletic shoes specifically designed for and labeled as aerobic are the best choice for safety.

20. Are the instructors well qualified? Do they have instructor certifications through a reputable organization?

21. Try a class to see how you like the format and instructor.

When Purchasing Home Exercise Equipment

22. Is the store knowledgeable and reputable in the fitness and exercise equipment industry?

23. Can the sales staff explain how each piece of equipment works and what the differences are between models within a line or from different manufacturers?

24. Can you try the equipment in the store?

25. What are the store polices regarding trial use of equipment at home or returns?

26. Are electrical and outlet requirements for electrically run equipment (such as a treadmill) fully explained before purchasing?

27. Are product guarantees or warranties explained?

28. Does the store deliver and set up the equipment?

29. Who would repair equipment—the store itself? Or do they send it out? Who pays for pickup and delivery? How long would you have to wait for repairs? Are repair charges explained?

When Purchasing Exercise/ Fitness Tapes

30. Is the workout appropriate for your fitness level?

31. Does the workout require any equipment such as a step or toning apparatus?

32. Do you have enough room to do routines safely?

33. If your floor surface carpeted to provide any shock absorption?

34. Is the instructor knowledgeable and reputable in the health and fitness industry? If not, does he or she credit someone with providing training for the workout? (This would apply, for example, to celebrity tapes.)

35. As your fitness level increases, can you vary the routine to keep it challenging? Does the instructor offer tips on varying the workout to suit different levels of fitness?

36. Video rental stores and libraries now offer exercise tapes; check one out and try it at home first.

THE FRAMEWORK— A HEALTHY ATTITUDE

The framework for your healthy body is formed by your attitude about eating and exercise. How you approach making changes, your ideas about weight management and how you manage special eating occasions all combine to help you decide whether your initial changes become permanent.

Lasting changes are truly important. Fluctuation back and forth between old and new habits not only may prevent you from ever reaching your goals but can even cause harm. For instance, constantly losing and regaining weight may add to health problems rather than help to alleviate them. Experts today support improving eating and exercise habits based on individual needs.

Gone are the days of preprinted diet and exercise plans. For long-term effectiveness, individual desires, obstacles and issues must be addressed. In short, the approach must be realistic, practical and tailored to each individual. Furthermore, experts advise a slow start to building new habits.

Focus on two or three major eating or exercise habits you wish to change. For example, you might decide to focus on reducing after-dinner snacking. And you might set a goal for three 20-minute walks a week. When you achieve those goals, you can address other areas you think need improvement. Nothing succeeds better than success, so set small, achievable goals along the way to your overall goal.

The best approach to managing your weight is to eat moderately following the Food Guide Pyramid and to exercise regularly. Quick weight-loss schemes, particularly those that advise eliminating any food group, can jeopardize both your nutritional status and your chances for success at weight management.

An effective approach to weight management also considers "healthy" weights. Healthy weights depend on the individual, and for some people, that's far from the fashion-model image popular today. Indeed, you may be healthy at a higher weight than your neighbor, even though you both are the same height. A realistic approach allows for a small amount of weight gain, maybe a few extra pounds, as we age.

Two simple measures of healthy weight include determining where excess fat is located (it's considered a greater health risk if fat is found primarily on the abdomen) and if you or your family has a history of health problems that may be aggravated by excess weight, such as diabetes or heart disease. Check to see if your weight falls within a healthy range as defined in the Suggested Healthy Weights for Adults table on the next page.

Being realistic during the food-filled holidays and other special celebrations is important as well. At those times, it seems that tasty, high-fat, high-calorie tidbits lurk in every corner, just waiting to sabotage our efforts. But there's really no need to throw in the towel at these times. You can have your cake and eat it too. All it takes is a little planning.

It helps tremendously to remember that healthful eating depends on balance, variety and moderation. All foods can fit within a healthy diet; what's important is how often and how much you eat of certain foods. To successfully navigate special occasions, anticipate meals high in fat or cholesterol. Offset them by eating low-fat, low-cholesterol foods the days before and after.

Remember, too, that one mistake does not destroy all your good efforts. If you overeat— for one meal, one day or even one week—you can still salvage your healthy eating efforts by returning to your plan. Compare this behavior with totally giving up because you've made a mistake, and you can see that over time you're more likely to reach your goals.

Finally, any discussion of healthful habits must include a word about exercise. Physical inactivity places more Americans at risk for coronary heart disease, or CHD—our number-one killer today—than any other factor. Although a slightly greater risk for the disease comes from cigarette smoking, high blood cholesterol or high blood pressure, the number of Americans who are physically inactive actually exceeds the number who face these other risks. Yet we really don't give exercise the attention it deserves when it comes to its ability to improve and protect our health.

The good news is that we're not necessarily talking about running marathons. Increasing evidence suggests that light to moderate physical activity can have significant health benefits, including a decreased risk of CHD. For inactive people, even relatively small increases in activity are associated with measurable health benefits. In addition, light to moderate physical activity is more readily adopted and maintained than vigorous physical activity.

As a result, experts today emphasize light to moderate physical activity as the goal for many Americans. Such activity requires sustained, rhythmic muscular movement and is performed at less than 60 percent of minimum heart rate for your age (subtract your age from 220 to get your maximum heart rate). Examples of such activity include walking, swimming, cycling, dancing, gardening, yardwork and even running after young children!

In short, today's advice for adopting healthy lifestyles is to be flexible. A flexible approach to healthy living forms a basic structure that can withstand the assaults of individual strengths and weaknesses. It allows us to live happily and healthily every day.

Suggested Healthy Weights for Adults

| Height* | Weight (lbs)** | |
	Age 19 to 34 years	Age 35 years and over
5'0"	97–128	108–138
5'1"	101–132	111–143
5'2"	104–137	115–148
5'3"	107–141	119–152
5'4"	111–146	122–157
5'5"	114–150	126–162
5'6"	118–155	130–167
5'7"	121–160	134–172
5'8"	125–164	138–178
5'9"	129–169	142–183
5'10"	132–174	146–188
5'11"	136–179	151–194
6'0"	140–184	155–199
6'1"	144–189	159–205
6'2"	148–195	164–210
6'3"	152–200	168–216
6'4"	156–205	173–222
6'5"	160–211	177–228
6'6"	164–216	182–234

*Without shoes.

**Without clothes.

The higher weights in the ranges generally apply to men, who tend to have more muscle and bone; the lower weights more often apply to women, who have less muscle and bone.

Appetizers

Chicken Pot Stickers (page 48)

(continued on next page)

Guacamole

2 1/4 cups dip

This versatile dip can be served with chips, or to top burgers, sandwiches or anything that needs a kick of flavor.

2 large ripe avocados, mashed
2 medium tomatoes, finely chopped
    (1 1/2 cups)
2 jalapeño chilis, seeded and chopped*
1 medium onion, chopped (1/2 cup)
1 clove garlic
2 tablespoons finely chopped fresh cilantro
2 tablespoons lime or lemon juice
1/2 teaspoon salt
Dash of pepper
Spicy Tortilla Chips (page 40), Baked Pita
    Chips (page 40), or tortilla chips,
    if desired

Mix all ingredients except Spicy Tortilla Chips in glass or plastic bowl. Cover and refrigerate 1 hour to blend flavors. Serve with tortilla chips.

1 TABLESPOON: Calories 15 (Calories from Fat 10); Fat 1g (Saturated 0g); Cholesterol 0mg; Sodium 30mg; Carbohydrate 1g (Dietary Fiber 0g); Protein 0g.

*2 tablespoons canned chopped green chilis can be substituted for the jalapeño chilis.

Mexican Dip

3 1/2 cups dip

This also makes a quick and appetizing dinner!

1/2 pound lean ground turkey breast
1/2 teaspoon ground mustard (dry)
1/4 to 1/2 teaspoon chili powder
1 small onion, finely chopped (1/4 cup)
1/4 cup finely chopped green bell pepper
1 can (15 ounces) black beans, rinsed and
    drained
1 can (8 ounces) tomato sauce
1 envelope (1 1/4 ounces) taco
    seasoning mix
Yogurt Topping (below)
1/2 cup finely shredded lettuce
1/2 cup shredded reduced-fat Cheddar
    cheese (2 ounces)
Baked Pita Chips (page 40) or tortilla chips,
    if desired

Cook turkey in 10-inch skillet over medium heat 8 to 10 minutes, stirring occasionally, until brown; drain. Stir in mustard, chili powder, onion, bell pepper, beans, tomato sauce and seasoning mix (dry). Heat to boiling, stirring constantly. Spread turkey mixture in ungreased pie plate, 9 × 1 1/4 inches. Prepare Yogurt Topping; spread over turkey mixture. Sprinkle with lettuce and cheese. Serve with Baked Pita Chips.

YOGURT TOPPING

1 cup plain nonfat yogurt
2 tablespoons shredded Cheddar cheese
1/4 teaspoon chili powder

Mix all ingredients.

1 TABLESPOON: Calories 20 (Calories from Fat 0); Fat 0g (Saturated 0g); Cholesterol 5mg; Sodium 85mg; Carbohydrate 2g (Dietary Fiber 0g); Protein 2g.

Yummy Black Bean Hummus

4 cups spread

Add a twist to traditional hummus, usually made with only garbanzo beans, by using black beans. Try it at your next fiesta.

**1 can (15 ounces) black beans, rinsed
    and drained
1 can (15 ounces) garbanzo beans, rinsed
    and drained
1/2 cup water or bean liquid
3 tablespoons lemon juice
2 tablespoons olive or vegetable oil
1 teaspoon sesame oil
1/4 teaspoon ground cumin
Salt and pepper to taste
2 cloves garlic, finely chopped
2 tablespoons chopped fresh parsley
Pita bread or raw vegetables, if desired**

Place all ingredients except parsley and pita bread in blender. Cover and blend on medium speed until smooth. Place in serving bowl. Sprinkle with parsley. Cover and refrigerate about 2 hours or until chilled. Serve with pita bread.

1 TABLESPOON: Calories 25 (Calories from Fat 9); Fat 1g (Saturated 0g); Cholesterol 0mg; Sodium 50mg; Carbohydrate 4g (Dietary Fiber 1g); Protein 1g.

Tangy Sunset Dip

about 1 cup dip and 64 chips

**1 extra-creamy plain nonfat yogurt
2 tablespoons chili sauce
1 to 2 teaspoons prepared horseradish
Baked Pita Chips (page 40) or raw
    vegetables**

Mix yogurt, chili sauce and horseradish. Cover and refrigerate at least 1 hour to blend flavors. Serve with Baked Pita Chips.

1 TABLESPOON DIP AND 4 CHIPS: Calories 50 (Calories from Fat 0); Fat 0g (Saturated 0g); Cholesterol 0mg; Sodium 115mg; Carbohydrate 10g (Dietary Fiber 1g); Protein 2g.

HEALTHY HINT

Flavored vinegars can add freshness and zing to cooked vegetables, pasta, soups, salads, dips and cooked meats. Good choices to experiment with include balsamic, seasoned rice, raspberry, tarragon and white wine vinegars.

Layered Black Bean Dip

12 servings

1 can (15 ounces) black beans, rinsed
    and drained
1 can (4 ounces) chopped ripe olives,
    drained
1 small onion, finely chopped (1/4 cup)
1 clove garlic, finely chopped
2 tablespoons vegetable oil
2 tablespoons lime juice
1/4 teaspoon salt
1/4 teaspoon crushed red pepper
1/4 teaspoon ground cumin
1/8 teaspoon pepper
1 package (8 ounces) cream cheese,
    softened
2 hard-cooked eggs, chopped
1/4 cup finely chopped red bell pepper
1 medium green onion, sliced
    (2 tablespoons)
Tortilla chips, if desired

Mix beans, olives, chopped onion, garlic, oil, lime juice, salt, crushed red pepper, cumin, and pepper in glass or plastic bowl. Cover and refrigerate 1 to 2 hours to blend flavors.

Spread cream cheese on serving plate. Spoon bean mixture evenly over cream cheese. Arrange eggs on bean mixture in ring around edge of plate. Sprinkle bell pepper and green onion over bean mixture. Serve with tortilla chips.

1 SERVING: Calories 150 (Calories from Fat 100); Fat 11g (Saturated 5g); Cholesterol 50mg; Sodium 250mg; Carbohydrate 10g (Dietary Fiber 2g); Protein 5g.

Cheese Tips

If you like cheese, substitute the light or reduced-fat counterpart to your favorite regular hard cheeses or choose lower-calorie cheeses. The following chart shows the calories in 1 ounce of cheese:

American	105
American, reduced-fat	70
Cheddar	115
Cheddar, reduced-fat	50
Cream cheese	100
Cream cheese (reduced-fat or Neufchâtel)	75
Monterey Jack	110
Monterey Jack, reduced-fat	80
Mozzarella, whole-milk	80
Mozzarella, part-skim	70
Swiss	105
Swiss, reduced-fat	70

Ginger-Eggplant Dip

2 1/4 cups dip

You'll find gingerroot in the produce section of your supermarket.

1 medium eggplant (about 1 1/2 pounds),
   cut lengthwise in half
1-inch piece of peeled gingerroot
1 to 2 cloves garlic
1/2 small onion
2 tablespoons packed brown sugar
2 tablespoons cider vinegar
Baked Pita Chips (page 40), if desired

Place eggplant, cut sides up, in rectangular microwavable dish, 22 × 7 × 1 1/2 inches. Cover with plastic wrap, folding back one corner to vent. Microwave on High 8 to 10 minutes, rotating dish 1/2 turn after 4 minutes, until tender.

Place gingerroot, garlic and onion in food processor. Cover and process until chopped. Scoop out eggplant pulp. Add eggplant pulp, brown sugar and vinegar to gingerroot mixture. Cover and process until smooth. Serve with Baked Pita Chips.

1 TABLESPOON: Calories 10 (Calories from Fat 0); Fat 0g (Saturated 0g); Cholesterol 0mg; Sodium 0mg; Carbohydrate 2g (Dietary Fiber 0g); Protein 0g.

Sun-Dried Tomato and Bell Pepper Spread

about 2 cups spread and 64 chips

1/4 cup sun-dried tomatoes (not oil-packed)
1/2 cup part-skim ricotta cheese
1/4 cup chopped fresh parsley
2 tablespoons chopped fresh or 2 teaspoons
   dried basil leaves
4 drops red pepper sauce
1 medium yellow bell pepper, chopped
1/2 package (8-ounce size) reduced-fat
   cream cheese (Neufchâtel)
Mini-sweet peppers, if desired
Baked Pita Chips (page 40), reduced-fat
   crackers or fresh vegetable dippers

Cover sun-dried tomatoes with hot water. Let stand at room temperature 10 minutes or until tender. Drain and chop. Mix sun-dried tomatoes and remaining ingredients except Baked Pita Chips. Garnish with mini-sweet peppers. Serve with Baked Pita Chips.

1 TABLESPOON SPREAD AND 2 CHIPS: Calories 55 (Calories from Fat 10); Fat 1g (Saturated 1g); Cholesterol 5mg; Sodium 110mg; Carbohydrate 9g (Dietary Fiber 0g); Protein 2g.

Sun-Dried Tomato and Bell Pepper Spread

Quick Tomato Salsa

about 4 cups salsa

2 cans (14 1/2 ounces each) Mexican-style
 stewed tomatoes, undrained
1 can (4 ounces) chopped green chilis,
 drained
8 medium green onions, chopped (1/2 cup)
1 small green bell pepper, chopped
 (1/2 cup)
1 clove garlic, finely chopped
1/2 cup chopped fresh cilantro
Dash of chili powder
Baked Pita Chips (page 40), Spicy Tortilla
 Chips (page 40), or tortilla chips,
 if desired

Place all ingredients except tortilla chips in
blender. Cover and blend on medium speed
until blended but still chunky. Cover and
refrigerate until serving. Serve with tortilla
chips.

1 TABLESPOON: Calories 5 (Calories from Fat 0); Fat 0g
(Saturated 0g); Cholesterol 0mg; Sodium 35mg;
Carbohydrate 1g (Dietary Fiber 0g); Protein 0g.

Do-Ahead Directions: Store tightly covered in
refrigerator up to 5 days.

Chicken-Apple Pâté

8 servings

1 pound chicken livers
1/2 pound skinless boneless chicken breasts
1 small onion, cut in half
1/4 cup half-and-half
1/4 cup bourbon or chicken broth
1 teaspoon salt
1/2 teaspoon ground nutmeg
2 eggs
1 cup shredded peeled apple (1 medium)
Red onion or apple slices, if desired
Bread slices or crackers, if desired

Heat oven to 350°. Grease loaf pan, 8 1/2 ×
4 1/2 × 2 1/2 inches, or 4-cup ovenproof glass
mold or porcelain terrine. Place chicken livers, chicken breasts and onion in food
processor. Cover and process until coarsely
ground. Add remaining ingredients except
shredded apple. Cover and process until well
blended. Stir in apple.

Pour chicken mixture into mold. Cover
tightly and bake 60 to 70 minutes or until
meat thermometer inserted in center reads
180°. Let stand uncovered 1 hour at room
temperature. Cover and refrigerate 2 hours
to set. Unmold onto serving platter. Garnish
with red onion or apple slices. Serve with
bread slices.

1 SERVING: Calories 125 (Calories from Fat 45); Fat 5g
(Saturated 3g); Cholesterol 290mg; Sodium 320mg;
Carbohydrate 4g (Dietary Fiber 1g); Protein 16g.

Chicken-Apple Pâté

Spicy Tortilla Chips

96 chips

2 tablespoons margarine, melted
1/2 teaspoon chili powder
8 corn or flour tortillas (8 inches in diameter)

Heat oven to 400°. Mix margarine and chili powder; brush on one side of tortillas. Cut each into 12 wedges. Place on ungreased jelly roll pan, 15 1/2×10 1/2×1 inch. Bake uncovered 8 to 10 minutes or until crisp and golden brown; cool. (Tortillas will continue to crisp as they cool.)

1 CHIP: Calories 10 (Calories from Fat 0); Fat 0g (Saturated 0g); Cholesterol 0mg; Sodium 3mg; Carbohydrate 1g (Dietary Fiber 0g); Protein 0g.

Baked Pita Chips

8 servings (8 chips each)

4 whole wheat pita breads (6 inches in diameter)

Heat oven to 400°. Cut around outside edges of pita breads to separate layers. Cut each layer into 8 wedges. Place in single layer on 2 ungreased cookie sheets. Bake about 9 minutes or until crisp and light brown; cool.

1 SERVING: Calories 115 (Calories from Fat 0); Fat 1g (Saturated 0g); Cholesterol 0mg; Sodium 240mg; Carbohydrate 23g (Dietary Fiber 3g); Protein 4g.

Crispy Chili Twists

16 servings (1/4 cup each)

Here's a spicy alternative to chips using pasta as a base. They also add some crunch and zip to a soup or sandwich meal.

2 cups uncooked rotini pasta (6 ounces)
Vegetable oil
2 tablespoons grated Parmesan cheese
1/2 teaspoon chili powder
1/4 teaspoon seasoned salt
1/8 teaspoon garlic powder

Cook and drain pasta as directed on package. Rinse with cold water; drain very thoroughly (excess water on pasta will cause oil to spatter). Heat oil (1 inch) in skillet to 375°. Fry pasta, about 1 cup at a time, about 2 minutes or until crisp and light golden brown, stirring if necessary to separate. Drain on paper towels. Mix remaining ingredients in large bowl; toss with pasta until evenly coated.

1 SERVING: Calories 80 (Calories from Fat 20); Fat 2g (Saturated 0g); Cholesterol 0mg; Sodium 35mg; Carbohydrate 13g (Dietary Fiber 0g); Protein 2g.

Crispy Chili Twists and Marinated Balsamic Pasta and Vegetables (page 44)

Shrimp Toast

10 servings (2 toasts each)

Baking these toasts on a rack allows the hot air in the oven to circulate around them so they are crispy, without fat-laden deep frying!

**1/2 pound uncooked shrimp, peeled,
    deveined and coarsely chopped**
1/2 cup chopped green onions (5 medium)
1/4 cup all-purpose flour
1/4 cup water
1 tablespoon cornstarch
1/2 teaspoon salt
1/2 teaspoon sesame oil
1/4 teaspoon sugar
Dash of white pepper
2 egg whites
**1 baguette (8 ounces), cut into 3/8-inch
    diagonal slices**

Heat oven to 425°. Place wire rack on cookie sheet; spray rack with nonstick cooking spray. Mix all ingredients except bread. Spread about 1 tablespoon shrimp mixture on each bread slice. Place slices on rack on cookie sheet. Spray lightly with cooking spray. Bake about 15 minutes or until edges of bread are deep golden brown and crisp.

1 SERVING: Calories 85 (Calories from Fat 10); Fat 1g (Saturated 0g); Cholesterol 20mg; Sodium 280mg; Carbohydrate 15g (Dietary Fiber 1g); Protein 5g.

Hot and Peppery Cocktail Shrimp

12 servings (about 5 shrimp each)

**1 1/2 pounds peeled and deveined raw
    medium shrimp (about 65)**
**1/4 cup chopped green onions
    (2 to 3 medium)**
1/4 cup lime juice
1 tablespoon reduced-sodium soy sauce
2 teaspoons grated lime peel
1/4 teaspoon pepper
1/8 teaspoon crushed red pepper
2 cloves garlic, finely chopped
2 teaspoons sesame oil

Mix all ingredients except oil in large glass or plastic bowl. Cover and refrigerate 4 hours. Heat oven to 400°. Spray rectangular pan, 13 × 9 × 2 inches, with nonstick cooking spray. Arrange shrimp in single layer in pan. Bake 10 to 12 minutes or until shrimp are pink. Drizzle with oil. Serve hot with toothpicks.

1 SERVING: Calories 50 (Calories from Fat 10); Fat 1g (Saturated 0g); Cholesterol 80mg; Sodium 140mg; Carbohydrate 1g (Dietary Fiber 0g); Protein 9g.

Hot and Peppery Cocktail Shrimp, Creamy Onion Tartlets (page 43)

Chicken Pot Stickers

16 servings (3 pot stickers each)

(photograph on page 28)

If you can't find ground chicken, you can substitute ground turkey.

1 1/2 pounds ground chicken
1/2 cup finely chopped red bell pepper
    (about 1 small)
1/2 cup shredded green cabbage
1/3 cup chopped green onions
    (about 3 medium)
2 teaspoons chopped gingerroot
1 teaspoon sesame oil
1/4 teaspoon white pepper
1 egg white
1 package (10 ounces) round wonton skins
2 cups chicken broth
4 teaspoons reduced-sodium soy sauce

Mix all ingredients except wonton skins, broth and soy sauce. Brush each wonton skin with water. Place 1 scant tablespoon chicken mixture on center of skin. Pinch 5 pleats on each of one half of circle. Fold circle in half over chicken mixture, pressing pleated edge to unpleated edge. Repeat with remaining skins and chicken mixture.

Spray 12-inch skillet with nonstick cooking spray. Heat over medium heat. Cook 12 pot stickers at a time in skillet 3 minutes or until light brown; turn. Stir in 1/2 cup of the broth and 1 teaspoon of the soy sauce. Cover and cook 5 minutes. Uncover and cook 1 minute longer or until liquid has evaporated. Repeat with remaining pot stickers, broth and soy sauce.

1 SERVING: Calories 125 (Calories from Fat 35); Fat 4g (Saturated 1g); Cholesterol 25mg; Sodium 240mg; Carbohydrate 11g (Dietary Fiber 0g); Protein 11g.

Chinese Barbecued Ribs

about 42 servings

Look for sake and hoisin sauce in the ethnic section of your supermarket.

1 1/2 to 2 pounds fresh pork spareribs
1/4 cup soy sauce
1/4 cup hoisin sauce or chili sauce
2 tablespoons honey
2 tablespoons sake or dry sherry
1 small clove garlic, crushed

Have butcher cut spareribs crosswise into 1 1/2-inch pieces. Place ribs in shallow glass or plastic dish. Mix remaining ingredients; spoon over ribs. Cover and refrigerate at least 2 hours but no longer than 24 hours.

Heat oven to 325°. Line broiler pan with aluminum foil. Remove ribs from marinade; reserve marinade. Arrange ribs, meaty sides up, in single layer on rack in broiler pan. Brush with reserved marinade. Cover and bake 1 hour. Brush ribs with marinade. Bake uncovered about 45 minutes longer, brushing occasionally with marinade, until tender.

1 SERVING: Calories 35 (Calories from Fat 20); Fat 2g (Saturated 1g); Cholesterol 10mg; Sodium 105mg; Carbohydrate 2g (Dietary Fiber 0g); Protein 2g.

Chicken Satay

12 servings

An authentic Asian satay consists of marinated meat or seafood grilled on skewers and served with a sauce. Hoisin and plum sauce replace the high-fat peanut sauce that usually accompanies satay.

1 pound boneless skinless chicken breasts
1/3 cup hoisin sauce
1/3 cup plum sauce
2 tablespoons sliced green onions
   (with tops)
1 tablespoon grated gingerroot
2 tablespoons dry sherry
2 tablespoons white vinegar

Trim fat from chicken breasts. Cut chicken lengthwise into 1/2-inch strips. Mix all ingredients except chicken in large glass or plastic bowl. Add chicken; toss to coat. Cover and refrigerate 2 hours.

Set oven control to broil. Remove chicken from marinade; drain. Reserve marinade. Thread 2 pieces chicken on each of twelve 10-inch skewers.* Place on rack in broiler pan. Broil with tops 3 to 4 inches from heat about 8 minutes, turning once, until done. Heat marinade to boiling in 1-quart saucepan; boil 1 minute. Serve with chicken.

1 SERVING: Calories 80 (Calories from Fat 20); Fat 2g (Saturated 1g); Cholesterol 25mg; Sodium 85mg; Carbohydrate 7g (Dietary Fiber 0g); Protein 8g.

*If using bamboo skewers, soak skewers in water at least 30 minutes before using to prevent burning.

Chicken-Stuffed Mushrooms

12 servings

For a deeper mushroom flavor, look for cultivated wild mushrooms, such as cremini, for this appetizer.

1/4 cup chopped onion (about 1 small)
2 tablespoons chopped fresh cilantro
3 tablespoons cholesterol-free egg product
   or egg white
1 tablespoon Dijon mustard
1 1/2 teaspoons finely chopped gingerroot
2 teaspoons reduced-sodium soy sauce
1 clove garlic, finely chopped
1/2 pound ground chicken
12 large mushrooms, stems removed

Heat oven to 450°. Spray cookie sheet with nonstick cooking spray. Mix all ingredients except mushrooms. Fill mushroom caps with chicken mixture. Place mushrooms, filled sides up, on cookie sheet. Bake 7 to 10 minutes or until tops are light brown and chicken mixture is done. Serve hot.

1 SERVING: Calories 35 (Calories from Fat 10); Fat 1g (Saturated 0g); Cholesterol 10mg; Sodium 70mg; Carbohydrate 2g (Dietary Fiber 0g); Protein 5g.

Glazed Chicken Wings

about 30 servings

3 pounds chicken wings (about 15)
2/3 cup soy sauce
1/2 cup honey
2 tablespoons vegetable oil
2 teaspoons five-spice powder
2 cloves garlic, crushed

Cut each chicken wing at joints to make 3 pieces; discard tip. Place chicken in shallow glass or plastic dish. Mix remaining ingredients; pour over chicken. Cover and refrigerate at least 1 hour but no longer than 4 hours, turning chicken occasionally.

Heat oven to 375°. Line broiler pan with aluminum foil. Remove chicken from marinade; reserve marinade. Arrange chicken on rack in broiler pan. Brush with reserved marinade. Bake 30 minutes. Turn chicken. Bake about 30 minutes longer, brushing occasionally with marinade, until juice of chicken is no longer pink when center of thickest pieces are cut. Discard any remaining marinade.

1 SERVING: Calories 70 (Calories from Fat 35); Fat 4g (Saturated 1g); Cholesterol 15mg; Sodium 380mg; Carbohydrate 5g (Dietary Fiber 0g); Protein 4g.

Do-Ahead Directions: After baking, chicken wings can be covered and refrigerated up to 24 hours. Bake uncovered in 375° oven about 15 minutes or until hot.

Mexicali Meatballs

30 servings

1 pound ground chicken or beef
1 medium onion, chopped (1/2 cup)
1 egg
1/3 cup dry bread crumbs
1/4 cup milk
1/4 teaspoon salt
1/8 teaspoon pepper
1 1/2 cups salsa
Thinly sliced green onions, if desired

Heat oven to 400°. Mix all ingredients except salsa and green onions. Shape into thirty 1-inch balls. Place in ungreased rectangular pan, $13 \times 9 \times 2$ inches. Bake uncovered about 15 minutes or until no longer pink in center; drain. Heat meatballs and salsa in 2-quart saucepan until salsa is hot. Sprinkle with green onions. Serve with wooden or plastic toothpicks.

1 SERVING: Calories 35 (Calories from Fat 10); Fat 1g (Saturated 0g); Cholesterol 15mg; Sodium 105mg; Carbohydrate 2g (Dietary Fiber g); Protein 4g.

Do-Ahead Directions: Place meatballs in single layer on ungreased cookie sheet. Freeze uncovered about 1 hour or until firm. Store tightly sealed in heavy-duty plastic food-storage bag or freezer container up to 2 months.

About 25 minutes before serving, place salsa and frozen meatballs in 2-quart saucepan. Heat to boiling, stirring occasionally; reduce heat. Cover and simmer about 20 minutes or until meatballs are hot.

Mexicali Meatballs

Steamed Vegetable Dumplings

10 servings (3 dumplings each)

Horseradish Dipping Sauce (right)
6 dried black (shiitake) mushrooms
4 cups coleslaw mix (8 ounces)
1/3 cup chopped green onions (4 medium)
1 teaspoon grated gingerroot
2 cloves garlic, finely chopped
2 tablespoons soy sauce
1/2 teaspoon sesame oil
30 wonton or siu mai skins

Prepare Horseradish Dipping Sauce. Soak mushrooms in hot water about 20 minutes or until soft; drain. Rinse with warm water; drain. Squeeze out excess moisture. Remove and discard stems; chop caps. Spray nonstick wok or 12-inch skillet with nonstick cooking spray; heat over medium-high heat until cooking spray starts to bubble. Add mushrooms, coleslaw mix, green onions, gingerroot and garlic; stir-fry about 4 minutes or until vegetables are very tender. Stir in soy sauce and sesame oil; cool.

Brush edges of 1 wonton skin with water. Place 1 scant tablespoon vegetable mixture on center of skin. (Cover remaining skins with plastic wrap to keep them pliable.) Fold bottom corner of wonton skin over filling to opposite corner, forming a triangle; pleat unfolded edges. (Cover filled dumplings with plastic wrap to keep them from drying out.) Repeat with remaining skins and vegetable mixture.

Place dumplings on heatproof plate; place plate on rack in steamer. Cover and steam over boiling water in wok or Dutch oven 15 minutes. Serve hot with dipping sauce.

HORSERADISH DIPPING SAUCE

1/4 cup soy sauce
2 tablespoons prepared horseradish
2 teaspoons grated gingerroot
1 teaspoon sugar
1 1/2 teaspoons rice vinegar

Mix all ingredients.

1 SERVING: Calories 110 (Calories from Fat 10); Fat 1g (Saturated 0g); Cholesterol 0mg; Sodium 780mg; Carbohydrate 22g (Dietary Fiber 1g); Protein 4g.

Stuffed Pattypan Squash

8 servings (2 squash each)

16 tiny pattypan squash (about 1 1/2 inches in diameter)*
1/2 cup soft bread crumbs
1/4 teaspoon dried thyme leaves
1/4 teaspoon salt
2 green onions (with tops), finely chopped
1 tablespoon grated Parmesan cheese

Heat oven to 350°. Heat 1 inch water to boiling. Add squash. Cook 6 to 8 minutes or until crisp-tender; drain. Cut off stem ends. Hollow out squash; reserve squash shells. Chop squash meat finely. Mix squash and remaining ingredients except cheese. Spoon 1 heaping teaspoon filling into each squash shell. Sprinkle with cheese. Place in ungreased square pan, 9 × 9 × 2 inches. Bake uncovered 10 to 12 minutes or until hot.

1 SERVING: Calories 15 (Calories from Fat 0); Fat 0g (Saturated 0g); Cholesterol 0mg; Sodium 95mg; Carbohydrate 3g (Dietary Fiber 2g); Protein 1g.

*8 small pattypan squash (about 2 1/2 inches in diameter) can be substituted for the tiny squash. Spoon 1 heaping tablespoon filling into each squash shell.

Chinese Firecrackers (page 53) and Stuffed Pattypan Squash

Chilled Spring Rolls

10 servings

2 green onions
5 cups bean sprouts (10 ounces)
10 cooked fresh crab legs, shelled,
    or imitation whole crab legs
    (each about 2 inches long)
1 teaspoon sesame oil
10 leaf lettuce leaves
10 ready-to-eat spring roll skins
    (8 1/2 inches square)
1/3 cup chopped fresh cilantro
Honey Sichuan Sauce (right)

Cut green onions into 2-inch pieces; cut pieces lengthwise into thin strips. Mix green onions and bean sprouts; divide mixture into 10 equal parts. Sprinkle crabmeat pieces with sesame oil. Tear each lettuce leaf into 3-inch squares.

Place 1 lettuce square on center of 1 spring roll skin. (Cover remaining skins with plastic wrap to keep them pliable.) Place 1 part bean sprout mixture on lettuce; top with 1 crabmeat piece and 1 1/2 teaspoons cilantro. Fold bottom corner of spring roll skin over filling, tucking the point under. Fold in and overlap the 2 opposite corners. Brush fourth corner generously with cold water; roll up to seal.

Repeat with remaining spring roll skins. (Cover filled spring rolls with plastic wrap to keep them from drying out.) Cover and refrigerate at least 2 hours but no longer than 8 hours. Cut in half if desired. Serve with Honey Sichuan Sauce.

HONEY SICHUAN SAUCE

1/3 cup honey
1/3 cup chili puree

Mix ingredients.

1 SERVING: Calories 130 (Calories from Fat 25); Fat 3g (Saturated 0g); Cholesterol 45mg; Sodium 220mg; Carbohydrate 15g (Dietary Fiber 1g); Protein 12g.

Tasty Appetizers and Snacks

- Use fruits and vegetables (steamed or uncooked) in place of chips and crackers.

- Make your own chips for saving on fat and calories. Or, try toasted thin bagel slices. Spicy Tortilla Chips (page 40) and Baked Pita Chips (page 40) are both delicious options.

- Always read the labels on commercial cracker and snack products. When choosing purchases, look for items without animal fats (lard or tallow) or saturated fats.

- Avoid fried and other fatty items. Potato chips and corn chips, of course, and deep-fat fried foods, cheese curds, and dips made with mayonnaise or cream cheese aren't diet-wise choices.

- Substitute low-fat or nonfat yogurt for sour cream or mayonnaise in your favorite recipes for dips and spreads. Cholesterol-free reduced-fat mayonnaise or salad dressing is a step in the right direction, but substitute some low-fat or nonfat yogurt for part of it.

- Don't forget that herbs and spices give wonderful flavor to dips and spreads without adding salt, as dry mixes can.

White Bean Pita Pizzas

4 servings

Who said pizza is junk food? Whole wheat pita bread, great northern beans and fresh vegetables make these appetizer pizzas a wholesome treat!

4 whole wheat pita breads (4 inches in diameter)
1 small onion, chopped (1/4 cup)
1 small clove garlic, finely chopped
1 can (15 to 16 ounces) great northern beans, drained and 1/4 cup liquid reserved
2 tablespoons chopped fresh or 2 teaspoons dried basil leaves
1 large tomato, seeded, cut into 1/4-inch pieces
1 large green bell pepper, cut into 16 thin rings
1 cup shredded reduced-fat mozzarella cheese (4 ounces)

Heat oven to 425°. Cut pita breads around edge with knife to split in half. Place in ungreased jelly roll pan 15 1/2 × 10 × 1 inch. Bake uncovered about 5 minutes or just until crisp.

Cook onion and garlic in reserved bean liquid in 10-inch nonstick skillet over medium heat 5 minutes, stirring occasionally. Stir in beans; heat through. Place bean mixture and basil in blender or food processor. Cover and blend, or process, until smooth.

Spread about 2 tablespoons bean mixture on each pita bread half. Top each with tomato, bell pepper and cheese. Bake in jelly roll pan 5 to 7 minutes or until cheese is melted.

1 SERVING: Calories 150 (Calories from Fat 0); Fat 3g (Saturated 2g); Cholesterol 10mg; Sodium 280mg; Carbohydrate 25g (Dietary Fiber 5g); Protein 11g.

White Bean Pita Pizzas

What Are You Craving?

Here's how to satisfy it for 100 calories or less!

CHEWY:

1 mini-bagel with 1 tablespoon reduced-fat cream cheese

1/2 English muffin with 2 teaspoons apple butter

8 dried apricot halves

3 gingersnaps

CREAMY:

1/2 cup nonfat soft-serve frozen yogurt

1/2 cup low-fat chocolate milk

1/2 cup sugar-free vanilla pudding (made with skim milk)

1/2 cup lemon nonfat yogurt

CRUNCHY:

50 thin pretzel sticks (2 1/4 inches)

8 fat-free saltine crackers

3 cups light microwave popcorn

2 cups raw vegetables

SPICY:

10 cooked medium shrimp with 3 tablespoons cocktail sauce

3 ounces smoked turkey breast with 2 teaspoons mustard

2 cups spicy vegetable juice cocktail

1/2 medium baked potato with 1/4 cup salsa

Garden Vegetable Appetizers

30 servings

These popular appetizers are perfect to tote to picnics. Pack the triangles in a flat container that will fit into your cooler.

1 package pie crust mix
1 package (0.4 ounce) ranch dressing mix
1 teaspoon baking soda
1/4 cup plus 1 tablespoon water
1 package (8 ounces) cream cheese, softened
1/2 cup sour cream
2 cups chopped vegetables
3 medium green onions, thinly sliced (1/3 cup)
6 slices bacon, crisply cooked and crumbled

Heat oven to 400°. Stir pie crust mix, 2 teaspoons of the dressing mix (dry), the baking soda and water until pastry forms a ball. Press mixture evenly in bottom of ungreased jelly roll pan, 15 1/2 × 10 1/2 × 1 inch, with floured hands. Bake 8 to 10 minutes or until golden brown; cool completely.

Beat cream cheese, sour cream and remaining dressing mix with electric mixer on medium speed until smooth. Spread evenly over pastry. Sprinkle evenly with vegetables, onions and bacon. Cover and refrigerate at least 2 hours but no longer than 24 hours. Cut into 3-inch squares. Cut each square diagonally in half to make triangles.

1 SERVING: Calories 105 (Calories from Fat 70); Fat 8g (Saturated 4g); Cholesterol 10mg; Sodium 200mg; Carbohydrate 6g (Dietary Fiber 0g); Protein 2g.

Zucchini Snackers

6 servings (2 appetizers each)

1 medium zucchini (1 1/2 inches in diameter)
1/3 cup fat-free cream cheese or reduced-fat cream cheese (Neufchâtel), softened
1/4 cup finely chopped red bell pepper
2 tablespoons chopped fresh parsley
1/2 teaspoon onion-and-herb seasoning mix or onion powder
2 drops red pepper sauce

Cut zucchini lengthwise into 6 strips. Cut each strip crosswise in half; trim each piece to 2 inches. Mix remaining ingredients. Spoon 2 to 3 teaspoons bell pepper spread on each piece of zucchini.

1 SERVING: Calories 50 (Calories from Fat 0); Fat 0g (Saturated 0g); Cholesterol 0mg; Sodium 200mg; Carbohydrate 6g (Dietary Fiber 1g); Protein 7g.

Bell Pepper Nachos

6 servings (6 strips each)

1/2 orange bell pepper, seeded and cut into
6 strips
1/2 red bell pepper, seeded and cut into
6 strips
1/2 yellow bell pepper, seeded and cut into
6 strips
3/4 cup shredded reduced-fat Monterey
Jack cheese (3 ounces)
2 tablespoons chopped ripe olives
1/4 teaspoon crushed red pepper

Cut bell pepper strips crosswise in half.
Arrange close together in ungreased broiler-
proof pie pan, 9 × 1 1/4 inches, or round pan,
9 × 1 1/2 inches. Sprinkle with cheese, olives
and crushed red pepper.

Set oven control to broil. Broil peppers
with tops 3 to 4 inches from heat about 3 minutes or until cheese is melted.

1 SERVING: Calories 50 (Calories from Fat 25); Fat 3g
(Saturated 2g); Cholesterol 10mg; Sodium 100mg;
Carbohydrate 2g (Dietary Fiber 0g); Protein 4g.

Black Bean–Corn Wonton Cups

36 servings

*This recipe is great when you need appetizers that
can be prepared ahead of time. Just bake the wonton cups ahead and mix up the filling. Fill and
garnish the wonton cups right before serving.*

36 wonton skins
2/3 cup thick-and-chunky salsa
1/4 cup chopped fresh cilantro
1/2 teaspoon ground cumin
1/2 teaspoon chili powder
1 can (15 1/4 ounces) whole kernel corn,
drained
1 can (15 ounces) black beans, rinsed
and drained
1/4 cup plus 2 tablespoons nonfat
sour cream
Cilanto sprigs, if desired

Heat oven to 350°. Gently fit 1 wonton skin
into each of 36 small muffin cups, 1 3/4 × 1
inch. Bake 8 to 10 minutes or until light
golden brown. Remove from pan; cool on
wire racks. Mix remaining ingredients except
sour cream and cilantro sprigs. Just before
serving, spoon bean mixture into wonton
cups. Top each with 1/2 teaspoon sour
cream. Garnish each with cilantro sprig.

1 SERVING: Calories 50 (Calories from Fat 0); Fat 0g
(Saturated 0g); Cholesterol 0mg; Sodium 120g;
Carbohydrate 11g (Dietary Fiber 1g); Protein 2g.

Black Bean–Corn Wonton Cups

Tortellini Kabobs

12 servings

**24 uncooked refrigerated or dried
    cheese-filled spinach tortellini**
1/2 cup reduced-fat Italian dressing
12 small whole mushrooms
12 small cherry tomatoes
Fresh mustard greens or parsley, if desired

Cook tortellini as directed on package; drain
and cool. Place dressing in shallow bowl.
Stir in tortellini, mushrooms and tomatoes.
Cover and refrigerate 1 to 2 hours, stirring
once to coat. Drain tortellini mixture. Thread
tortellini, mushrooms and tomatoes alternately on each of twelve 6-inch skewers. Serve
on bed of mustard greens.

1 SERVING: Calories 50 (Calories from Fat 9); Fat 1g
(Saturated 0g); Cholesterol 0mg; Sodium 125mg;
Carbohydrate 10g (Dietary Fiber 1g); Protein 1g.

Cucumbers, Carrots and Smoked Salmon Crudités

24 servings

*Isn't it great to know that appetizers don't always
have to be fat traps? And, by using carrot or
cucumber slices instead of crackers, this healthful
appetizer is even lower in fat and calories!*

2 ounces salmon lox, finely chopped
1/2 cup fat-free soft cream cheese, softened
**3/4 teaspoon chopped fresh or
    1/4 teaspoon dried dill weed**
**2 large cucumbers or carrots, cut into
    1/4-inch slices (24 slices)**
Dill weed sprigs, if desired.

Mix lox, cream cheese and chopped dill
weed. Place lox mixture in decorating bag
fitted with large star tip, and pipe 1 heaping
teaspoonful onto each carrot slice; or spoon
lox mixture onto each carrot slice. Garnish
each with dill weed sprig.

1 SERVING: Calories 10 (Calories from Fat 0); Fat 0g
(Saturated 0g); Cholesterol 0mg; Sodium 55mg;
Carbohydrate 1g (Dietary Fiber 0g); Protein 1g.

Cucumbers, Carrots and Smoked Salmon Crudités

Apple Cinnamon Popcorn

6 servings (about 2 cups each)

1 bag 94% fat-free butter or natural flavor
    microwave popcorn, popped (12 cups)
1 cup Apple-Cinnamon Cheerios®
1/2 cup dried apple pieces
1 teaspoon ground cinnamon

Toss all ingredients in large bowl. Store loosely covered.

1 SERVING: Calories 100 (Calories from Fat 20); Fat 2g (Saturated 1g); Cholesterol 0mg; Sodium 160mg; Carbohydrate 19g (Dietary Fiber 0g); Protein 1g.

Hot and Spicy Popcorn

6 servings (about 2 cups each)

1 bag (3 ounces) fat-free microwave
    popcorn, popped (12 cups)
1 cup fat-free pretzel sticks
1 tablespoon reduced-fat margarine, melted
1/4 teaspoon paprika
1/8 teaspoon garlic powder
1/8 teaspoon ground red pepper (cayenne)

Mix popcorn and pretzels in large bowl. Mix remaining ingredients. Drizzle over popcorn and pretzels; toss until evenly coated.

1 SERVING: Calories 55 (Calories from Fat 10); Fat 1g (Saturated 0g); Cholesterol 0mg; Sodium 200mg; Carbohydrate 10g (Dietary Fiber 0g); Protein 1g.

Southwest Snack

8 servings (about 2 cups each)

1 bag 94% fat-free butter or natural flavor
    microwave popcorn, popped (12 cups)
3 cups light Cheddar cheese–flavored
    corn snacks
1 cup fat-free pretzel sticks
1 tablespoon reduced-fat margarine, melted
1/2 teaspoon chili powder
1/4 teaspoon ground cumin
1/4 teaspoon garlic powder
2 tablespoons grated Parmesan cheese

Heat oven to 300°. Mix popcorn, corn snacks and pretzels in 2-gallon plastic food-storage bag. Mix margarine, chili powder, cumin and garlic powder; pour over mixture in bag. Seal bag; shake to coat. Sprinkle with cheese. Seal bag; shake to coat.

Pour mixture into ungreased rectangular pan, 13 × 9 × 2 inches. Bake 10 minutes; cool. Store in airtight container.

1 SERVING: Calories 85 (Calories from Fat 20); Fat 2g (Saturated 0g); Cholesterol 0mg; Sodium 280mg; Carbohydrate 15g (Dietary Fiber 1g); Protein 2g.

Jungle Fun Toss

20 servings (about 1/2 cup each)

(photograph on page 71)

6 cups frosted Cheerios®
1 1/2 cups animal crackers
1 1/2 cups small pretzel twists
1 1/2 cups cheese-flavored snack crackers
1/2 package (9-ounce size) chewy fruit snack

Mix all ingredients. Store in airtight container.

1 SERVING: Calories 100 (Calories from Fat 20); Fat 2g (Saturated 1g); Cholesterol 0mg; Sodium 160mg; Carbohydrate 19g (Dietary Fiber 0g); Protein 1g.

Date Balls

about 6 dozen balls

3/4 cup sugar
1/2 cup margarine or butter
1 pound pitted dates, cut up
1 tablespoon skim milk
1 teaspoon vanilla
1/2 teaspoon salt
1/4 cup fat-free cholesterol-free egg product
    or 1 egg, well beaten
1/2 cup chopped nuts
4 cups Wheaties®, crushed
Finely chopped nuts or shredded coconut,
    if desired

Mix sugar, margarine and dates in 2-quart saucepan. Cook over low heat, stirring constantly, until margarine is melted; remove from heat. Mix in milk, vanilla, salt and egg. Cook over very low heat about 4 minutes, stirring constantly, until slightly thickened; remove from heat. Stir in 1/2 cup nuts. Cool 5 minutes. Stir in cereal. Shape mixture into 1-inch balls. Roll balls in finely chopped nuts.

1 BALL: Calories 50 (Calories from Fat 20); Fat 2g (Saturated 0g); Cholesterol 0mg; Sodium 4mg; Carbohydrate 8g (Dietary Fiber 0g); Protein 0g.

Granola Candy

12 candies

These low-fat candies are perfect for children. Kids can snack on them and get a little nutrition at the same time.

1/2 cup fat-free granola or low-fat
    fruit granola
1/2 cup crispy corn puff cereal
2 tablespoons raisins or dried cranberries,
    if desired
1/2 cup miniature marshmallows
1 tablespoon honey
1 tablespoon reduced-fat peanut butter

Line cookie sheet with waxed paper. Mix granola, corn puff cereal and raisins in medium bowl. Heat remaining ingredients in 1-quart nonstick saucepan over low heat, stirring constantly, until marshmallows are melted. Immediately pour over cereal mixture; stir until evenly coated. Shape mixture into 1 1/2-inch balls, using wet hands. Place on waxed paper. Refrigerate at least 10 minutes.

1 CANDY: Calories 40 (Calories from Fat 10); Fat 1g (Saturated 0g); Cholesterol 0mg; Sodium 2mg; Carbohydrate 7g (Dietary Fiber 0g); Protein 1g.

Cool Chocolate-Coffee Shake

2 servings

This shake gives you the treat of a classic milk-shake, but puts the freeze on fat by using ice milk, which has 3 grams of fat per serving. In contrast, premium ice cream can weigh in at 17 grams of fat per 1/2-cup serving!

**1 1/2 cups chocolate low-fat ice cream
    or frozen yogurt**
1/4 cup prepared espresso or strong coffee
1/4 cup skim milk
Dash of ground cinnamon
Dash of cocoa

Place all ingredients except cocoa in blender. Cover and blend on high speed until smooth and frothy. Pour into 2 glasses. Sprinkle with cocoa.

1 SERVING: Calories 185 (Calories from Fat 36); Fat 4g (Saturated 2g); Cholesterol 15mg; Sodium 110mg; Carbohydrate 31g (Dietary Fiber 1g); Protein 7g.

Mocha Whip

2 servings

1 medium banana
1 cup skim milk
1 tablespoon sugar
2 teaspoons cocoa
1 teaspoon powdered instant coffee
1/2 teaspoon vanilla
3 or 4 ice cubes, cracked

Place all ingredients except ice cubes in blender. Cover and blend on high speed about 15 seconds or until smooth. Add ice cubes. Cover and blend about 15 seconds more or until blended. Serve immediately.

1 SERVING: Calories 130 (Calories from Fat 9); Fat 1g (Saturated 1g); Cholesterol 2mg; Sodium 65mg; Carbohydrate 27g (Dietary Fiber 2g); Protein 5g.

Mocha Whip, Brown Sugar Strawberries (page 406)

Morning Parfaits

2 servings

For extra crunch and texture, add 1/2 cup low-fat granola to the yogurt before layering this eye-opening parfait.

1 cup vanilla nonfat yogurt
1/8 teaspoon almond extract
1/3 cup chopped cantaloupe
1/3 cup chopped strawberries
1/3 cup chopped kiwifruit
2 tablespoons sliced almonds, toasted

Mix yogurt and almond extract. Alternate layers of fruit and 1/4 cup yogurt mixture in 2 goblets or parfait glasses, beginning and ending with fruit. Top with almonds.

1 SERVING: Calories 160 (Calories from Fat 23); Fat 4g (Saturated 1g); Cholesterol 2mg; Sodium 55mg; Carbohydrate 26g (Dietary Fiber 2g); Protein 7g.

Double Fruit Shake

4 servings

1 container (16 ounces) extra-creamy plain or vanilla nonfat yogurt (2 cups)
1 package (10 ounces) frozen sweetened strawberries or raspberries, partially thawed
1 medium banana, sliced (1 cup)

Place all ingredients in blender. Cover and blend on medium speed about 30 seconds or until smooth.

1 SERVING: Calories 155 (Calories from Fat 0); Fat 0g (Saturated 0g); Cholesterol 2mg; Sodium 95mg; Carbohydrate 34g (Dietary Fiber 2g); Protein 7g.

Orange Frost

6 servings

1/4 cup milk
3/4 cup water
1 can (6 ounces) frozen orange juice concentrate
8 ice cubes
1/4 cup sugar
1 teaspoon vanilla

Place all ingredients in order listed in blender. Cover and blend on high speed about 30 seconds or until mixture is smooth and frothy. Serve immediately. Or pour mixture into square baking dish, 8 × 8 × 2 inches. Cover and freeze about 2 hours or until firm. Let stand at room temperature about 30 minutes before serving. Stir until smooth.

1 SERVING: Calories 95 (Calories from Fat 10); Fat 1g (Saturated 0g); Cholesterol 2mg; Sodium 15mg; Carbohydrate 21g (Dietary Fiber 0g); Protein 1g.

Eat More, Lose More

One of the easiest ways to cut down on high-fat snacks (and calories) is to eat a minimum of five servings of fruits and/or vegetables every day. Because fruits and vegetables are bulky (so they fill you up) and are low in calories, you can actually eat more food and feel more satisfied.

Orange Frost, Jungle Fun Toss (page 66)

Ginger Mint Iced Tea

4 servings

The secret to this flavorful tea is the gingerroot. The more gingerroot you use and the longer the tea stands, the stronger the ginger flavor will be.

4 cups water
4 tea bags
3- to 4-inch piece gingerroot, thinly sliced
1 to 2 tablespoons grated orange peel
4 sprigs mint

Heat water to boiling. Add tea bags, gingerroot and orange peel; remove from heat. Steep 10 minutes; remove tea bags. Let stand 30 to 60 minutes. Place mint in ice-filled glasses. Strain tea over ice. Strain and refrigerate any remaining tea.

1 SERVING: Calories 5 (Calories from Fat 0); Fat 0g (Saturated 0g); Cholesterol 0mg; Sodium 5mg; Carbohydrate 1g (Dietary Fiber 0g); Protein 0g.

Cranberry Raspberry Iced Tea

8 servings

4 cups iced tea
4 cups chilled cranberry-raspberry drink
1 cup raspberries
Fresh mint leaves, if desired

Mix tea and cranberry-raspberry drink. Pour over ice. Top with raspberries. Garnish with mint.

1 SERVING: Calories 80 (Calories from Fat 0); Fat 0g (Saturated 0g); Cholesterol 0mg; Sodium 5mg; Carbohydrate 20g (Dietary Fiber 1g); Protein 0g.

HEALTHY HINT

Take a 100-calorie banana to the office so that when the urge for a sweet pick-me-up hits in midafternoon, you won't be tempted to buy a 200- or 300-calorie candy bar.

Frosty Pink Lemonade Pops

7 pops

A real crowd pleaser for kids! You can also use apple juice instead of the lemonade.

1 cup cranberry juice cocktail
1/2 cup water
1 can (6 ounces) frozen lemonade
    concentrate, thawed
7 paper cups (3-ounce size)
7 wooden ice-cream sticks

Mix cranberry juice cocktail, water and lemonade concentrate. Pour into paper cups. Freeze about 1 hour or until mixture is thick and slushy. Place wooden stick in center of each pop. Freeze about 7 hours or until pops are solid. Peel paper cups from frozen pops before eating.

1 POP: Calories 80 (Calories from Fat 0); Fat 0g (Saturated 0g); Cholesterol 0mg; Sodium 5mg; Carbohydrate 20g (Dietary Fiber 0g); Protein 0g.

Chocolate Pudding Yogurt Pops

6 pops

You can also make sandwich cookies by spreading 1 tablespoon of the pudding-yogurt mixture between graham crackers or 1 teaspoon of the mixture between vanilla wafers. Then freeze 2 hours and enjoy!

1 container (16 ounces) extra-creamy plain
    nonfat yogurt (2 cups)
1 package (4-serving size) chocolate instant
    pudding and pie filling
6 paper cups (3 ounce size)
6 wooden ice-cream sticks

Beat yogurt and pudding and pie filling (dry) with wire whisk or hand beater until smooth. Spoon into six 3-ounce paper cups; insert wooden ice-cream sticks in center of yogurt mixture in each cup. Freeze about 4 hours or until firm. Peel off paper cups before serving.

1 POP: Calories 95 (Calories from Fat 0); Fat 0g (Saturated 0g); Cholesterol 2mg; Sodium 290mg; Carbohydrate 20g (Dietary Fiber 0g); Protein 4g.

Meat

Beef and Broccoli with Garlic Sauce (page 96)

(continued on next page)

Vegetable Beef Soup

6 servings

1 pound ground beef
1 medium onion, chopped (1/2 cup)
1 package Betty Crocker Hamburger
    Helper® mix for beef pasta
5 cups water
1/4 teaspoon salt
1/8 teaspoon pepper
1 bay leaf
1 can (16 ounces) whole tomatoes,
    undrained
1 package (10 ounces) frozen mixed
    vegetables

Cook beef and onion in Dutch oven over medium heat, stirring occasionally, until beef is brown; drain. Stir in sauce mix, water, salt, pepper, bay leaf and tomatoes, breaking up tomatoes. Heat to boiling, stirring constantly; reduce heat. Cover and simmer 10 minutes, stirring occasionally. Stir in pasta and vegetables. Cover and simmer 10 minutes longer. Remove bay leaf before serving.

1 SERVING: Calories 290 (Calories from Fat 110); Fat 12g (Saturated 5g); Cholesterol 45mg; Sodium 990mg; Carbohydrate 36g (Dietary Fiber 3g); Protein 20g.

Easy Burgundy Stew

8 servings

2 pounds beef boneless bottom or top
    round, tip or chuck steak
4 medium carrots, sliced (2 cups)
2 medium stalks celery, sliced
2 medium onions, sliced
1 can (8 ounces) sliced water chestnuts,
    drained
1 can (8 ounces) mushroom stems and
    pieces, drained
3 tablespoons all-purpose flour
1 tablespoon chopped fresh or 1 teaspoon
    dried thyme leaves
1 teaspoon ground mustard (dry)
1/2 teaspoon salt
1/4 teaspoon pepper
1 cup water
1 cup dry red wine or beef broth
1 can (16 ounces) whole tomatoes,
    undrained

Heat oven to 325°. Trim fat from beef. Cut beef into 1-inch cubes. Mix beef, carrots, celery, onions, water chestnuts and mushrooms in Dutch oven. Mix flour, thyme, mustard, salt and pepper; stir into beef mixture. Stir in remaining ingredients, breaking up tomatoes. Cover and bake about 4 hours or until beef is tender and stew is thickened.

1 SERVING: Calories 180 (Calories from Fat 35); Fat 4g (Saturated 2g); Cholesterol 55mg; Sodium 400mg; Carbohydrate 16g (Dietary Fiber 3g); Protein 23g.

Beef-Barley Stew

6 servings

This easy, hearty stew requires next to no kitchen preparation.

1 pound extra-lean ground beef
1/2 cup chopped onion (about 1 medium)
2 cups beef broth
2/3 cup uncooked barley
2 teaspoons chopped fresh or 1/2 teaspoon
    dried oregano leaves
1/4 teaspoon salt
1/4 teaspoon pepper
1 can (16 ounces) whole tomatoes,
    undrained
1 can (8 ounces) sliced water chestnuts,
    undrained
1 package (10 ounces) frozen mixed
    vegetables

Heat oven to 350°. Spray 10-inch nonstick skillet with nonstick cooking spray. Cook ground beef and onion in skillet over medium heat, stirring occasionally, until beef is brown; drain. Mix beef mixture and remaining ingredients except frozen mixed vegetables in 3-quart casserole; break up tomatoes. Cover and bake 30 minutes. Stir in mixed vegetables. Cover and bake 30 to 40 minutes longer or until barley is done.

1 SERVING: Calories 215 (Calories from Fat 22g); Fat 4g (Saturated 2g); Cholesterol 50mg; Sodium 545mg; Carbohydrate 21g (Dietary Fiber g); Protein 22g.

Cut the Fat

To reduce fat and calories:

- Trim visible fat from meat before and after cooking.

- Chill stews, soups and braised dishes, then remove fat from the surface. Use a baster to remove fat during cooking.

- Use a gravy separator to separate fat from meat juices.

- Use nonstick cooking utensils to reduce the amount of added fat or oil.

- Roast or broil meat on a rack so fat drips away from the meat.

Spicy Burgers

4 servings

Top this burger with some Guacamole (page 31) for a special treat.

1 pound extra-lean ground beef
1/2 teaspoon chili powder
1/2 teaspoon pepper
1/4 teaspoon salt
1/4 teaspoon ground red pepper (cayenne)
1 clove garlic, finely chopped

Mix all ingredients thoroughly. Shape mixture into 4 patties, each 1/2 inch thick. Heat 10-inch nonstick skillet until hot. Place patties in skillet; reduce heat to medium. Cover and cook 6 to 8 minutes, turning once, until desired doneness.

1 SERVING: Calories 165 (Calories from Fat 45); Fat 5g (Saturated 3g); Cholesterol 75mg; Sodium 205mg; Carbohydrate 1g (Dietary Fiber 0g); Protein 27g.

Broiled Dijon Burgers

6 servings

2 slices bread, torn into 1-inch pieces
1/4 cup fat-free cholesterol-free egg product
**   or 2 egg whites**
2 tablespoons skim milk
3/4 pound extra-lean ground beef
1/4 teaspoon salt
1/8 teaspoon pepper
1/4 cup finely chopped onion
**   (about 1 small)**
2 teaspoons Dijon mustard
6 sourdough or plain English muffins,
**   split and lightly toasted**
6 leaves lettuce
6 slices tomato
Dijon-Yogurt Sauce (below)

Set oven control to broil. Spray broiler pan rack with nonstick cooking spray. Mix bread, egg product and milk in medium bowl. Stir in ground beef, salt, pepper, onion and mustard. Shape by about 1/3 cupfuls into 6 patties, about 3 1/2 × 1/2 inch. Place on rack in broiler pan. Broil with tops 3 to 4 inches from heat about 5 minutes or until brown. Turn patties. Broil 3 to 4 minutes longer or until no longer pink in center. Serve on English muffins with lettuce, tomato and Dijon-Yogurt Sauce.

DIJON-YOGURT SAUCE

1/2 cup plain nonfat yogurt
1 teaspoon sweet pickle relish
1/2 teaspoon Dijon mustard

Mix all ingredients.

1 SERVING: Calories 300 (Calories from Fat 90); Fat 10g (Saturated 4g); Cholesterol 35mg; Sodium 530mg; Carbohydrate 35g (Dietary Fiber 2g); Protein 19g.

Broiled Dijon Burgers

Meat Tips

If you love meat, you probably noticed the new types of beef and pork sold in supermarkets. Since more consumers are concerned about fat and cholesterol, animals are now being bred to be leaner. And while in the past you may have seen up to 1/2 inch of fat covering a beef or pork cut, today those same cuts will only have 1/8 to 1/4 inch of fat covering.

For the fewest calories per serving, trim all visible fat before cooking and use lean-cooking methods such as broiling, pan broiling, roasting, grilling or microwaving.

These leaner meats are more sensitive to cooking and especially to overcooking. Watch meats carefully and cook them just until tender or to the temperatures indicated. With less fat within the muscle tissue, even a few degrees over the specified temperature can overcook meats and cause them to toughen.

To avoid any food safety problems, ground beef should be cooked to at least medium doneness (160°, which may be very slightly pink) or well-done (170°), whichever you prefer. The lower temperatures allow the leaner meats to retain their juiciness and tenderness.

Hamburger Cabbage Casserole

6 servings

Serve with mashed potatoes on the side, or spoon beef mixture over mashed potatoes.

1 pound ground beef
1 large onion, chopped (1 cup)
1/2 cup uncooked instant rice
1/2 teaspoon salt
1/2 teaspoon pepper
1 can (10 3/4 ounces) condensed
    tomato soup
1/4 cup water
4 cups coleslaw mix or shredded cabbage

Heat oven to 400°. Cook beef and onion in 10-inch skillet over medium heat 8 to 10 minutes, stirring occasionally, until beef is brown; drain. Stir in rice, salt, pepper, soup and water.

Place coleslaw mix in ungreased 2-quart casserole. Spoon beef mixture over coleslaw mix. Cover and bake about 45 minutes or until hot and bubbly.

1 SERVING: Calories 245 (Calories from Fat 110); Fat 12g (Saturated 5g); Cholesterol 45mg; Sodium 540mg; Carbohydrate 20g (Dietary Fiber 2g); Protein 16g.

Hamburger Cabbage Casserole

Chinese Tacos with Tomato-Ginger Salsa

10 servings

Tomato-Ginger Salsa (right)
1 pound lean ground beef
1/4 cup hoisin sauce
3 tablespoons water
2 tablespoons soy sauce
1/8 teaspoon ground red pepper (cayenne)
10 taco shells
1/4 cup sesame seed
2 cups shredded napa (Chinese) cabbage (8 ounces)
1 medium carrot, shredded (3/4 cup)
Plum sauce, if desired

Prepare Tomato-Ginger Salsa. Cook ground beef in 10-inch skillet, stirring frequently, until brown; drain. Stir in hoisin sauce, 2 tablespoons of the water, 1 tablespoon of the soy sauce and the red pepper. Heat to boiling, stirring constantly. Boil and stir 2 minutes.

Heat oven to 350°. Mix remaining 1 tablespoon water and 1 tablespoon soy sauce. Brush taco shells with mixture; sprinkle with sesame seed. Place on ungreased cookie sheet. Bake 5 to 7 minutes or until heated through. Fill taco shells with beef mixture. Top with cabbage, carrot and salsa. Serve with plum sauce.

TOMATO-GINGER SALSA

1 large tomato, finely chopped (1 cup)
1 tablespoon chopped fresh cilantro
1 teaspoon finely chopped gingerroot

Mix all ingredients.

1 SERVING: Calories 170 (Calories from Fat 90); Fat 10g (Saturated 3g); Cholesterol 25mg; Sodium 180mg; Carbohydrate 12g (Dietary Fiber 2g); Protein 10g.

Soft Shell Tacos

10 servings

If you can't find jicama in your produce section, you can use water chestnuts instead.

1/2 pound extra-lean ground beef
1 can (15 to 16 ounces) kidney beans, rinsed and drained
1 can (11 ounces) whole kernel corn with red and green peppers, drained
1 can (14 1/2 ounces) Mexican-style stewed tomatoes, undrained
10 nonfat flour tortillas (8 inches in diameter)
1 cup shredded carrots (about 1 1/2 medium)
1 cup shredded jicama
Salsa, if desired
Nonfat sour cream, if desired

Cook ground beef in 10-inch nonstick skillet over medium-high heat, stirring occasionally, until brown; drain. Stir in beans, corn and tomatoes, breaking up tomatoes. Cook, stirring occasionally, until hot. Spoon about 1/2 cup bean mixture onto each tortilla. Top each with about 2 tablespoons carrots and jicama; roll up. Serve with salsa and sour cream.

1 SERVING: Calories 220 (Calories from Fat 25); Fat 3g (Saturated 1g); Cholesterol 15mg; Sodium 420mg; Carbohydrate 42g (Dietary Fiber 6g); Protein 12g.

Teriyaki Beef Stir-fry

6 servings

1 pound ground beef
2 teaspoons soy sauce
1 teaspoon finely chopped gingerroot
1/4 cup sliced green onions (3 medium)
1 clove garlic, finely chopped
1 small red bell pepper, thinly sliced
1/2 large red onion, thinly sliced
2 stalks bok choy, cut into 1-inch slices (1 cup)
1 cup teriyaki barbecue marinade
1 package (8 ounces) uncooked Chinese noodles or spaghetti

Mix beef, soy sauce, 1/2 teaspoon of the gingerroot, the green onions and garlic. Shape mixture into 1-inch balls. Cook over medium-high heat about 6 minutes, turning occasionally, until beef is no longer pink in center and juice is clear. Remove meatballs from skillet; keep warm. Drain drippings from skillet, reserving 1 tablespoon.

Cook remaining 1/2 teaspoon gingerroot in drippings in skillet over medium-high heat 30 seconds. Add bell pepper, red onion and bok choy. Cook, stirring occasionally, until crisp-tender. Stir in teriyaki barbecue marinade. Stir in meatballs; cook until hot. Cook and drain noodles as directed on package. Serve meatball mixture over noodles.

1 SERVING: Calories 285 (Calories from Fat 100); Fat 11g (Saturated 4g); Cholesterol 45mg; Sodium 2,000mg; Carbohydrate 30g (Dietary Fiber 1g); Protein 18g.

Cajun Beef and Rice

4 servings

1/2 pound ground beef
1 medium stalk celery, chopped (1/2 cup)
1 medium onion, chopped (1/2 cup)
2 teaspoons Cajun or Creole seasoning
2 cups uncooked instant rice
1 cup water
8 medium fresh okra, sliced, or 1 cup
    frozen (thawed) cut okra
2 medium tomatoes, chopped (1 1/2 cups)
1 small green bell pepper, chopped
    (1/2 cup)
2 cans (11 1/2 ounces each) lightly tangy
    eight-vegetable juice

Heat 12-inch nonstick skillet over medium-high heat. Cook beef, celery, onion and Cajun seasoning in skillet about 4 minutes, stirring frequently, until beef is brown and vegetables are tender. Stir in remaining ingredients. Reduce heat to medium-low. Cover and cook about 5 minutes or until rice is tender.

1 SERVING: Calories 385 (Calories from Fat 80); Fat 9g (Saturated 4g); Cholesterol 30mg; Sodium 640mg; Carbohydrate 63g (Dietary Fiber 4g); Protein 17g.

Garlicky Meatballs over Rice

4 servings

If you love garlic and chilis, these are the meatballs for you!

3/4 pound extra-lean ground beef
1 slice whole wheat bread, crumbled
1/4 cup salsa
4 cloves garlic, finely chopped
2 cans (8 ounces each) tomato sauce
3 cups hot cooked rice

Mix all ingredients except tomato sauce and rice. Shape into sixteen 1 1/2-inch meatballs. Spray 10-inch nonstick skillet with nonstick cooking spray; heat over medium-high heat. Place meatballs in skillet; spray meatballs with nonstick cooking spray. Cook until meatballs are brown on all sides. Stir in tomato sauce. Heat to boiling; reduce heat to low. Cover and simmer about 20 minutes, stirring occasionally until meatballs are no longer pink in center. Serve over rice.

1 SERVING: Calories 355 (Calories from Fat 90); Fat 10g (Saturated 4g); Cholesterol 50mg; Sodium 810mg; Carbohydrate 47g (Dietary Fiber 3g); Protein 22g.

Garlicky Meatballs over Rice

Raita Pasta with Spicy Steak

4 servings

This Indian-influenced dish takes raita—the typical yogurt-chopped vegetable accompaniment—and adds a pasta twist.

Spicy Rub (right)
1/2 pound beef flank steak
1 1/2 cups uncooked gemelli (twists) pasta
   (6 ounces)
1 cup plain yogurt
1/2 large tomato, seeded and diced
   (1/2 cup)
1/2 medium cucumber, seeded and diced
   (1/2 cup)
1/4 cup chopped fresh cilantro or parsley
1/4 teaspoon salt

Prepare Spicy Rub; rub mixture on both sides of beef. Cover and refrigerate 1 hour. Cook and drain pasta as directed on package. Mix yogurt, tomato, cucumber, cilantro and salt in large bowl; toss with pasta.

Set oven control to broil. Grease broiler pan rack. Place beef on rack in broiler pan. Broil with top about 3 inches from heat about 5 minutes or until brown. Turn beef; broil 4 to 6 minutes longer for medium doneness or until desired doneness. Cut beef diagonally into very thin slices. Serve with pasta mixture.

SPICY RUB

1 1/2 teaspoons olive or vegetable oil
1/2 teaspoon ground cumin
1/4 teaspoon crushed red pepper
1/4 teaspoon salt
1/8 teaspoon ground red pepper (cayenne)
1/8 teaspoon chili powder
1 clove garlic, finely chopped

Mix all ingredients.

1 SERVING: Calories 295 (Calories from Fat 65); Fat 7g (Saturated 2g); Cholesterol 35mg; Sodium 340mg; Carbohydrate 39g (Dietary Fiber 1g); Protein 20g.

Grilling Directions: Heat coals or gas grill. Grill rubbed beef uncovered 4 to 5 inches from medium heat 6 to 8 minutes on each side for medium doneness, turning occasionally, or until desired doneness.

Peppered Beef with Pasta

2 servings

1/2 pound beef boneless sirloin steak,
    about 1/2 inch thick
1/2 teaspoon coarsely ground pepper
2 tablespoons tomato paste
1 tablespoon red wine vinegar
1 teaspoon chopped fresh or 1/2 teaspoon
    dried thyme leaves
1 medium bell pepper, chopped (1 cup)
1 small onion, chopped (1/4 cup)
2 cups hot cooked farfalle (bow-tie) pasta
    or soba noodles (2 ounces)

Cut beef into 2 serving pieces. Rub both sides of beef with coarsely ground pepper. Heat 10-inch nonstick skillet over medium-high heat. Cook beef in skilled 4 minutes on each side, turning once. Stir in remaining ingredients except pasta. Reduce heat to medium-low. Cook uncovered about 5 minutes, stirring occasionally, until beef is medium doneness (160°). Serve sauce over beef and pasta.

1 SERVING: Calories 330 (Calories from Fat 35); Fat 4g (Saturated 2g); Cholesterol 55mg; Sodium 170mg; Carbohydrate 49g (Dietary Fiber 4g); Protein 28g.

Zesty Beef with Bow-tie Pasta

6 servings

1 1/2 pounds beef boneless sirloin steak
1 pound asparagus, cut into 2-inch pieces
    (3 cups), or 2 packages (10 ounces each)
    frozen asparagus cuts, thawed
2 medium onions, sliced
1 1/2 cups beef broth
4 cups cooked farfalle (bow-tie) pasta
1 cup tomato puree
3 tablespoons chopped fresh or
    1 tablespoon dried basil leaves
3 tablespoons chopped sun-dried tomatoes
    (not oil-packed)
1/4 teaspoon pepper
2 tablespoons grated Parmesan cheese

Trim fat from beef. Cut beef across grain into 2-inch strips; cut strips crosswise into 1/8-inch slices. Spray 12-inch skillet with nonstick cooking spray; heat over medium heat. Cook asparagus, onions and 1 cup of the broth in skillet 5 to 7 minutes, stirring occasionally, until liquid has evaporated; remove mixture from skillet.

Cook beef in skillet over medium heat about 2 minutes, stirring frequently, until no longer pink. Return vegetable mixture to skillet. Stir in remaining 1/2 cup broth and remaining ingredients except cheese. Cook about 2 minutes, stirring frequently until hot. Sprinkle with cheese.

1 SERVING: Calories 295 (Calories from Fat 45); Fat 5g (Saturated 2g); Cholesterol 55mg; Sodium 430mg; Carbohydrate 37g (Dietary Fiber 3g); Protein 2g.

Gingered Beef Lo Mein

6 servings

Chili oil is vegetable oil that has been steeped or infused with hot chilis. It adds a hot, spicy "kick" to this recipe.

1 cup water
3 tablespoons cornstarch
1 tablespoon packed brown sugar
3 tablespoons low-sodium soy sauce
3 teaspoons grated gingerroot
1 teaspoon low-sodium beef bouillon
    granules
4 ounces uncooked vermicelli
2 teaspoons chili oil
1 pound beef boneless sirloin steak,
    cut into 2×1/4-inch strips
1 clove garlic, crushed
1 medium red bell pepper, cut into
    2×1/4-inch strips
1 cup 1/4-inch slices mushrooms
    (about 3 ounces)
1 cup Chinese pea pods
1 tablespoon sesame seed, toasted

Mix water, cornstarch, brown sugar, soy sauce, 2 teaspoons of the gingerroot and the bouillon granules; set aside. Cook and drain vermicelli as directed on package.

While vermicelli is cooking, heat wok or 12-inch nonstick skillet until 1 or 2 drops of water bubble and skitter when sprinkled in wok. Add oil; rotate wok to coat sides. Add beef, remaining 1 teaspoon gingerroot and the garlic; stir-fry about 3 minutes or until beef is brown. Add bell pepper, mushrooms and pea pods; stir-fry 1 minute. Stir in cornstarch mixture. Cook and stir about 1 minute or until thickened. Stir in vermicelli. Sprinkle with sesame seed.

1 SERVING: Calories 270 (Calories from Fat 110); Fat 12g (Saturated 4g); Cholesterol 60mg; Sodium 420mg; Carbohydrate 24g (Dietary Fiber 2g); Protein 19g.

Gingered Beef Lo Mein

Beef and Broccoli with Garlic Sauce

4 servings

(photograph on page 74)

By using a nonstick pan and nonstick cooking spray, you don't need to add any oil to stir-fry the sirloin.

1/2 pound beef boneless sirloin or
    round steak
1/4 teaspoon salt
Dash of white pepper
1 pound broccoli, cut into flowerets
    and 1×1/2-inch pieces (4 cups)
1 teaspoon cornstarch
1 teaspoon soy sauce
1 teaspoon sesame oil
1/4 cup fat-free reduced-sodium
    chicken broth
1 teaspoon vegetable oil
1 tablespoon finely chopped garlic (6 cloves)
1 teaspoon finely chopped gingerroot
2 tablespoons brown bean paste
1 can (8 ounces) sliced bamboo shoots,
    drained
2 cups hot cooked rice

Trim fat from beef. Cut beef lengthwise into 2-inch strips. Cut strips crosswise into 1/8-inch slices. Toss beef with salt and white pepper. Place broccoli in 1 inch boiling water; heat to boiling. Cover and cook 2 minutes. Immediately rinse with cold water; drain. Mix cornstarch and soy sauce; stir in sesame oil and broth.

Spray nonstick wok or 12-inch skillet with nonstick cooking spray; heat over medium-high heat until cooking spray starts to bubble. Add beef; stir-fry about 2 minutes or until brown. Remove beef from wok. Cool wok slightly. Wipe clean and respray. Add oil and rotate wok to coat sides. Heat over medium-high heat. Add garlic, gingerroot and bean paste; stir-fry 30 seconds. Add bamboo shoots; stir-fry 20 seconds. Stir in beef and broccoli. Stir in cornstarch mixture; cook and stir about 30 seconds or until thickened. Serve over rice.

1 SERVING: Calories 215 (Calories from Fat 45); Fat 5g (Saturated 1g); Cholesterol 25mg; Sodium 270mg; Carbohydrate 30g (Dietary Fiber 3g); Protein 15g.

HEALTHY HINT

Adding a small amount of diced fresh or canned chilis to foods can really perk up the flavor. Try adding chilis to spaghetti sauce, soups, stews, stir-fries and casseroles. Many varieties are available, from sweet to hot to mild.

Korean Barbecued Beef

4 servings

This is probably the most popular Korean meat dish. The meat is tenderized by a soy sauce and sesame oil marinade.

1 pound beef boneless top loin or sirloin steak
1/4 cup soy sauce
3 tablespoons sugar
2 tablespoons sesame or vegetable oil
1/4 teaspoon pepper
3 green onions, finely chopped
2 cloves garlic, chopped

Trim fat from beef steak. Cut beef diagonally across grain into 1/8-inch slices. (Beef is easier to cut if partially frozen, about 1 1/2 hours.) Mix remaining ingredients in medium glass or plastic bowl. Stir in beef until well coated. Cover and refrigerate 30 minutes. Drain beef. Heat wok or 10-inch skillet over medium heat until hot. Add beef; stir-fry 2 to 3 minutes or until brown. Serve beef with hot cooked rice if desired.

1 SERVING: Calories 175 (Calories from Fat 80); Fat 9g (Saturated 3g); Cholesterol 55mg; Sodium 310mg; Carbohydrate 3g (Dietary Fiber 0g); Protein 21g.

Meat Main Dishes

- Rather than make floury sauces and gravies, just reduce pan juices to the desired consistency and concentration of flavor. Remove the fat from meat cooking juices; pour the juices into a fat separator (which has a spout coming from the bottom of the container—below the fat line, because fat rises to the liquid surface) or refrigerate the cooking juices, then skim off the congealed fat.

- Select lean cuts of meat and trim off all visible fat before cooking. Refrigerate, then skim soups and stews.

- The higher the designated grade of meat, the more fat it contains. "Prime," the highest grade, is the most thoroughly marbled with fat. "Choice" is next, and the leanest is "Select."

- Avoid frying meats, a cooking method that only adds fat to a fatty situation. Use nonstick cookware so less added fat is needed in cooking.

- Baste meats with their own juices, broth or water rather than margarine. Meat roasted on a rack can't cook in (and reabsorb) its own fat.

- Marinades don't have to be oil based. Use flavored vinegars, herbs and spices.

- Rib cuts of beef, pork, veal and lamb are fatty; loin cuts are leaner. Beef and veal flank and round cuts are relatively lean; leg and shoulder cuts should be examined for leanness before buying.

- When buying ground beef, choose extra-lean.

Indian Beef with Cucumber Rice

6 servings

Here are many of the classic flavors of far-away India: cardamom, cloves, nutmeg, ginger, coriander, cumin and turmeric. The Indians love their cooling raita, yogurt with cucumber. We've stirred crunchy cucumber right into the rice.

1 1/2 pounds lean beef boneless chuck roast
1 1/4 cups plain nonfat yogurt
1 teaspoon cardamom seeds (removed from pods), crushed
1/4 teaspoon ground cloves
1/8 teaspoon ground nutmeg
1 tablespoon reduced-fat margarine
2 cups chopped onions (about 2 large)
1 tablespoon grated gingerroot
2 cloves garlic, finely chopped
3/4 teaspoon coriander seed, crushed
1/2 teaspoon cumin seed
1/4 teaspoon ground turmeric
3/4 teaspoon salt
Cucumber Rice (right)
1/4 cup cold water
1 tablespoon cornstarch
1 tablespoon all-purpose flour
Chopped fresh cilantro

Trim fat from beef roast; cut beef into 1-inch cubes. Mix 1 cup of the yogurt, the cardamom, cloves and nutmeg in glass or plastic bowl or heavy plastic bag; stir in beef. Cover and refrigerate at least 4 hours.

Heat margarine in 10-inch nonstick skillet over medium heat until melted. Cook and stir onions, gingerroot and garlic about 2 minutes. Stir in beef mixture, coriander, cumin, turmeric and salt. Heat to boiling; reduce heat. Cover and cook, stirring occasionally, until meat is tender, about 1 1/2 hours.

Prepare Cucumber Rice. Shake water, cornstarch and flour in tightly covered container; gradually stir into beef mixture. Heat to boiling, stirring constantly. Boil and stir 1 minute. Serve beef mixture over Cucumber Rice; drizzle with remaining 1/4 cup yogurt and sprinkle with cilantro.

CUCUMBER RICE

2 cups hot cooked rice
1 cup chopped seeded cucumber (about 1 medium)
2 tablespoons lemon juice

Mix all ingredients; heat if necessary.

1 SERVING: Calories 330 (Calories from Fat 90); Fat 10g (Saturated 3g); Cholesterol 85mg; Sodium 650mg; Carbohydrate 28g (Dietary Fiber 1g); Protein 32g.

Beefy Skillet Calzone

4 servings

Lean ground beef could be easily substituted for the beef sirloin strips. Shaved Parmesan cheese scattered over each serving adds a rich, tangy flavor.

**8 diagonally cut slices French bread,
    1/2 inch thick**
2 tablespoons grated Parmesan cheese
**3/4 pound beef sirloin or flank steak,
    cut into thin strips**
1 tablespoon olive or vegetable oil
1 small green bell pepper, sliced
1 or 2 cloves garlic, finely chopped
**1 can (14 1/2 ounces) diced tomatoes with
    Indian-style herbs, undrained**
1 can (8 ounces) pizza sauce
**1 jar (4 1/2 ounces) sliced mushrooms,
    drained**

Set oven control to broil. Place bread slices on ungreased cookie sheet. Spray bread with cooking spray; sprinkle with cheese. Broil with tops 4 to 6 inches from heat 1 to 2 minutes or until light brown; set aside.

Cut beef into thin strips (beef is easier to cut if partially frozen, about 1 1/2 hours). Heat oil in 10-inch nonstick skillet over medium-high heat. Cook beef, bell pepper and garlic in oil, stirring occasionally, until beef is brown. Stir in tomatoes, pizza sauce and mushrooms. Cook 2 to 4 minutes or until hot.

Place 2 toasted bread slices on each of 4 serving plates; top with beef mixture.

1 SERVING: Calories 335 (Calories from Fat 100); Fat 11g (Saturated 3g); Cholesterol 45mg; Sodium 1,020mg; Carbohydrate 39g (Dietary Fiber 4g); Protein 24g.

Easy Beef Casserole

6 servings

1 1/2 cups cut-up cooked lean beef
**1 1/2 cups uncooked elbow macaroni
    (about 6 ounces)**
1 cup sliced celery (about 2 medium stalks)
1/2 cup skim milk
1/4 cup chopped onion (about 1 small)
1 1/2 teaspoons dried basil leaves
1/2 teaspoon garlic powder
1/8 teaspoon pepper
**1 jar (8 ounces) mushroom stems and
    pieces, undrained**
1 can (8 ounces) tomato sauce

Heat oven to 350°. Mix all ingredients in ungreased 2-quart casserole. Cover and bake 30 minutes; stir. Cover and bake until macaroni is tender, about 20 minutes longer.

1 SERVING: Calories 265 (Calories from Fat 90); Fat 10g (Saturated 4g); Cholesterol 35mg; Sodium 255mg; Carbohydrate 29g (Dietary Fiber 1g); Protein 14g.

Microwave Directions: Mix all ingredients in 3-quart microwavable casserole; pour 1/2 cup water over top. Cover tightly and microwave on High, stirring every 6 minutes, until macaroni is tender, 15 to 18 minutes. Let stand covered 5 minutes.

Beef in Creamy Mushroom Sauce

6 servings

Choose this meal when you're in the mood for hearty comfort food.

2 tablespoons cornstarch
1 cup water
1 pound lean beef boneless sirloin steak, about 1/2 inch thick
1 small onion, chopped (about 1/4 cup)
1 clove garlic, crushed
1/4 teaspoon salt
1/8 teaspoon pepper
1 medium red bell pepper, cut into bite-size pieces
3 cups sliced mushrooms (about 8 ounces)
1/4 cup brandy or water
1 teaspoon low-sodium beef bouillon granules
2 tablespoons nonfat sour cream
3 tablespoons chopped fresh chives
3 cups hot cooked mostaccioli

Stir cornstarch into water; set aside. Trim fat from beef steak. Cut beef into thin strips, about 1 1/2 × 1/2 inch.

Spray 10-inch skillet with nonstick cooking spray; heat over medium-high heat. Cook onion, garlic, salt and pepper in skillet about 3 minutes, stirring frequently, until onion is tender. Stir in beef and bell pepper. Cook about 4 minutes, stirring frequently until beef is no longer pink. Stir in mushrooms.

Add brandy to skillet; sprinkle bouillon granules over beef mixture. Heat to boiling; reduce heat. Cover and simmer 1 minute. Stir in sour cream. Stir in cornstarch mixture. Cook over medium-high heat about 2 minutes, stirring frequently, until thickened. Stir in chives. Serve over mostaccioli.

1 SERVING: Calories 205 (Calories from Fat 30); Fat 3g (Saturated 1g); Cholesterol 40mg; Sodium 220mg; Carbohydrate 27g (Dietary Fiber 2g); Protein 19g.

HEALTHY HINT

If you're a fast eater and tend to overeat, try following this rule: Never have a spoon or fork in your hand when you have food in your mouth. Setting down your spoon or fork between bites will naturally slow you down and help you savor your food more.

French-Style Beef Roast

8 servings

3 pounds beef boneless chuck or rolled
    rump roast
1 teaspoon salt
1 tablespoon chopped fresh or 1 teaspoon
    dried thyme leaves
1 bay leaf
1 large clove garlic, cut into fourths
6 whole cloves
5 peppercorns
4 cups water
4 medium carrots, cut crosswise in half
2 medium onions, cut into fourths
2 medium turnips, cut into fourths
2 medium stalks celery, cut into 1-inch
    pieces

Place beef roast, salt, thyme, bay leaf, garlic, cloves and peppercorns in 4-quart Dutch oven; add water. Heat to boiling; reduce heat. Cover and simmer 2 1/2 hours. Add remaining ingredients. Cover and simmer about 30 minutes or until beef and vegetables are tender. Remove beef; cut into 1/4-inch slices. Serve vegetables with beef. Strain broth; serve with beef and vegetables.

1 SERVING: Calories 250 (Calories from Fat 70); Fat 8g (Saturated 4g); Cholesterol 105mg; Sodium 390mg; Carbohydrate 9g (Dietary Fiber 1g); Protein 36g.

Roast Beef Pocket Sandwiches

4 servings

These are terrific take-along sandwiches when the yogurt mixture is packed separately and added just before serving.

1 cup plain nonfat yogurt
1 1/2 teaspoons snipped fresh or
    1/2 teaspoon dried dill weed
1 teaspoon mustard
1 cup chopped bell pepper
    (about 1 medium)
2 pita breads (6 inches in diameter),
    cut into halves
1/3 pound thinly sliced lean roast beef
1 cup alfalfa sprouts

Mix yogurt, dill weed and mustard; stir in bell pepper. Fill each pita bread half with 1/3 cup yogurt mixture and 1/4 of the beef and alfalfa sprouts.

1 SERVING: Calories 195 (Calories from Fat 35); Fat 4g (Saturated 2g); Cholesterol 35mg; Sodium 85mg; Carbohydrate 24g (Dietary Fiber 1g); Protein 17g.

Broiled Veal and Onions

4 servings

If the onions won't stand upright, cut a thin slice off the small end of each one.

4 veal rib or loin chops, about 3/4 inch thick
1 tablespoon Dijon mustard
1 teaspoon mustard seed
1/4 teaspoon salt
1/2 teaspoon pepper
2 large yellow onions (about 3 inches in
    diameter), cut into halves
4 teaspoons reduced-fat margarine, softened
2 tablespoons packed brown sugar

Set oven control to broil. Brush both sides of veal chops lightly with mustard; sprinkle with mustard seed, salt and 1/4 teaspoon of the pepper. Place veal and onions, cut sides down, on rack in broiler pan. Broil with tops of veal about 3 inches from heat about 6 minutes or until veal is brown; turn veal and onions.

Spread 1 teaspoon margarine over each onion half; sprinkle with brown sugar and remaining 1/4 teaspoon pepper. Broil about 6 minutes longer or until veal is brown and onions are tender.

1 SERVING: Calories 340 (Calories from Fat 110); Fat 12g (Saturated 4g); Cholesterol 130mg; Sodium 300mg; Carbohydrate 13g (Dietary Fiber 0g); Protein 45g.

Is Fat-Free Always Best?

Fact: Fat-free and low-fat foods are low in calories.

False: Just because fat has been removed from food doesn't necessarily mean the calories have been reduced. When food manufacturers remove fat, other components, usually carbohydrates, are added to improve the taste and texture of the reduced-fat food. Check the labels on these products to be sure you're not overindulging on these foods.

Fact: Fat-free and low-fat foods are always healthier than regular foods.

False: Foods with less fat often appear to be a better choice than their regular counterparts. However, read nutrition labels on packaged products to be sure. Often, when fat is removed, so is flavor. And to make up for the loss in flavor, extra calories, sugar and salt may be added to boost the taste.

Veal Cutlets with Mushrooms

6 servings

Try substituting fresh shiitake mushrooms in this dish for a slightly more exotic taste.

6 veal cutlets (about 1/4 pound each)
1/2 teaspoon paprika
1/4 teaspoon salt
6 cups sliced mushrooms (1 pound)
1/3 cup water
1 teaspoon grated lemon peel
1 tablespoon lemon juice
1 clove garlic, finely chopped
2 teaspoons cornstarch
1 tablespoon cold water
1 cup beef broth
Hot cooked noodles, if desired

Spray 10-inch nonstick skillet with nonstick cooking spray. Trim fat from veal. Sprinkle veal with paprika and salt. Cook veal in skillet over medium heat, turning once, until brown on both sides. Add mushrooms. Mix 1/3 cup water, the lemon peel, lemon juice and garlic; pour over veal and mushrooms. Heat to boiling; reduce heat. Cover and simmer about 30 minutes or until veal is tender.

Mix cornstarch and 1 tablespoon cold water. Stir broth and cornstarch mixture into veal mixture. Heat to boiling, stirring constantly. Boil and stir 1 minute. Serve over noodles.

1 SERVING: Calories 130 (Calories from Fat 35); Fat 4g (Saturated 2g); Cholesterol 75mg; Sodium 260mg; Carbohydrate 5g (Dietary Fiber 1g); Protein 20g.

Veal Sauté

4 servings

1 pound veal round steak, about 1/2 inch thick
2 tablespoons all-purpose flour
1/2 teaspoon paprika
1/2 teaspoon salt
1/8 teaspoon pepper
2 teaspoons olive or vegetable oil
1/2 cup dry white wine or chicken broth
1/4 cup water
1 teaspoon chopped fresh or 1/4 teaspoon dried rosemary or thyme leaves
3/4 cup peeled tiny pearl onions (4 ounces)
2 medium carrots, cut into julienne strips

Trim fat from veal. Cut veal into 4 serving pieces. Mix flour, paprika, 1/4 teaspoon of the salt and the pepper. Coat veal with flour mixture. Flatten veal to 1/4-inch thickness between waxed paper or plastic wrap.

Heat oil in 10-inch nonstick skillet over medium-high heat. Cook veal in oil, turning once, until brown; drain. Add wine, water, rosemary, remaining 1/4 teaspoon salt, the onions and carrots. Heat to boiling; reduce heat. Cover and simmer about 45 minutes, adding water if necessary, until veal and vegetables are tender. Place veal and vegetables on platter; pour pan drippings over top.

1 SERVING: Calories 160 (Calories from Fat 55); Fat 6g (Saturated 2g); Cholesterol 75mg; Sodium 340mg; Carbohydrate 9g (Dietary Fiber 2g); Protein 19g.

Veal Sauté

Crispy Pork with Sweet-and-Sour Vegetables

4 servings

Rice cracker crumbs are used in place of the traditional deep-fried batter coating to create a low-fat crisp-crumb coating. Using a skillet rather than a wok allows for all of the pork to come in contact with the surface of the pan so it browns evenly. It's best to brown the meat with a minimum of turning.

1/2 pound pork tenderloin
1 egg white, lightly beaten
1 teaspoon water
34 crisp rice crackers, crushed (1/2 cup)
1/4 teaspoon garlic powder
1/4 teaspoon ground mustard (dry)
1 teaspoon sesame or vegetable oil
1 package (1 pound 5 ounces) frozen stir-fry vegetables with sweet-and-sour sauce and pineapple*

Trim fat from pork. Cut pork crosswise into 1/4-inch slices; stack slices and cut lengthwise into 1/2-inch strips. Mix egg white and water in medium bowl. Stir in pork until well coated. Mix crushed crackers, garlic powder and mustard in plastic bag or glass bowl. Add a few pork strips at a time; toss to coat evenly.

Spray 12-inch nonstick skillet with nonstick cooking spray; heat over medium-high heat until cooking spray starts to bubble. Add sesame oil; rotate skillet to coat bottom. Reduce heat to medium. Place pork strips flat in skillet; cook 2 to 3 minutes or until brown on bottom. Turn pork. Cook 2 to 3 minutes more or until no longer pink in center.

Remove pork from skillet. Wipe skillet clean. Add frozen vegetables and sauce. Cover and cook 7 to 10 minutes, stirring frequently, until vegetables are crisp-tender and sauce is hot. Gently stir in pork strips just until well coated with sauce. Serve immediately.

1 SERVING: Calories 240 (Calories from Fat 55); Fat 6g (Saturated 2g); Cholesterol 35mg; Sodium 710mg; Carbohydrate 33g (Dietary Fiber 4g); Protein 17g.

Frozen stir-fry vegetables without sauce and 1/2 cup purchased sweet-and-sour sauce can be substituted for the vegetables with sauce.

Crispy Pork with Sweet-and-Sour Vegetables

Pork Fajit

4 servings

3/4 pound lean
2 tablespoons lin
1 tablespoon veg
2 cloves garlic, sl
2 teaspoons chili
1 teaspoon garlic
1/2 teaspoon salt
1/4 teaspoon pe
4 flour tortillas (8
1 medium onion,
1 medium green
    1/4-inch strip
3/4 cup chopped
    (about 1 medi
1/4 cup reduced-

Trim fat from por
into 2-inch strips.
1/4-inch slices. (F
freeze pork, about
oil, garlic, chili pov
pepper in glass or
bag. Place pork in
and refrigerate at
than 24 hours, turi

Heat oven to
and heat until w
Remove from over
pork from marina
skillet or wok ove
drops of water bub
kled in skillet. Ad
Add onion and bel
etables are crisp-ter

For each servin
pork mixture, ch
cream in center of
filling; serve with li

1 SERVING: Calories 300
(Saturated 4g); Cholester
Carbohydrate 30g (Dietar

Sausage-Mushroom Pasta Calzones

6 servings

Stuff egg roll wrappers with delicious fillings, and you've got individual pasta pockets without a lot of work!

1/2 pound bulk pork sausage
1 small onion, chopped (1/4 cup)
1 cup spaghetti sauce
6 square egg roll wrappers (about
    6 1/2 inches square)
1/2 cup sliced mushrooms
1 cup shredded mozzarella cheese
    (4 ounces)
1/4 cup crumbled Gorgonzola cheese,
    if desired

Heat oven to 400°. Grease rectangular baking dish, 13 × 9 × 2 inches. Cook sausage and onion in 10-inch skillet over medium-high heat, stirring occasionally, until sausage is no longer pink; drain. Stir in spaghetti sauce; cook until hot. Spoon sausage mixture on half of each egg roll wrapper to within 1/2 inch of edge. Top with mushrooms, 1/2 cup of the mozzarella cheese and the Gorgonzola cheese. Moisten edges of wrappers lightly with water. Fold over filling; press edges to seal. Place in baking dish. Sprinkle with remaining mozzarella cheese. Bake uncovered 15 to 20 minutes or until calzones are hot and cheese begins to brown. Serve with additional spaghetti sauce if desired.

1 SERVING: Calories 295 (Calories from Fat 110); Fat 12g (Saturated 5g); Cholesterol 30mg; Sodium 1,030mg; Carbohydrate 34g (Dietary Fiber 2g); Protein 15g.

Sausage-Mushroom Pasta Calzones

Warm Ham and Spinach Salad

6 servings

Use leftover ham or pick up a small amount of ham from the deli for this quick, light main-dish salad.

10 ounces spinach, torn into bite-size pieces
    (8 cups)
6 slices bacon
1 cup cubed fully cooked smoked ham
2 medium zucchini, cut into julienne strips
1/3 cup chopped green onions (4 medium)
Hot Dressing (right)

Place spinach in large serving bowl. Cook bacon in 10-inch skillet over medium-high heat about 5 minutes or until crisp; drain and crumble. Drain fat from skillet. Cook ham, zucchini and green onions in same skillet about 2 minutes, stirring occasionally, until onions are crisp-tender. Add bacon and ham mixture to spinach; toss. Prepare Hot Dressing in same skillet. Pour dressing over spinach mixture; toss. Serve warm.

HOT DRESSING

1/2 cup water
1/4 cup cider vinegar
1 tablespoon sugar
1 tablespoon all-purpose flour
1 teaspoon Dijon mustard
1/2 teaspoon celery seed

Heat water and vinegar in skillet until hot. Stir in remaining ingredients. Cook about 1 minute, stirring constantly, until slightly thickened.

1 SERVING: Calories 125 (Calories from Fat 65); Fat 7g (Saturated 2g); Cholesterol 20mg; Sodium 350mg; Carbohydrate 7g (Dietary Fiber 2g); Protein 9g.

Poultry

Oven-Fried Chicken (page 133)

(continued on next page)

White Bean and Chicken Chili

4 servings

Keep cans of chunk chicken on the shelf to use when you don't have time to cook chicken. Or just add another can of beans in place of the chicken and enjoy a vegetarian chili.

2 cups chopped cooked chicken breast
1 1/2 cups chicken broth
1 can (15 to 16 ounces) cannellini or great northern beans, rinsed and drained
1 package (9 ounces) frozen shoepeg white corn
1 can (7 ounces) salsa verde or 3/4 cup green taco sauce
1/4 cup chopped fresh cilantro
Sour cream, if desired
Salsa, if desired

Mix chicken, broth, beans, corn and salsa verde in 3-quart saucepan. Heat to boiling; reduce heat. Cover and simmer 15 minutes. Stir in cilantro. Top each serving with sour cream and salsa.

1 SERVING: Calories 310 (Calories from Fat 35); Fat 4g (Saturated 1g); Cholesterol 55mg; Sodium 860mg; Carbohydrate 39g (Dietary Fiber 6g); Protein 35g.

Chicken 'n' Pepper Stir-fry

4 servings

The secret to a perfect stir-fry is to make sure the skillet or wok is hot before you add the oil and food. To ensure even cooking, keep the food moving by stirring constantly.

2 tablespoons soy sauce
2 tablespoons ketchup
1/2 teaspoon ground ginger
2 cloves garlic, finely chopped
3 skinless boneless chicken breast halves (about 3/4 pound), thinly sliced
2 tablespoons vegetable oil
6 green onions, cut into 1-inch pieces
1 medium green bell pepper, thinly sliced
1 medium red bell pepper, thinly sliced
4 cups hot cooked Chinese noodles or rice

Mix soy sauce, ketchup, ginger and garlic in resealable heavy-duty plastic bag. Add chicken; seal bag and turn to coat with marinade. Let stand 15 minutes. Heat 1 tablespoon of the oil in 10-inch skillet or wok over medium-high heat. Add green onions and bell peppers; stir-fry until crisp-tender. Remove from skillet. Heat remaining 1 tablespoon oil in skillet. Add chicken; stir-fry 4 to 5 minutes or until no longer pink in center. Stir in bell pepper mixture. Serve with noodles.

1 SERVING: Calories 315 (Calories from Fat 80); Fat 9g (Saturated 2g); Cholesterol 45mg; Sodium 650mg; Carbohydrate 40g (Dietary Fiber 2g); Protein 21g.

Super-Easy Chicken Stir-fry

4 servings

2 tablespoons vegetable oil
1 pound skinless boneless chicken breast halves or thighs, cut into 1-inch pieces
3 cups cut-up assorted vegetables (bell pepper, broccoli flowerets, shredded carrots)
1 clove garlic, finely chopped
1/2 cup stir-fry sauce
Hot cooked vermicelli or rice, if desired

Heat 1 tablespoon of the oil in 12-inch skillet or wok over high heat. Add chicken; stir-fry about 3 minutes or until no longer pink in center. Remove from skillet. Heat remaining 1 tablespoon oil in skillet. Add vegetables and garlic; stir-fry about 2 minutes or until vegetables are crisp-tender. Add chicken and stir-fry sauce. Cook and stir about 2 minutes or until heated through. Serve with vermicelli.

1 SERVING: Calories 230 (Calories from Fat 90); Fat 10g (Saturated 2g); Cholesterol 60mg; Sodium 980mg; Carbohydrate 10g (Dietary Fiber 2g); Protein 27g.

Spicy Mexican Skillet Chicken

4 servings

1/2 to 1 teaspoon chili powder
1/4 teaspoon salt
1/4 teaspoon pepper
4 skinless boneless chicken breast halves (about 1 pound)
1 tablespoon vegetable oil
1 cup frozen (thawed) corn or canned (drained) whole kernel corn
1/3 cup chunky salsa
2 tablespoons chopped fresh cilantro
1 large tomato, chopped (about 1 cup)
1 can (15 ounces) black beans, rinsed and drained

Mix chili powder, salt and pepper. Sprinkle evenly over both sides of chicken. Heat oil in 10-inch skillet over medium-high heat. Cook chicken in oil 10 minutes or until brown on both sides. Stir in remaining ingredients. Heat to boiling; reduce heat Cover and simmer 3 to 5 minutes or until juice of chicken is no longer pink when centers of thickest pieces are cut and vegetables are heated through.

1 SERVING: Calories 325 (Calories from Fat 70); Fat 8g (Saturated 2g); Cholesterol 65mg; Sodium 560mg; Carbohydrate 36g (Dietary Fiber 9g); Protein 36g.

Spicy Mexican Skillet Chicken

Thai Chicken Skillet

4 servings

Leftover Thai Seasoning Mix? Brush 4 skinless boneless chicken breast halves with oil, rub with about 2 tablespoons seasoning mix and bake for 35 to 45 minutes.

1/4 cup Thai Seasoning Mix (below)
4 skinless boneless chicken breast halves
    (about 1 pound)
1 tablespoon vegetable oil
1 can (15 ounces) lychees, drained
1/4 cup sliced green onions (3 medium)
2 jalapeño or red chilis, seeded and chopped
1/4 cup chopped dry-roasted peanuts

Sprinkle seasoning mix evenly over both sides of chicken. Heat oil in 12-inch skillet over medium-high heat. Cook chicken in oil about 4 minutes or until chicken is brown on both sides. Add remaining ingredients except peanuts; reduce heat. Cover and cook 10 to 15 minutes or until juice of chicken is no longer pink when centers of thickest pieces are cut. Sprinkle with peanuts.

THAI SEASONING MIX

1/3 cup chopped fresh lemongrass
3 tablespoons grated lemon peel
1 tablespoon five-spice powder
3/4 teaspoon salt
1/2 teaspoon garlic powder

Mix all ingredients in storage container with tight-fitting lid. Refrigerate up to 5 days. Stir to mix before each use.

1 SERVING: Calories 280 (Calories from Fat 100); Fat 11g (Saturated 2g); Cholesterol 60mg; Sodium 300mg; Carbohydrate 19g (Dietary Fiber 4g); Protein 30g.

Italian Chicken Skillet

4 servings

1 tablespoon olive or vegetable oil
4 skinless boneless chicken breast halves
    (about 1 pound)
2 cloves garlic, finely chopped
2 large bell peppers, cut into 1-inch pieces
1 medium onion, thinly sliced
2 medium zucchini, sliced
1/4 cup 1/4-inch strips sliced pepperoni
    (about 1 ounce)
1/4 cup chicken broth or dry red wine
    (or nonalcoholic)
1 1/2 teaspoons chopped fresh or
    1/4 teaspoon dried thyme leaves
1 1/2 teaspoons chopped fresh or
    1/4 teaspoon dried rosemary leaves
1/4 teaspoon salt
1/8 teaspoon pepper
4 cups hot cooked vermicelli, fettuccine
    or linguine
1 tablespoon grated Parmesan cheese

Heat oil in 10-inch nonstick skillet over medium-high heat. Add chicken and garlic. Cook 15 to 20 minutes, turning once, until juice of chicken is no longer pink when centers of thickest pieces are cut. Remove chicken mixture from skillet; keep warm. Heat remaining ingredients except vermicelli and cheese to boiling in same skillet. Cook and stir 3 to 4 minutes or until vegetables are crisp-tender. Stir in vermicelli; cook until hot. Serve chicken over vermicelli mixture. Sprinkle with cheese.

1 SERVING: Calories 365 (Calories from Fat 90); Fat 10g (Saturated 3g); Cholesterol 50mg; Sodium 350mg; Carbohydrate 45g (Dietary Fiber 3g); Protein 26g.

Italian Chicken Skillet

Baked Lemon Chicken

4 servings

4 skinless boneless chicken breast halves
(about 1 pound)
1 egg white
1 teaspoon water
1/4 cup all-purpose flour
1 teaspoon baking soda
1/4 to 1/2 teaspoon ground red pepper
(cayenne), if desired
Chinese Lemon Sauce (right)
Chopped green onions and lemon slices

Cut breasts crosswise in half. Mix egg white and water in medium bowl. Add chicken; turn chicken to coat. Let stand 10 minutes. Heat oven to 450°. Spray nonstick cookie sheet with nonstick cooking spray. Remove chicken from egg white mixture; discard mixture. Mix flour, baking soda and red pepper in plastic bag. Add 1 chicken piece at a time. Seal bag and shake to coat chicken. Place chicken on cookie sheet; spray with cooking spray about 5 seconds or until surface of chicken appears moist.

Bake uncovered 20 to 25 minutes or until juice of chicken is no longer pink when centers of thickest pieces are cut. Meanwhile, prepare Chinese Lemon Sauce. Let chicken stand 5 minutes; cut each piece crosswise into about 5 slices. Pour sauce over chicken. Garnish with green onion and lemon slices.

CHINESE LEMON SAUCE

1/3 cup fat-free reduced-sodium
chicken broth
1/4 cup sugar
1 1/2 teaspoons grated lemon peel
3 tablespoons lemon juice
2 tablespoons rice vinegar
2 tablespoons light corn syrup
1 clove garlic, finely chopped, or
1/2 teaspoon garlic powder
1/4 teaspoon salt
2 teaspoons cornstarch
2 teaspoons cold water

Heat broth, sugar, lemon peel, lemon juice, vinegar, corn syrup, garlic and salt to boiling in 1-quart saucepan, stirring occasionally. Mix cornstarch and cold water; stir into sauce. Cook and stir about 30 seconds or until thickened. Serve warm, or cover and refrigerate up to 2 weeks.

1 SERVING: Calories 250 (Calories from Fat 30); Fat 3g (Saturated 1g); Cholesterol 60mg; Sodium 590mg; Carbohydrate 29g (Dietary Fiber 0g); Protein 27g.

Oven-Fried Chicken

6 servings

(photograph on page 124)

2 1/2- to 3 1/2-pound cut-up broiler-fryer
   chicken
1 tablespoon margarine or butter
2/3 cup Bisquick® Reduced Fat or Original
   baking mix
1 1/2 teaspoons paprika
1 1/4 teaspoons salt
1/4 teaspoon pepper

Heat oven to 425°. Remove skin from chicken if desired. Heat margarine in rectangular baking dish or pan 13×9×2 inches in oven until melted. Mix baking mix, paprika, salt and pepper; coat chicken. Place skin sides down (meaty sides down if skinned) in pan (pan and margarine should be hot). Bake 35 minutes. Turn; bake about 15 minutes longer or until juice of chicken is no longer pink when centers of thickest pieces are cut.

1 SERVING: Calories 210 (Calories from Fat 80); Fat 9g (Saturated 3g); Cholesterol 70mg; Sodium 720mg; Carbohydrate 8g (Dietary Fiber 0g); Protein 24g.

Oven-Barbecued Chicken

6 servings

3- to 3 1/2-pound cut-up broiler-fryer
   chicken
3/4 cup chili sauce
2 tablespoons honey
1 tablespoon soy sauce
1 teaspoon ground mustard (dry)
1/2 teaspoon prepared horseradish
1/2 teaspoon red pepper sauce

Heat oven to 375°. Place chicken, skin sides up, in ungreased rectangular pan, 13×9×2 inches. Mix remaining ingredients; pour over chicken. Cover and bake 30 minutes. Spoon sauce in pan over chicken. Bake uncovered about 30 minutes longer or until juice of chicken is no longer pink when centers of thickest pieces are cut.

1 SERVING: Calories 270 (Calories from Fat 110); Fat 12g (Saturated 4g); Cholesterol 85mg; Sodium 600mg; Carbohydrate 14g (Dietary Fiber 0g); Protein 27g.

Low-Fat Frying

Love fried foods but not the calories and fat? Change to oven-fried! Dip pieces of poultry or meat into low-fat or fat-free liquids such as buttermilk, yogurt or skim milk. Roll in a crunchy coating such as corn flakes or low-fat cracker crumbs. Place in a pan sprayed with nonstick cooking spray. Bake at 425° until done.

Chicken Breasts with Sun-Dried Tomato Sauce

4 servings

Sun-dried tomatoes add a rich flavor to this low-fat chicken and pasta dish.

1/4 cup coarsely chopped sun-dried
　　tomatoes (not oil-packed)
1/2 cup chicken broth
4 skinless boneless chicken breast halves
　　(about 1 pound)
1/2 cup sliced mushrooms (1 1/2 ounces)
2 tablespoons chopped green onions
　　(2 medium)
2 cloves garlic, finely chopped
2 tablespoons dry red wine or apple juice
1 teaspoon vegetable oil
1/2 cup skim milk
2 teaspoons cornstarch
2 teaspoons chopped fresh or 1/2 teaspoon
　　dried basil leaves
3 cups hot cooked fettuccine

Mix tomatoes and broth. Let stand 30 minutes. Trim fat from chicken. Cook mushrooms, green onions and garlic in wine in 10-inch nonstick skillet over medium heat about 3 minutes, stirring occasionally, until mushrooms are tender; remove mixture from skillet.

Add oil to skillet. Cook chicken in oil over medium heat until brown on both sides. Add tomato mixture. Heat to boiling; reduce heat. Cover and simmer about 10 minutes, stirring occasionally, until juice of chicken is no longer pink when centers of thickest pieces are cut. Remove chicken from skillet; keep warm.

Mix milk, cornstarch and basil; stir into tomato mixture. Heat to boiling, stirring constantly. Boil and stir 1 minute. Stir in mushroom mixture, heat through. Serve over chicken and fettuccine.

1 SERVING: Calories 335 (Calories from Fat 65); Fat 7g (Saturated 2g); Cholesterol 105mg; Sodium 250mg; Carbohydrate 36g (Dietary Fiber 2g); Protein 34g.

Chicken Safety

To prevent salmonella contamination, which can cause food poisoning, follow these simple guidelines:

- Wash your hands before and after handling uncooked poultry.

- Thaw chicken in the refrigerator or microwave—never on the countertop.

- Scrub the countertop, cutting board and cutlery with hot, soapy water before you use them to prepare other foods.

Chicken Breasts with Sun-Dried Tomato Sauce

Chicken with Fennel

6 servings

6 bone-in chicken breast halves
    (about 3 1/2 pounds)
1/4 cup (1/2 stick) margarine or butter,
    softened
1 1/2 tablespoons chopped fresh or
    1 1/2 teaspoons dried basil leaves
1 tablespoon chopped fresh parsley or
    1 teaspoon dried parsley flakes
1/2 teaspoon fennel seed
1/8 teaspoon pepper

Heat oven to 375°. Place chicken, skin sides up, on rack in shallow roasting pan. Mix remaining ingredients. Gently loosen skin from chicken with fingers. Spread margarine mixture between breast meat and skin. Cover breast with skin. Bake uncovered 50 to 60 minutes or until juice of chicken is no longer pink when centers of thickest pieces are cut.

1 SERVING: Calories 205 (Calories from Fat 100); Fat 11g (Saturated 3g); Cholesterol 65mg; Sodium 150mg; Carbohydrate 0g (Dietary Fiber 0g); Protein 26g.

HEALTHY HINT

Cooking chicken with the skin on adds to the flavor, not the fat. Research has found that the fat does not transfer to the meat during cooking. So go ahead and leave the skin on—it helps keep the juices in, creates a moister, more tender meat and boosts the flavor. If you're watching your calories, cholesterol and fat, remove the skin after cooking and discard it.

Tequila Chicken with Fettuccine

6 servings

This is guaranteed to be a big hit at your next gathering! Toss the fettuccine with 1 teaspoon of the grated lime peel to add vibrant color.

1/4 cup tequila or chicken broth
1/4 cup frozen (thawed) limeade
1 tablespoon grated lime peel
1 1/2 pounds skinless boneless
    chicken breast halves, cut into
    1 1/2×1/2-inch strips
1 small orange or yellow bell pepper,
    cut into 1/4-inch strips
1 1/2 cups sliced mushrooms (4 ounces)
1 clove garlic, finely chopped
1 package (16 ounces) uncooked
    spinach fettuccine
1/2 cup grated Parmesan cheese

Mix tequila, limeade and lime peel in medium glass or plastic bowl. Stir in chicken. Cover and refrigerate 30 minutes. Place chicken and marinade in 12-inch skillet. Stir in bell pepper, mushrooms and garlic. Cook over medium-high heat 10 to 12 minutes, stirring occasionally, until chicken is no longer pink in center. Cook and drain fettuccine as directed on package. Divide fettuccine among 6 serving plates. Spoon chicken mixture over fettuccine. Sprinkle with cheese. Garnish with additional grated lime peel if desired.

1 SERVING: Calories 375 (Calories from Fat 65); Fat 7g (Saturated 3g); Cholesterol 115mg; Sodium 180mg; Carbohydrate 52g (Dietary Fiber 4g); Protein 30g.

Tequila Chicken with Fettuccine

Rosemary-Mustard Chicken

6 servings

Serve with roasted new potatoes and steamed asparagus for a meal that's sure to say, "Welcome, spring."

3 tablespoons reduced-fat sour cream
3 tablespoons Dijon mustard
1 teaspoon dried rosemary leaves, crushed
1/4 teaspoon white pepper
12 skinless boneless chicken thighs
    (about 2 1/4 pounds)

Mix all ingredients except chicken in large glass or plastic dish. Add chicken; turn to coat with marinade. Cover and refrigerate at least 3 hours but no longer than 24 hours.

Heat oven to 400°. Spray rectangular pan, 13 × 9 × 2 inches, with nonstick cooking spray. Place chicken in pan. Bake uncovered about 20 minutes or until juice of chicken is no longer pink when centers of thickest pieces are cut.

1 SERVING: Calories 220 (Calories from Fat 90); Fat 10g (Saturated 3g); Cholesterol 95mg; Sodium 190mg; Carbohydrate 2g (Dietary Fiber 0g); Protein 30g.

Roast Chicken with Spiced Yogurt

6 servings

3- to 3 1/2-pound broiler-fryer chicken
1/4 cup plus 1/2 teaspoon water
1/4 teaspoon ground mustard (dry)
1 cup plain nonfat yogurt
1/4 cup lemon juice
1/2 teaspoon salt
1/2 teaspoon ground cardamom
1/4 teaspoon ground ginger
1/4 teaspoon ground cumin
1/4 teaspoon crushed red pepper
1/4 teaspoon pepper
1 clove garlic, chopped

Fold wings of chicken across back with tips touching. Tie or skewer drumsticks to tail. Place chicken in large glass or plastic bowl. Mix 1/2 teaspoon of the water with the mustard in small bowl. Stir in remaining ingredients except 1/4 cup water; pour over chicken. Turn chicken to coat well with marinade. Cover and refrigerate at least 12 hours but no longer than 24 hours.

Heat oven to 375°. Remove chicken from marinade; reserve marinade. Place chicken on rack in shallow roasting pan. Insert thermometer so tip is in the thickest part of inside thigh muscle and does not touch bone. Roast uncovered 1 to 1 1/4 hours, brushing marinade over chicken during last 30 minutes of roasting, until thermometer reads 180° and juice is no longer pink when center of thigh is cut. Remove chicken from pan; keep warm. Stir 1/4 cup water into pan drippings; heat just until hot. Remove and discard chicken skin. Serve chicken with sauce.

1 SERVING: Calories 160 (Calories from Fat 45); Fat 5g (Saturated 2g); Cholesterol 65mg; Sodium 270mg; Carbohydrate 4g (Dietary Fiber 0g); Protein 25g.

Chicken Ratatouille

6 servings

Sprinkle lightly with freshly grated Parmesan cheese for extra flavor at only a few calories!

1 tablespoon all-purpose flour
1 teaspoon salt
1 teaspoon paprika
1/4 plus 1/8 teaspoon pepper
3- to 3 1/2-pound cut-up broiler-fryer
    chicken
1 tablespoon vegetable oil
1/4 cup water
3 cloves garlic, finely chopped
1 tablespoon chopped fresh or 1 teaspoon
    dried basil leaves
4 cups 1-inch pieces eggplant
    (about 1 pound)
2 cups sliced zucchini (about 2 small)
1 medium green bell pepper, cut into
    1-inch pieces
1/2 cup chopped onion (about 1 medium)
3 medium tomatoes, cut into wedges

Mix flour, 1/2 teaspoon of the salt, the paprika and 1/8 teaspoon of the pepper; sprinkle over chicken. Heat oil in 12-inch nonstick skillet or 4-quart Dutch oven. Cook chicken over medium heat about 15 minutes or until brown on all sides; add water. Heat to boiling; reduce heat. Cover and simmer 20 minutes.

Mix garlic, basil and remaining 1/4 teaspoon pepper. Add eggplant to skillet; sprinkle with half of the garlic mixture. Add zucchini, bell pepper and onion; sprinkle with remaining garlic mixture. Add 1 to 2 tablespoons water if necessary. Cover and simmer 10 to 15 minutes, stirring occasionally, until juices of thickest pieces of chicken run clear and vegetables are crisp-tender. Add tomato wedges; sprinkle with remaining 1/2 teaspoon salt. Cover and simmer about 5 minutes or until tomatoes are hot.

1 SERVING: Calories 320 (Calories from Fat 115); Fat 13g (Saturated 4g); Cholesterol 125mg; Sodium 490mg; Carbohydrate 12g (Dietary Fiber 4g); Protein 43g.

HEALTHY HINT

Instead of sautéing in butter, margarine or oil, use a small amount of broth (chicken, vegetable or beef), rice vinegar, fruit juice or wine. All of these add flavor with little or no added fat.

Chicken and Asparagus Roulades

4 servings

This dish is a taste of spring anytime of the year. Slice the roulades crosswise and arrange the slices in a shallow pool of sauce.

**4 small skinless boneless chicken breast
  halves (about 2 pounds)**
1/4 teaspoon salt
1/4 teaspoon onion powder
1/4 teaspoon dried dill weed
**1 package (10 ounces) frozen asparagus
  spears, thawed and drained**
**1/2 medium red bell pepper, cut into
  1/4-inch strips**
Mock Hollandaise Sauce (right)
Fresh dill weed sprigs, if desired

Heat oven to 375°. Remove excess fat from chicken; flatten each chicken breast half to 1/4-inch thickness between plastic wrap or waxed paper. Mix salt, onion powder and dill weed; sprinkle over chicken. Place 1/4 of asparagus spears and pepper strips crosswise on large end of each chicken breast half. Roll tightly and secure with wooden picks. Place chicken, seam sides down, in square pan, 8×8×2 inches, sprayed with nonstick cooking spray. Cover and bake until chicken is done, about 30 minutes. Prepare Mock Hollandaise Sauce; serve with chicken. Garnish with fresh dill weed sprigs.

MOCK HOLLANDAISE SAUCE

2 tablespoons reduced-fat margarine
1 tablespoon all-purpose flour
1/4 teaspoon salt
2/3 cup skim milk
1 egg yolk
1/2 teaspoon grated lemon peel
2 teaspoons lemon juice

Heat margarine in 1-quart nonstick saucepan over low heat until melted. Stir in flour and salt. Cook over low heat until mixture is smooth and bubbly, stirring constantly; remove from heat. Mix milk and egg yolk until smooth; stir into flour mixture. Heat to boiling, stirring constantly. Boil and stir 1 minute. Remove from heat; stir in lemon peel and lemon juice.

1 SERVING: Calories 265 (Calories from Fat 90); Fat 10g (Saturated 3g); Cholesterol 145mg; Sodium 420mg; Carbohydrate 7g (Dietary Fiber 3g); Protein 36g.

Chicken with Garden Vegetables

4 servings

Celebrate good nutrition with this healthful chicken dish! Bell peppers provide vitamin C; carrots provide lots of vitamin A; and the rice, wheat germ and vegetables provide extra flavor.

1/4 cup wheat germ
1 teaspoon chopped fresh or 1/4 teaspoon
 dried basil leaves
4 skinless boneless chicken breast halves
 (about 1 pound)
1/4 cup hot water
1/2 teaspoon chicken bouillon granules
1/4 cup water
1 tablespoon lemon juice
1 clove garlic, crushed
1 cup cut-up broccoli
2 medium carrots, cut into julienne strips
1 medium red bell pepper, cut into julienne
 strips
1 small onion, sliced and separated into rings
1 teaspoon chopped fresh or 1/4 teaspoon
 dried basil leaves, if desired
Salt and pepper to taste, if desired
2 cups hot cooked wild and brown rice mix

Mix wheat germ and 1 teaspoon basil in plastic bag. Add 1 chicken breast half at a time and shake until evenly coated. Spray 10-inch nonstick skillet with nonstick cooking spray; heat skillet over medium heat. Cook chicken in skillet 10 minutes, turning once, until golden brown. Mix 1/4 cup hot water and the bouillon granules; pour into skillet. Cover and cook 5 to 10 minutes longer or until juice of chicken is no longer pink when centers of thickest pieces are cut. Remove chicken from skillet; keep warm.

Remove any chicken coating from skillet. Heat 1/4 cup water to boiling in skillet; add lemon juice. Cook garlic in liquid in skillet 30 seconds. Stir in remaining ingredients except rice. Cover and cook over medium heat about 5 minutes, stirring occasionally, until vegetables are crisp-tender. Spoon vegetables over rice. Serve with chicken.

1 SERVING: Calories 280 (Calories from Fat 45); Fat 5g (Saturated 1g); Cholesterol 60mg; Sodium 240mg; Carbohydrate 32g (Dietary Fiber 4g); Protein 31g.

HEALTHY HINT

The best way to judge the doneness of a whole chicken is to use a meat thermometer. Insert the meat thermometer so the tip is in the thickest part of the outside thigh muscle and does not touch the bone. Roast the chicken until the thermometer reads 180° and the juice of the chicken is no longer pink when the center of the thigh is cut.

Chicken with Orange Glaze

6 servings

This quick honey-orange glaze is an adaptation of the more time-consuming classic French orange sauce.

3- to 3 1/2-pound broiler-fryer chicken
1/2 cup honey
2 tablespoons orange juice
1 tablespoon lemon juice
1/4 teaspoon ground nutmeg

Heat oven to 375°. Fold wings of chicken across back with tips touching. Tie or skewer drumsticks to tail. Place chicken, breast side up, on rack in shallow roasting pan. Insert meat thermometer so tip is in thickest part of inside thigh muscle and does not touch bone. Roast uncovered 1 hour 15 minutes. Mix remaining ingredients; reserve half of the orange mixture. Brush some of remaining orange mixture on chicken. Roast uncovered about 15 minutes longer, brushing once or twice with remaining orange mixture, until thermometer reads 180° and juice of chicken is no longer pink when center of thigh is cut. Serve chicken with reserved orange juice mixture.

1 SERVING: Calories 310 (Calories from Fat 110); Fat 12g (Saturated 4g); Cholesterol 85mg; Sodium 75mg; Carbohydrate 24g (Dietary Fiber 0g); Protein 27g.

Sun-Dried Tomato and Apricot Chicken

6 servings

If you prefer to use sun-dried tomatoes that aren't packed in oil, pour enough hot water over the dried tomatoes to cover them. Let them stand 10 to 15 minutes to soften; drain. You'll need 1 1/2 cups of the softened tomatoes.

1/2 cup orange juice
2 tablespoons balsamic vinegar
3- to 3 1/2-pound cut-up broiler-fryer chicken
1/2 teaspoon salt
1/4 teaspoon pepper
1/3 cup orange marmalade
1 jar (8 ounces) sun-dried tomatoes in oil, drained
1 package (6 ounces) dried apricots
3 tablespoons packed brown sugar

Heat oven to 375°. Mix orange juice and vinegar in ungreased rectangular pan, 13 × 9 × 2 inches. Arrange chicken, skin sides up, in pan. Spoon orange juice mixture over chicken. Sprinkle with salt and pepper. Spread marmalade over chicken. Bake uncovered 30 minutes.

Spoon orange juice mixture over chicken. Sprinkle tomatoes and apricots around chicken; toss with orange juice mixture. Sprinkle brown sugar over tomatoes and apricots. Bake uncovered 35 to 40 minutes, spooning orange juice mixture frequently over chicken, until juice of chicken is no longer pink when centers of thickest pieces are cut. (Cover pan loosely with aluminum foil when chicken begins to brown.)

1 SERVING: Calories 375 (Calories from Fat 110); Fat 12g (Saturated 4g); Cholesterol 85mg; Sodium 270mg; Carbohydrate 41g (Dietary Fiber 3g); Protein 29g.

Chicken Breasts Dijon

6 servings

Try honey Dijon mustard for a flavor twist!

**6 small skinless boneless chicken breast
    halves (about 3 pounds)**
1/4 cup Dijon mustard
1 teaspoon vegetable oil
2 tablespoons dry white wine
Freshly ground pepper
2 tablespoons mustard seed
Chopped parsley, if desired

Heat oven to 400°. Remove excess fat from
chicken. Place chicken, meaty sides up, in
rectangular pan, 13×9×2 inches, sprayed
with nonstick cooking spray. Mix mustard, oil
and wine; brush over chicken. Sprinkle with
pepper and mustard seed. Bake uncovered
until chicken is done, about 30 minutes.
Sprinkle with chopped parsley.

1 SERVING: Calories 255 (Calories from Fat 65); Fat 7g
(Saturated 2g); Cholesterol 120mg; Sodium 230mg;
Carbohydrate 2g (Dietary Fiber 0g); Protein 46g.

Quick Chicken Ideas

- Slice skinless boneless chicken breasts
  or thighs and combine with cut-up
  vegetables from the produce section,
  salad bar or deli for a quick stir-fry.

- For a tasty chicken salad, mix equal
  parts of chopped cooked chicken with
  your favorite bottled salad dressing
  or marinade. For a healthy crunch,
  add thawed frozen or cut-up fresh
  vegetables.

- Cook a couple of extra pieces of
  chicken when grilling. They make
  flavorful leftovers for salads and
  sandwiches.

- If you like chicken but are trying to
  cut calories, there's a good chance
  you've passed up preparing or eating
  greasy fried chicken. However, you can
  indulge in fried chicken occasionally if
  you remove the skin before eating.

- Making the switch from a fried chicken
  breast to a skinless broiled chicken
  breast saves about 80 calories for a
  3-ounce portion. You save about 40
  calories by broiling instead of frying
  and another 40 calories by removing
  the skin. You'll also find that the same
  size serving of light chicken meat has
  less fat than dark chicken meat.

- Chicken can be purchased in a variety
  of ways: whole or cut-up whole, specific
  parts, skinned and boned, canned and
  cooked from the deli. It's versatile
  enough to be used at any meal, healthful and low in calories, and you'll find
  plenty of tempting flavorful recipes for
  this favorite right here.

Italian Chicken Stir-fry

4 servings

Pepperoni cut into strips rather than left in slices makes that marvelous flavor go further.

1 pound skinless boneless chicken breasts
1 tablespoon olive or vegetable oil
1/4 cup 1/4-inch strips thinly sliced
    pepperoni (about 1 ounce)
2 cloves garlic, finely chopped
2 large bell peppers, cut into 1-inch pieces
1 medium onion, thinly sliced
2 cups 1/4-inch slices zucchini
    (about 2 medium)
1/4 cup dry red wine
1 teaspoon chopped fresh or 1/2 teaspoon
    dried thyme leaves
1 teaspoon chopped fresh or 1/2 teaspoon
    dried rosemary leaves
1/4 teaspoon salt
1/8 teaspoon pepper
1 tablespoon grated Parmesan cheese

Remove excess fat from chicken; cut chicken into 2-inch pieces. Heat oil in 10-inch non-stick skillet or wok over medium-high heat. Add chicken, pepperoni and garlic; stir-fry until chicken is almost done, 3 to 4 minutes. Remove chicken mixture from skillet; keep warm. Heat remaining ingredients except cheese to boiling in skillet; stir-fry until vegetables are crisp-tender, 3 to 4 minutes. Stir in chicken; heat through. Sprinkle with cheese.

1 SERVING: Calories 290 (Calories from Fat 90); Fat 10g (Saturated 3g); Cholesterol 95mg; Sodium 370mg; Carbohydrate 10g (Dietary Fiber 3g); Protein 37g.

Chicken with Bell Peppers

4 servings

2 tablespoons vegetable oil
2 medium bell peppers, cut into
    1/4-inch strips
1 small onion, chopped (1/4 cup)
1 clove garlic, finely chopped
1 pound skinless boneless chicken breasts,
    cut into 1-inch pieces
1 teaspoon salt
1/8 teaspoon pepper
1/2 lemon
4 cups hot cooked couscous or rice

Heat oil in 10-inch skillet over medium-high heat. Cook bell peppers, onion and garlic in oil about 5 minutes, stirring occasionally, until peppers are almost tender. Stir in chicken, salt and pepper. Cook about 8 minutes, stirring occasionally, until chicken is no longer pink in center. Squeeze juice from lemon over chicken mixture. Serve with couscous.

1 SERVING: Calories 395 (Calories from Fat 90); Fat 10g (Saturated 2g); Cholesterol 60mg; Sodium 1,000mg; Carbohydrate 46g (Dietary Fiber 2g); Protein 32g.

Garlic Chicken Kiev

6 servings

3 tablespoons reduced-fat margarine,
    softened
1 tablespoon snipped fresh chives
    or parsley
1/8 teaspoon garlic powder
6 small skinless boneless chicken breast
    halves (about 3 pounds)
2 cups corn flakes, crushed
    (about 1 cup)
2 tablespoons chopped fresh parsley
1/2 teaspoon paprika
1/4 cup buttermilk or skim milk

Mix margarine, chives and garlic powder; shape into rectangle, 3 × 2 inches. Cover and freeze until firm, about 30 minutes. Remove excess fat from chicken; flatten each chicken breast half to 1/4-inch thickness between waxed paper or plastic wrap.

Heat oven to 425°. Cut margarine mixture crosswise into 6 pieces. Place 1 piece on center of each chicken breast. Fold long sides over margarine; fold up ends and secure with wooden pick. Mix corn flakes, parsley and paprika. Dip chicken into buttermilk; lightly and evenly coat with corn flake mixture. Place chicken breasts, seam sides down, in square pan, 9 × 9 × 2 inches, sprayed with nonstick cooking spray. Bake uncovered until chicken is done, about 35 minutes.

1 SERVING: Calories 190 (Calories from Fat 55); Fat 7g (Saturated 2g); Cholesterol 60mg; Sodium 210mg; Carbohydrate 9g (Dietary Fiber 0g); Protein 23g.

Microwave Directions: Prepare chicken as directed. Arrange coated chicken breasts, seam sides down, on microwavable rack in microwavable dish. Microwave uncovered on High 4 minutes; rotate dish 1/2 turn. Microwave until chicken is done, 4 to 6 minutes longer. Let stand uncovered 5 minutes.

Garlic Chicken and Mushrooms

4 servings

Without chicken, this becomes a delicious side dish, especially with grilled meat.

2 1/4 cups uncooked mafalde (mini-lasagna noodles) pasta (4 1/4 ounces)
2 tablespoons olive or vegetable oil
1 pound skinless boneless chicken breast halves, cut into 1/2-inch slices
8 cloves garlic, finely chopped
8 ounces whole mushrooms, cut into fourths
1/2 cup sliced green onions (5 medium)
1 can (14 1/2 ounces) diced tomatoes, undrained
1/2 cup chicken broth
1/2 teaspoon crushed red pepper
1/2 teaspoon cornstarch
1/2 teaspoon salt
1/2 cup chopped fresh cilantro or parsley

Cook and drain pasta as directed on package. Heat 1 tablespoon of the oil in 12-inch skillet over medium-high heat. Cook chicken in oil 3 to 4 minutes, stirring occasionally, until light brown. Remove from skillet; keep warm.

Heat remaining 1 tablespoon oil in skillet over medium-high heat. Cook garlic in oil, stirring occasionally, until golden. Stir in mushrooms and green onions. Cook 2 minutes, stirring occasionally. Stir in tomatoes, broth, red pepper, cornstarch and salt. Heat to boiling; reduce heat to medium. Cook 4 to 5 minutes, stirring occasionally, until thickened. Stir in pasta, chicken and cilantro.

1 SERVING: Calories 395 (Calories from Fat 100); Fat 11g (Saturated 2g); Cholesterol 60mg; Sodium 600mg; Carbohydrate 44g (Dietary Fiber 3g); Protein 33g.

Cholesterol Myths

Fact: Margarine, vegetable oil and peanut butter contain a lot of cholesterol.

False: These foods from vegetable sources don't provide cholesterol; however, they do provide a concentrated source of fat and calories. Only animal foods contain cholesterol.

Fact: Chicken and fish are cholesterol free.

False: Contrary to popular belief, chicken and fish do contain cholesterol. These foods supply less fat and saturated fat in general than do red meats, such as beef and pork.

Fact: Foods low in cholesterol are low in fat too.

False: Whether or not a food contains cholesterol doesn't have any bearing on the amount of fat that's present in the food. Cholesterol is only found in foods of animal origin: meats, fish, poultry, some seafood and dairy products. But fat is found in both plant and animal foods.

Spicy Shredded Chicken and Vegetables

6 servings

Using precut vegetables, such as broccoli slaw or coleslaw mix, is a real time-saver.

1/3 cup fat-free reduced-sodium
     chicken broth
1/2 pound skinless boneless chicken
     breast halves
2 cups broccoli slaw or coleslaw mix
1/2 medium red bell pepper, cut into
     2×1/4-inch pieces (1/2 cup)
2 tablespoons brown bean sauce*
2 teaspoons sugar
2 teaspoons chili puree with garlic
1 teaspoon finely chopped gingerroot
4 cups hot cooked rice

Heat broth to boiling in 10-inch skillet. Add chicken; reduce heat to medium-low. Cover and cook about 8 minutes or until juice of chicken is no longer pink when centers of thickest pieces are cut. Remove chicken from broth; reserve broth. Cool chicken 5 minutes. Cut chicken into 2-inch pieces. Shred pieces with 2 knives or forks.

Spray nonstick wok or 12-inch skillet with nonstick cooking spray; heat over medium-high heat until cooking spray starts to bubble. Add broccoli slaw; stir-fry about 2 minutes or until crisp-tender. Add bell pepper and chicken; stir-fry 1 minute. Stir bean sauce, sugar, chili puree and gingerroot into reserved broth. Pour into wok; stir-fry about 1 minute or until heated through. Serve over rice.

1 SERVING: Calories 185 (Calories from Fat 10); Fat 1g (Saturated 0g); Cholesterol 20mg; Sodium 110mg; Carbohydrate 34g (Dietary Fiber 1g); Protein 11g.

Hoisin sauce can be substituted for the brown bean sauce. Decrease sugar to 1 teaspoon.

Flavor Boosters

For ultra flavor, ultra fast:

- Rub boneless, skinless chicken breasts with a paste of finely chopped garlic, olive oil, salt, pepper and chopped fresh herbs, such as thyme, oregano, tarragon or basil. Grill or broil in the usual way.

- Season chicken with a premixed spice blend.

- Brush chicken with steak sauce, barbecue sauce, flavored mustard or chutney.

- Poach chicken in fruit juice or wine for mellow flavors.

Spicy Shredded Chicken and Vegetables

Cilantro Pesto Chicken

4 servings

You can make the Cilantro Pesto ahead of time and keep it covered in the refrigerator. It will keep up to 3 days.

Cilantro Pesto (right)
6 ounces uncooked fettuccine
2 teaspoons vegetable oil
1 cup 1-inch diagonal slices asparagus
    (4 ounces)
1 cup sliced fresh mushrooms (3 ounces)
1 medium onion, chopped (1/2 cup)
1 1/2 cups cut-up cooked chicken

Prepare Cilantro Pesto. Cook and drain fettuccine as directed on package. While fettuccine is cooking, heat oil in 10-inch nonstick skillet over high heat. Cook asparagus, mushrooms and onion in oil 4 minutes, stirring frequently, until asparagus is crisp-tender; reduce heat. Stir in chicken. Heat through; remove from heat. Add hot fettuccine and pesto to skillet; toss. Serve immediately.

CILANTRO PESTO

1/4 cup reduced-sodium chicken broth
2 tablespoons olive or vegetable oil
2 teaspoons lemon juice
1/4 cup grated Parmesan cheese
1 tablespoon pine nuts
2 cloves garlic
1 cup firmly packed fresh cilantro

Place all ingredients in blender or food processor in the order listed. Cover and blend on medium speed, stopping occasionally to scrape sides, until almost smooth.

1 SERVING: Calories 375 (Calories from Fat 155); Fat 17g (Saturated 4g); Cholesterol 85mg; Sodium 180mg; Carbohydrate 34g (Dietary Fiber 4g); Protein 25g.

Chicken-Rice Casserole

6 servings

1/4 cup reduced-fat margarine
1/3 cup all-purpose flour
3/4 teaspoon salt
1/8 teaspoon pepper
1 1/2 cups skim milk
1 cup chicken broth
2 cups cut-up cooked chicken or turkey
    (about 10 ounces)
1 1/2 cups cooked white rice or wild rice
1/3 cup chopped green bell pepper
1/4 cup slivered almonds
2 tablespoons chopped pimiento
1 can (4 ounces) mushroom stems and
    pieces, drained
Parsley, if desired

Heat oven to 350°. Heat margarine in 2-quart saucepan over medium heat. Stir in flour, salt and pepper. Cook, stirring constantly, until bubbly; remove from heat. Stir in milk and broth. Heat to boiling, stirring constantly. Boil and stir 1 minute. Stir in remaining ingredients. Pour into ungreased 2-quart casserole or square baking dish, 8 × 8 × 2 inches. Bake uncovered 40 to 45 minutes or until bubbly. Garnish with parsley.

1 SERVING: Calories 280 (Calories from Fat 110); Fat 12g (Saturated 3g); Cholesterol 40mg; Sodium 520mg; Carbohydrate 25g (Dietary Fiber 1g); Protein 19g.

Sauerkraut and Chicken Casserole

4 servings

Four fully cooked smoked pork loin chops can be used in place of the chicken. Reduce baking time to about 30 minutes, or until pork and sauerkraut are hot. Serve with buttered, boiled potatoes and string beans.

1 can (16 ounces) sauerkraut, drained
4 skinless boneless chicken breast halves
    (about 1 pound)
1 teaspoon garlic powder
3/4 cup barbecue sauce

Heat oven to 350°. Spread sauerkraut evenly in bottom of ungreased rectangular baking dish, 11 × 7 × 1 1/2 inches. Place chicken on sauerkraut; sprinkle with garlic powder. Spread barbecue sauce over chicken. Cover and bake about 1 hour or until juice of chicken is no longer pink when centers of thickest pieces are cut.

1 SERVING: Calories 190 (Calories from Fat 45); Fat 5g (Saturated 1g); Cholesterol 70mg; Sodium 1190mg; Carbohydrate 11g (Dietary Fiber 3g); Protein 27g.

Coconut Curry Chicken

4 servings

Toasted coconut adds an exotic tropical flavor, but just 2 tablespoons contain 4 grams of fat. By limiting the amount of coconut you use and using reduced-fat coconut milk, you can enjoy this favorite taste without excess fat and calories.

3/4 pound skinless boneless chicken breast halves
1 tablespoon curry powder
1 teaspoon vegetable oil
1 small onion, cut into 2 × 1/4-inch slices
1 small zucchini, cut into 1/4-inch slices
1 medium green bell pepper, cut into 3/4-inch pieces
1/3 cup reduced-fat (lite) coconut milk
1 tablespoon brown bean sauce
1 teaspoon grated gingerroot
1/2 teaspoon salt
2 tablespoons shredded coconut, toasted*
Hot cooked rice, if desired

Trim fat from chicken. Rub curry powder on chicken. Cut chicken into 3/4-inch pieces. Let stand 10 minutes. Spray 12-inch nonstick skillet or wok with nonstick cooking spray; heat over medium-high heat. Add chicken; stir-fry 2 minutes. Move chicken to side of skillet. Add oil to center of skillet. Add onion, zucchini and bell pepper; stir-fry 2 minutes. Add coconut milk, bean sauce, gingerroot and salt; cook and stir until sauce coats vegetables and chicken and is heated through. Sprinkle with coconut. Serve over rice.

1 SERVING: Calories 150 (Calories from Fat 55); Fat 6g (Saturated 0g); Cholesterol 45mg; Sodium 380mg; Carbohydrate 7g (Dietary Fiber 2g); Protein 19g.

*To toast coconut, heat oven to 350°. Bake in ungreased pan 5 to 7 minutes, stirring occasionally, until golden brown.

Shopping Smart

- Turkey and chicken franks are not necessarily low in fat. Check their food labels.

- Half of chicken's calories are in the skin. Buy skinless parts or remove skin before eating.

- For the leanest ground turkey available, buy ground turkey breast. Most butchers will grind it for you.

Coconut Curry Chicken

Chinese Chicken Salad with Peanut Dressing

4 servings

Leftover egg roll skins can be used to make the crispy wonton strips. They are also great for low-fat snacking!

Crispy Wonton Strips (right)
Warm Peanut Dressing (right)
1 can (8 ounces) pineapple tidbits in juice, drained and juice reserved
1/2 pound Chinese pea pods (2 cups)
6 cups shredded romaine lettuce
1 large red bell pepper, cut lengthwise into fourths and sliced crosswise
1 cup shredded cooked chicken breast
1/4 cup sliced green onions (3 medium)

Prepare Crispy Wonton Strips and Warm Peanut Dressing, using reserved pineapple juice for the dressing recipe. Remove strings from pea pods. Place pea pods in boiling water. Cover and cook 1 minute; drain. Immediately rinse with cold water; drain. Cut pea pods in half. Toss romaine, pea pods, bell pepper and pineapple. Divide among 4 plates. Top with chicken, peanut dressing and green onions. Garnish with wonton strips.

CRISPY WONTON STRIPS

1 tablespoon water
1 tablespoon soy sauce
Dash of garlic powder
12 wonton skins
Sesame seed, if desired

Heat oven to 350°. Spray cookie sheet with nonstick cooking spray. Mix water, soy sauce and garlic powder; brush on wonton skins. Cut each skin into 3/8-inch strips. Place strips on cookie sheet. Sprinkle with sesame seed. Bake 6 to 8 minutes or until golden brown; cool.

WARM PEANUT DRESSING

1/3 cup unsweetened pineapple juice
1/4 cup water
1 1/4 teaspoons ground coriander
1 teaspoon cornstarch
2 cloves garlic, finely chopped
2 tablespoons creamy peanut butter
1 1/2 tablespoons cider vinegar
2 teaspoons soy sauce
1 1/2 teaspoons grated gingerroot

Heat all ingredients to boiling in 1-quart saucepan, stirring constantly. Stir until smooth; remove from heat. Let stand 5 minutes.

1 SERVING: Calories 285 (Calories from Fat 65); Fat 7g (Saturated 1g); Cholesterol 25mg; Sodium 650mg; Carbohydrate 39g (Dietary Fiber 4g); Protein 20g.

Chinese Chicken Salad with Peanut Dressing

Jamaican Jerk Chicken

4 servings

The tradition of "jerking" meat is unique to Jamaica. Originally, the hot spicy seasonings were applied to wild boar to make it more edible. The tradition was then extended to meat and chicken. This recipe is spicy, hot and very colorful with its papaya, mango, red onion and yellow pepper.

2 tablespoons chopped fresh or 2 teaspoons
    dried thyme leaves
1/2 teaspoon crushed red pepper
1/2 teaspoon salt
1/4 teaspoon ground allspice
4 skinless boneless chicken breast halves
    (about 1 pound)
1 cup sliced papaya
1 cup sliced mango
1 medium red onion, sliced
1 medium yellow bell pepper, cut into
    1/4-inch strips

Heat oven to 375°. Mix thyme, red pepper, salt and allspice. Rub chicken breast halves with thyme mixture. Place chicken in greased rectangular pan, 13 × 9 × 2 inches. Cover and bake 30 minutes. Turn chicken; arrange remaining ingredients around chicken in pan. Bake uncovered 20 to 30 minutes longer or until juice is no longer pink when centers of thickest pieces are cut.

1 SERVING: Calories 190 (Calories from Fat 35); Fat 4g (Saturated 1g); Cholesterol 65mg; Sodium 330mg; Carbohydrate 15g (Dietary Fiber 3g); Protein 27g.

Spicy Curried Chicken with Couscous

4 servings

4 small skinless boneless chicken breast
    halves (about 2 pounds)
3 teaspoons vegetable oil
1/4 teaspoon salt
1/8 teaspoon ground red pepper (cayenne)
1 cup chopped unpeeled green apple
    (about 1 medium)
1/2 cup chopped onion (about 1 medium)
1 clove garlic, finely chopped
2 teaspoons curry powder
2 teaspoons grated orange peel
1 cup chicken broth or water
1/4 cup raisins
1 tablespoon cornstarch
1/4 cup cold water
2 cups hot cooked couscous or rice

Remove excess fat from chicken; cut chicken into 1-inch pieces. Heat 2 teaspoons of the oil in 10-inch nonstick skillet until hot. Cook and stir chicken, salt and red pepper in oil over medium heat until chicken is done, about 5 minutes; remove chicken. Add remaining 1 teaspoon oil, the apple, onion, garlic, curry powder and orange peel; cook and stir until apple is tender, about 7 minutes.

Stir in chicken broth and raisins. Heat to boiling, stirring constantly. Mix cornstarch and water; stir into chicken mixture. Boil and stir 1 minute. Serve over couscous.

1 SERVING: Calories 370 (Calories from Fat 65); Fat 7g (Saturated 2g); Cholesterol 85mg; Sodium 790mg; Carbohydrate 42g (Dietary Fiber 2g); Protein 37g.

Sweet-and-Sour Chicken

6 servings

We baked crumb-coated chicken in a very hot oven to keep the crispness of the original deep-fried recipe without the fat. Stir the crisp chicken into the sauce just before serving.

**1 pound skinless boneless chicken breast
    halves or thighs**
1 egg white
1 teaspoon water
2 tablespoons all-purpose flour
**2 tablespoons crushed rice crackers,
    cornmeal or soft bread crumbs**
1/4 teaspoon baking soda
1/4 cup cold water
2 tablespoons cornstarch
**1 can (8 ounces) pineapple chunks in juice,
    drained and juice reserved**
1/2 cup sugar
1/3 cup seasoned rice vinegar
2 teaspoons dark soy sauce
1 clove garlic, finely chopped
1/4 teaspoon salt
**2 medium Roma (plum) tomatoes,
    cut into eighths**
**1 medium green bell pepper, cut into
    1-inch pieces**

Cut chicken into 3/4-inch pieces. Mix egg white and 1 teaspoon water; toss with chicken in medium glass or plastic bowl. Let stand 10 minutes.

Heat oven to 425°. Spray nonstick cookie sheet with nonstick cooking spray. Mix flour, crushed crackers and baking soda in medium bowl. Remove chicken pieces from egg mixture; dip into flour mixture, turning to coat. Place chicken on cookie sheet; spray with cooking spray about 10 seconds or until surface of chicken appears moist. Bake 10 to 15 minutes, turning once, until brown and no longer pink in center.

Mix 1/4 cup cold water and the cornstarch. Heat reserved pineapple juice, the sugar, vinegar, soy sauce, garlic and salt to boiling in nonstick wok or 12-inch skillet, stirring frequently. Stir in cornstarch mixture; cook and stir about 1 minute or until thickened. Add tomatoes, bell pepper and pineapple; cook and stir 1 minute. Stir in chicken.

1 SERVING: Calories 235 (Calories from Fat 45); Fat 5g (Saturated 2g); Cholesterol 40mg; Sodium 310mg; Carbohydrate 32g (Dietary Fiber 1g); Protein 16g.

HEALTHY HINT

Marinating chicken adds flavor and makes for juicy chicken. Marinate boneless, skinless chicken breasts 1 to 2 hours. Bone-in chicken pieces can be marinated up to 24 hours.

Chicken Lo Mein

5 servings

Low-fat boiled vegetables and noodles soak up maximum flavor when they are stir-fried in a fresh gingerroot sauce.

1/2 pound skinless boneless chicken
    breast halves
1/2 pound snap pea pods, strings removed
    (2 cups)
6 ounces baby-cut carrots, cut lengthwise
    into 1/4-inch sticks (1 cup)
1/2 package (9-ounce size) refrigerated
    linguine, cut into 2-inch pieces
2 teaspoons cornstarch
1 teaspoon sugar
2 teaspoons water
1/3 cup fat-free reduced-sodium
    chicken broth
1 tablespoon soy sauce
4 cloves garlic, finely chopped
2 teaspoons finely chopped gingerroot
Toasted sesame seed, if desired

Cut chicken breast halves lengthwise into 2-inch pieces; cut pieces crosswise into 1/2-inch strips. Heat 2 quarts water to boiling in 3-quart saucepan. Add pea pods, carrots and linguine; heat to boiling. Boil 2 to 3 minutes or until linguine is just tender; drain. Mix cornstarch, sugar and water. Mix broth, soy sauce, garlic and gingerroot; stir in cornstarch mixture.

Spray nonstick wok or 12-inch skillet with nonstick cooking spray; heat over medium-high heat until cooking spray starts to bubble. Add chicken; stir-fry about 2 minutes or until chicken is white. Stir broth mixture; stir into chicken mixture. Stir in pea pods, carrots and linguine. Cook 2 minutes, stirring occasionally. Sprinkle with toasted sesame seed.

1 SERVING: Calories 185 (Calories from Fat 20); Fat 2g (Saturated 1g); Cholesterol 25mg; Sodium 270mg; Carbohydrate 29g (Dietary Fiber 2g); Protein 15g.

Chicken Gazpacho Salad

6 servings

1 package (14 ounces) uncooked fusilli pasta
2 cups cubed cooked chicken
1 cup chopped cucumber (about 1 small)
1 cup chopped yellow or red bell pepper
    (about 1 medium)
1 cup chopped tomato (about 1 large)
3/4 cup spicy eight-vegetable juice
1/4 cup lemon juice
1/2 teaspoon pepper
1/4 teaspoon salt
1 clove garlic, finely chopped

Cook pasta as directed on package; drain. Mix pasta and remaining ingredients. Serve immediately.

1 SERVING: Calories 350 (Calories from Fat 35); Fat 4g (Saturated 2g); Cholesterol 40mg; Sodium 510mg; Carbohydrate 58g (Dietary Fiber 2g); Protein 23g.

Chicken Gazpacho Salad

Hot Chicken Salad with Plum Sauce

4 servings

2 teaspoons olive or vegetable oil
4 skinless boneless chicken breast halves
    (about 1 pound)
1 can (16 ounces) purple plums in juice,
    rinsed, drained and pitted
1 tablespoon lemon juice
2 teaspoons packed brown sugar
1/4 teaspoon ground ginger
1/8 teaspoon crushed red pepper
1 clove garlic
4 cups shredded Chinese cabbage
1 cup bean sprouts (about 2 ounces)
1 tablespoon thinly sliced green onion
    with top (about 1/2 medium)

Heat oil in 10-inch nonstick skillet over medium heat. Cook chicken breast halves, turning once, about 10 minutes or until done. Place remaining ingredients except cabbage, bean sprouts and green onion in blender or food processor. Cover and blend on high speed or process about 30 seconds or until smooth. Heat sauce if desired. Arrange cabbage, bean sprouts and green onion on 4 serving plates. Top with chicken. Spoon plum sauce over chicken.

1 SERVING: Calories 205 (Calories from Fat 35); Fat 4g (Saturated 2g); Cholesterol 65mg; Sodium 140mg; Carbohydrate 16g (Dietary Fiber 2g); Protein 28g.

Warm Thai Chicken Salad

4 servings

Be sure to wear rubber or plastic gloves when seeding and chopping the jalapeño chili to prevent irritating your skin.

1 tablespoon vegetable oil
1 clove garlic, finely chopped
1 jalapeño chili, seeded and finely chopped
1 pound skinless boneless chicken breast
    halves, cut into 1/2-inch strips
1 large red bell pepper, cut into 1-inch pieces
1 medium cucumber, cut lengthwise in half
    then crosswise into 1/4-inch slices (2 cups)
2 green onions, sliced
1/4 cup lime juice
2 tablespoons soy sauce
1 tablespoon chopped fresh cilantro
2 teaspoons sugar
1/4 teaspoon pepper
Salad greens
Dry roasted peanuts, if desired
Lime slices, if desired

Heat oil in 10-inch skillet or wok over medium-high heat. Cook garlic and chili in oil 30 seconds, stirring frequently. Stir in chicken. Cook, stirring occasionally, until chicken is no longer pink in center. Add bell pepper, cucumber and green onions; toss with chicken mixture. Stir in remaining ingredients except salad greens. Heat to boiling, stirring constantly; boil and stir 30 seconds. Remove from heat.

Divide salad greens among 4 dinner plates. Spoon chicken mixture over salad greens, using slotted spoon. Drizzle liquid from skillet over chicken mixture and salad greens. Garnish with peanuts and lime slices.

1 SERVING: Calories 200 (Calories from Fat 65); Fat 7g (Saturated 2g); Cholesterol 60mg; Sodium 580mg; Carbohydrate 9g (Dietary Fiber 1g); Protein 26g.

Chicken and Tortellini Salad

4 servings

1 package (8 ounces) cheese-filled tortellini
1 1/2 cups cut-up cooked chicken or turkey
(about 8 ounces)
1/3 cup dry white wine or chicken broth
2 tablespoons olive or vegetable oil
2 tablespoons lemon juice
1 tablespoon chopped fresh or 1 teaspoon
dried tarragon leaves
1 teaspoon sugar
1/2 teaspoon salt
1/4 teaspoon pepper
3 cups bite-size pieces of salad greens
(spinach, leaf lettuce, romaine)
1 small red or green bell pepper, cut into
1/2-inch pieces

Cook tortellini as directed on package; drain. Rinse with cold water; drain. Mix tortellini and chicken in large bowl. Shake wine, oil, lemon juice, tarragon, sugar, salt and pepper in tightly covered container. Stir into tortellini mixture. Cover and refrigerate at least 2 hours. Toss tortellini mixture with salad greens and bell pepper just before serving.

1 SERVING: Calories 250 (Calories from Fat 70); Fat 8g (Saturated 4g); Cholesterol 30mg; Sodium 220mg; Carbohydrate 31g (Dietary Fiber 1g); Protein 15g.

Curried Chicken-Rice Salad

6 servings

1/2 cup reduced-fat mayonnaise or
salad dressing
1/2 cup plain nonfat yogurt
3/4 teaspoon curry powder
1/2 teaspoon ground ginger
1/4 teaspoon salt
1/4 teaspoon ground red pepper (cayenne)
3 cups cold cooked rice
2 cups cut-up cooked chicken
2 medium stalks celery, sliced (1 cup)
1 small bell pepper, chopped (1/2 cup)
1 can (15 1/4 ounces) pineapple chunks
in juice, drained
Salad greens
2 medium tomatoes, cut into wedges

Mix mayonnaise, yogurt, curry powder, ginger, salt and red pepper in large bowl. Stir in rice, chicken, celery, bell pepper and pineapple. Cover and refrigerate about 2 hours or until chilled. Just before serving, line 6 salad plates with salad greens. Divide salad evenly among plates. Garnish with tomato wedges.

1 SERVING: Calories 310 (Calories from Fat 90); Fat 10g (Saturated 2g); Cholesterol 40mg; Sodium 270mg; Carbohydrate 39g (Dietary Fiber 2g); Protein 18g.

Stir-fried Chicken Pitas

6 servings

3/4 pound skinless boneless chicken breast,
    cut into 1-inch pieces
1 small zucchini, sliced
1 medium carrot, shredded
1 small onion, sliced and separated
    into rings
1 teaspoon chopped fresh or 1/4 teaspoon
    dried basil leaves
1/4 teaspoon chopped fresh or
    1/4 teaspoon dried oregano leaves
1/4 teaspoon pepper
1 medium tomato, chopped (3/4 cup)
3 pita breads (6 inches in diameter),
    cut in half to form pockets
1/3 cup shredded mozzarella cheese

Spray 10-inch nonstick skillet with nonstick cooking spray; heat skillet over medium-high heat until hot. Add chicken; stir-fry 3 to 4 minutes or until no longer pink in center. Add zucchini, carrot, onion, basil, oregano and pepper; stir-fry 2 to 3 minutes or until vegetables are crisp-tender. Stir in tomato. Fill pita breads with chicken mixture. Sprinkle with cheese.

1 SERVING: Calories 200 (Calories from Fat 30); Fat 3g (Saturated 1g); Cholesterol 35mg; Sodium 270mg; Carbohydrate 35g (Dietary Fiber 2g); Protein 18g.

Chicken-Artichoke Toss

6 servings

3 cups uncooked radiatore (nugget) pasta
    (9 ounces)
1 jar (6 ounces) marinated artichoke hearts,
    undrained
1 pound skinless boneless chicken breast
    halves, cut into 1/2-inch slices
3 cups sliced mushrooms (8 ounces)
1 jar (7 ounces) roasted red peppers, sliced
3/4 cup chicken broth
1/2 cup dry white wine (or nonalcoholic)
    or apple juice
1 tablespoon cornstarch
1/2 teaspoon salt
1/4 teaspoon pepper
1 tablespoon chopped fresh parsley

Cook and drain pasta as directed on package. Drain liquid from artichokes into 10-inch skillet; heat over medium-high heat. Cook chicken in liquid 3 minutes, stirring occasionally. Stir in mushrooms. Cook 4 to 6 minutes, stirring occasionally, until chicken is light brown and no longer pink. Stir in artichokes and peppers.

Shake broth, wine, cornstarch, salt and pepper in tightly covered container. Gradually stir into chicken mixture. Heat to boiling, stirring constantly. Boil and stir 1 minute. Toss with pasta. Sprinkle with parsley.

1 SERVING: Calories 370 (Calories from Fat 35); Fat 4g (Saturated 1g); Cholesterol 40mg; Sodium 400mg; Carbohydrate 59g (Dietary Fiber 3g); Protein 27g.

Chicken-Artichoke Toss

Honey-Glazed Turkey with Roasted Pineapple

16 servings

4 1/2- to 5-pound turkey breast
1 pineapple
1/2 cup dry white wine or apple juice
2 tablespoons honey
2 tablespoons soy sauce
1 teaspoon finely chopped gingerroot
   or 1/2 teaspoon ground ginger
1 large clove garlic, finely chopped
2 teaspoons cornstarch
2 tablespoons cold water

Heat oven to 325°. Place turkey breast, skin side up, on rack in shallow roasting pan. Insert meat thermometer so tip is in thickest part of meat and does not touch bone. Roast uncovered 1 hour.

Peel pineapple. Cut lengthwise into 16 wedges; remove core. Cut each wedge in half crosswise to make 32 wedges. Mix wine, honey, soy sauce, gingerroot and garlic. Arrange pineapple on rack around turkey. Brush turkey and pineapple with wine mixture. Roast uncovered about 1 hour, brushing turkey and pineapple frequently with wine mixture, until thermometer reads 170° and juice is no longer pink when center is cut. Remove turkey and pineapple; keep warm.

Pour drippings into measuring cup; skim off any excess fat. Add enough water to drippings to measure 1 cup. Heat drippings to boiling in 1-quart saucepan. Mix cornstarch and cold water; stir into drippings. Boil and stir 1 minute. Serve with turkey.

1 SERVING: Calories 210 (Calories from Fat 80); Fat 9g (Saturated 2g); Cholesterol 70mg; Sodium 190mg; Carbohydrate 7g (Dietary Fiber 0g); Protein 25g.

Turkey Pie

6 servings

2 cups cut-up cooked turkey or chicken
1 jar (4 1/2 ounces) sliced mushrooms,
   drained
1/2 cup sliced green onions
1 cup shredded natural Swiss cheese
   (4 ounces)
1 1/3 cups skim milk
3/4 cup Bisquick baking mix
2 eggs
2 egg whites

Heat oven to 400°. Sprinkle turkey, mushroom, green onions and cheese in pie plate, 10 × 1 1/2 inches, sprayed with nonstick cooking spray. Beat remaining ingredients until smooth, 15 seconds in blender on high speed or 1 minute with hand beater. Pour into pie plate. Bake until golden brown and knife inserted halfway between center and edge comes out clean, 30 to 35 minutes. Let stand 5 minutes before cutting.

1 SERVING: Calories 240 (Calories from Fat 90); Fat 10g (Saturated 4g); Cholesterol 140mg; Sodium 320mg; Carbohydrate 14g (Dietary Fiber 0g); Protein 23g.

Curried Turkey Spaghetti

4 servings

Curry is a catchall term used to refer to many types of sauces, all of which have curry powder as a dominant ingredient. To vary this curry, try spinach or whole wheat pasta.

1/2 pound ground turkey or lean
　　ground beef
1/2 cup chopped onion (about 1 medium)
1 clove garlic, finely chopped
3/4 cup chopped unpeeled tart eating apple
　　(about 1 medium)
1/4 cup chopped fresh parsley
1 1/2 teaspoons curry powder
1/2 teaspoon ground cumin
1/8 teaspoon ground red pepper (cayenne)
1/4 cup unsweetened apple juice
1 can (16 ounces) whole tomatoes,
　　undrained
6 ounces uncooked spaghetti
2 tablespoons chopped dry-roasted peanuts

Cook ground turkey, onion and garlic in 10-inch nonstick skillet over medium heat, stirring frequently, until turkey is no longer pink; drain. Stir in remaining ingredients except spaghetti and peanuts; break up tomatoes. Heat to boiling; reduce heat. Simmer uncovered about 5 minutes or until apple is tender, stirring occasionally. Cook spaghetti as directed on package; drain. Serve sauce over spaghetti. Sprinkle with peanuts.

1 SERVING: Calories 350 (Calories from Fat 70); Fat 8g (Saturated 2g); Cholesterol 35mg; Sodium 260mg; Carbohydrate 50g (Dietary Fiber 2g); Protein 21g.

Spicy Mexican Torte

8 servings

1/2 pound turkey Italian sausage links
2 medium onions, chopped (1 cup)
2 cloves garlic, finely chopped
1 can (4 ounces) chopped green chilis,
　　drained
8 flour tortillas (8 to 10 inches in diameter)*
2 cups shredded reduced-fat Monterey Jack
　　cheese (8 ounces)
1 can (16 ounces) fat-free refried beans
1 jar (7 ounces) roasted red bell peppers,
　　drained
Salsa, sour cream or guacamole, if desired

Remove casings from sausage links. Cut sausages into 1/4-inch slices. Cook sausage, onions and garlic in 10-inch nonstick skillet over medium heat, stirring occasionally, until sausage is brown; drain. Stir in chilis; set aside.

Heat oven to 400°. Grease pie plate, 10 × 1 1/2 inches. Place 2 tortillas in pie plate. Spread with half of the sausage mixture; sprinkle with 1 cup of the cheese. Place 2 tortillas on cheese; spread with beans. Place 2 tortillas on beans; top with bell peppers. Place 2 tortillas on peppers; spread with remaining sausage mixture. Sprinkle with remaining 1 cup cheese. Cover and bake 40 minutes or until cheese is melted and center is hot. Cool 10 minutes before cutting. Serve with salsa.

1 SERVING: Calories 320 (Calories from Fat 100); Fat 11g (Saturated 4g); Cholesterol 35mg; Sodium 1,030mg; Carbohydrate 39g (Dietary Fiber 5g); Protein 21g.

*16 corn tortillas (5 to 6 inches in diameter) can be substituted for the flour tortillas. Overlap 4 corn tortillas for each layer.

Chimichangas

8 servings

1 pound lean ground turkey
1 small onion, finely chopped (1/4 cup)
1 clove garlic, finely chopped
1/4 cup slivered almonds
1/4 cup raisins
1 tablespoon red wine vinegar
1 teaspoon ground red chilis or chili powder
1/2 teaspoon salt
1/4 teaspoon ground cinnamon
1/8 teaspoon ground cloves
1 medium tomato, chopped (3/4 cup)
1 can (4 ounces) chopped green chilis
8 flour tortillas (8 to 10 inches in diameter), warmed
1 egg, beaten
Salsa, if desired

Cook turkey, onion and garlic in 10-inch non-stick skillet over medium heat 8 to 10 minutes, stirring occasionally, until turkey is no longer pink; drain. Stir in almonds, raisins, vinegar, ground red chilis, salt, cinnamon, cloves, tomato and green chilis. Heat to boiling; reduce heat. Simmer uncovered 20 minutes, stirring occasionally.

Spoon about 1/2 cup turkey mixture onto center of each tortilla. Fold one end of tortilla up about 1 inch over turkey mixture; fold right and left sides over folded end, overlapping. Fold remaining end down. Brush edges with egg to seal.

Heat oven to 400°. Spray chimichangas with cooking spray. Place seam sides down in ungreased jelly roll pan, 15 1/2 × 10 1/2 × 1 inch. Bake 8 to 10 minutes or until tortillas begin to brown and filling is hot. Serve chimichangas with salsa.

1 SERVING: Calories 285 (Calories from Fat 100); Fat 11g (Saturated 3g); Cholesterol 65mg; Sodium 540mg; Carbohydrate 31g (Dietary Fiber 2g); Protein 17g.

Turkey Teriyaki Meatballs

4 servings

You can substitute angel hair pasta for the Japanese curly noodles in this recipe.

1 package (5 ounces) Japanese curly noodles
3/4 pound ground turkey breast
1/4 cup seasoned dry bread crumbs
1 egg white
1 cup chicken broth
1/4 cup teriyaki sauce
1 tablespoon rice wine vinegar
2 cups sliced shiitake or other mushrooms (6 ounces)
1 medium red bell pepper, cut into 1-inch pieces (1 cup)
1 large zucchini, cut into 1/4-inch slices (2 cups)
1 tablespoon cornstarch
2 tablespoons water

Cook and drain noodles as directed on package. While noodles are cooking, mix turkey, bread crumbs and egg white. Divide mixture into 12 equal pieces; roll each into a ball with palm of hand. Cook meatballs in 12-inch non-stick skillet over medium-high heat 5 minutes or until brown on all sides; reduce heat.

Mix broth, teriyaki sauce and vinegar; pour into skillet. Cover and simmer 10 minutes. Stir in mushrooms, bell pepper and zucchini. Cook 3 minutes, stirring occasionally, until bell pepper is crisp-tender and meatballs are no longer pink in center. Move meatballs to side of skillet. Mix cornstarch and water; stir into sauce in skillet. Cook 1 to 2 minutes, stirring constantly, until thickened and bubbly. Serve over noodles.

1 SERVING: Calories 220 (Calories from Fat 45); Fat 5g (Saturated 2g); Cholesterol 50mg; Sodium 1,160mg; Carbohydrate 20g (Dietary Fiber 2g); Protein 26g.

Turkey Teriyaki Meatballs

Turkey with Chipotle Sauce

4 servings

Chipotle chilis are ripened, dried and smoked jalapeño chilis. These wrinkled brown chilis have a smoky flavor and can be purchased in specialty food shops and in the gourmet section of many supermarkets.

Chipotle Sauce (below)
2 teaspoons vegetable oil
1 pound boneless turkey breast slices,
    cutlets or turkey tenderloin steaks
    (1/4 to 1/2 inch thick)*
3/4 cup chopped seeded tomato
    (about 1 medium)
2 tablespoons sliced green onion tops

Prepare Chipotle Sauce; keep warm. Heat oil in 10-inch nonstick skillet over medium-high until hot. Cook turkey in oil, turning once, until no longer pink, 8 to 10 minutes. Arrange on serving plate; top with Chipotle Sauce. Sprinkle with tomato and green onion tops.

CHIPOTLE SAUCE

1/2 cup plain nonfat yogurt
2 tablespoons chopped green onions
1 to 2 tablespoons chopped, seeded
    and drained canned chipotle chilis in
    adobo sauce
2 tablespoons creamy peanut butter
1/8 teaspoon salt

Place all ingredients in blender container. Cover and blend on medium speed, stopping blender occasionally to scrape sides, until well blended, about 20 seconds. Heat sauce over low heat until hot, stirring occasionally.

1 SERVING: Calories 210 (Calories from Fat 65); Fat 7g (Saturated 2g); Cholesterol 75mg; Sodium 180mg; Carbohydrate 6g (Dietary Fiber 0g); Protein 31g.

*If turkey pieces are too thick, flatten each piece to 1/4- to 1/2-inch thickness between plastic wrap or waxed paper.

Storing Uncooked and Cooked Turkey

Uncooked Turkey: Refrigerate uncooked, thawed turkey up to 2 days before roasting. Stuff turkey just before roasting.

Leftovers: Remove stuffing from turkey as soon as possible after serving. Promptly refrigerate turkey meat, stuffing and gravy separately.

Use turkey meat within 3 days or freeze up to 3 weeks. Use stuffing and gravy within 2 days and reheat thoroughly before serving.

Turkey with Chipotle Sauce

Eating Out

If you like to eat out, here are a few tips to help cut main dish calories at your favorite restaurants.

- Go to restaurants that you know broil, grill or bake foods. Ask how foods are prepared so you can make a low-calorie choice.

- Consider ordering an appetizer and a tossed green salad instead of a full meal.

- Some restaurants pride themselves on the amount of food they serve, but don't be tempted by the 1-pound steak, the 1/2-pound hamburger or the half chicken. When ordering meat, choose the smallest size piece of meat. A 3-ounce serving, a portion about the size of a deck of playing cards, is satisfying as well as nutritious.

- If portions are large, split your dinner with a friend or take half of it home for another meal.

- When ordering pasta, choose an appetizer portion, preferably without cream sauce—tomato sauces usually have fewer calories. Also avoid pesto sauces, which are oil-based.

Eat slowly and enjoy your meal fully. Cutting calories doesn't mean cutting out good food!

Turkey with Red Wine Sauce

4 servings

Boneless chicken breasts can easily be substituted for the turkey in this recipe.

1 tablespoon margarine or butter
1 clove garlic, finely chopped
1 pound boneless turkey breast slices, cutlets or turkey breast tenderloins (1/4 to 1/2 inch thick)*
1/2 cup dry red wine or chicken broth
1 tablespoon tomato paste or ketchup
3 cups sliced mushrooms (8 ounces)
2 medium green onions, chopped (2 tablespoons)

Heat margarine and garlic in 10-inch non-stick skillet over medium heat until margarine is melted and garlic begins to brown. Cook turkey in melted margarine 8 to 10 minutes, turning once, until no longer pink in center. Remove turkey from skillet; keep warm. Mix wine and tomato paste in skillet; stir in mushrooms. Cook uncovered over medium heat 3 to 5 minutes, stirring occasionally, until mushrooms are tender. Serve mushroom mixture over turkey. Sprinkle with onions.

1 SERVING: Calories 180 (Calories from Fat 55); Fat 6g (Saturated 2g); Cholesterol 65mg; Sodium 130mg; Carbohydrate 4g (Dietary Fiber 1g); Protein 28g.

*If turkey pieces are too thick, flatten each piece to 1/4- to 1/2-inch thickness between plastic wrap or waxed paper.

Turkey Pasta with Pesto

6 servings

Use a flavorful olive oil to make this pesto. Calories have been cut dramatically here, but the wonderful distinctive flavor remains.

Pesto (below)
2 cups uncooked rigatoni pasta
    (about 4 ounces)
2 cups 1/4-inch slices zucchini
    (about 2 medium)
1/3 cup chopped onion
1 medium carrot, cut into julienne strips
1 teaspoon olive or vegetable oil
3 cups cut-up cooked turkey or chicken

Prepare Pesto. Cook pasta as directed on package; drain. Cook and stir zucchini, onion and carrot in oil in 10-inch nonstick skillet over medium heat until zucchini is crisp-tender, 3 to 4 minutes. Stir in turkey; heat just until turkey is hot, about 3 minutes. Stir in pasta and pesto; toss until well coated. Heat until hot.

PESTO

2 tablespoons olive oil
1 tablespoon plain nonfat yogurt
2 teaspoons lemon juice
1/4 cup grated Parmesan cheese
1 tablespoon pine nuts
2 to 3 cloves garlic
1 cup firmly packed fresh basil leaves

Place all ingredients in blender container in order listed. Cover and blend on medium speed, stopping blender occasionally to scrape sides, until almost smooth, about 2 minutes.

1 SERVING: Calories 305 (Calories from Fat 110); Fat 6g (Saturated 2g); Cholesterol 40mg; Sodium 490mg; Carbohydrate 26g (Dietary Fiber 2g); Protein 19g.

Turkey Soft Tacos

4 servings

For a more healthful alternative, try using whole wheat flour tortillas.

1/2 cup chicken broth
1 medium onion, chopped (1/2 cup)
1 small red or green bell pepper, diced
    (1/2 cup)
1/2 cup whole kernel corn
1/2 pound lean ground turkey breast
4 cloves garlic, finely chopped
1/2 cup salsa
1/4 cup chopped fresh cilantro
8 flour tortillas (8 to 10 inches in diameter),
    warmed*
Nonfat sour cream, if desired

Heat broth to boiling in nonstick wok or 10-inch skillet. Add onion, bell pepper and corn; stir-fry 2 to 3 minutes or until vegetables are crisp-tender. Add turkey and garlic; stir-fry 2 minutes. Stir in salsa; cook about 5 minutes or until desired consistency. Stir in cilantro. Spoon scant 1/2 cup turkey mixture down center of each tortilla; roll up tortilla. Serve with sour cream.

1 SERVING: Calories 375 (Calories from Fat 70); Fat 8g (Saturated 2g); Cholesterol 35mg; Sodium 720mg; Carbohydrate 57g (Dietary Fiber 4g); Protein 23g.

To warm tortillas, heat them in a hot ungreased skilled or griddle for 30 seconds to 1 minute. Or wrap desired number of tortillas tightly in aluminum foil and heat in 250° oven for 15 minutes. Or place 2 tortillas at a time between dampened microwavable paper towels or microwavable plastic wrap and microwave on High for 15 to 20 seconds or until warm.

Seafood

Red Snapper Teriyaki (page 202)

(continued on next page)

Creamy Fish Chowder

8 servings

This rich-looking chowder is light on calories but full of flavor.

2 cups cubed potatoes (about 2 medium)
1 cup 1/4-inch slices carrots (about
    2 medium)
1/2 cup chopped onion (about 1 medium)
1 cup clam juice
1 cup water
1 tablespoon reduced-fat margarine
1/2 teaspoon salt
1/4 teaspoon pepper
1 pound haddock or other lean fish fillets,
    cut into 1-inch pieces
1 can (6 1/2 ounces) whole clams,
    undrained
1 can (12 ounces) evaporated skim milk
2 tablespoons chopped fresh chives
1 teaspoon paprika

Heat potatoes, carrots, onion, clam juice, water, margarine, salt and pepper to boiling in 3-quart saucepan; reduce heat. Cover and simmer 15 to 20 minutes or until potatoes are almost tender. Stir in fish and clams. Cover and heat to boiling; reduce heat. Simmer about 5 minutes or until fish flakes easily with fork. Stir in milk, chives, and paprika; heat through.

1 SERVING: Calories 220 (Calories from Fat 20); Fat 2g (Saturated 1g); Cholesterol 35mg; Sodium 1,070mg; Carbohydrate 32g (Dietary Fiber 1g); Protein 19g.

Crunchy Baked Fish

4 servings

1 pound flounder, sole or orange roughy
    fillets
1/3 cup finely crushed reduced-fat cheese
    crackers
1 teaspoon dried parsley flakes
3 tablespoons fat-free Western or French
    dressing

Heat oven to 450°. Spray cookie sheet with nonstick cooking spray. If fish fillets are large, cut into 4 serving pieces. Mix crackers and parsley. Brush both sides of fish with dressing; coat one side of fish with cracker mixture. Place fish, cracker sides up, on cookie sheet. Bake uncovered 10 to 15 minutes or until fish flakes easily with fork.

1 SERVING: Calories 145 (Calories from Fat 35); Fat 4g (Saturated 1g); Cholesterol 55mg; Sodium 290mg; Carbohydrate 8g (Dietary Fiber 1g); Protein 20g.

Baked Halibut with Tomatoes and Spices

4 servings

1 large onion, sliced
2 cloves garlic, chopped
2 jalapeño chilis, seeded and chopped
1 can (16 ounces) whole tomatoes, drained
    and chopped
2 tablespoons white vinegar
1 1/4 teaspoons ground cumin
3/4 teaspoon ground coriander
4 halibut or other lean fish steaks, about
    1 inch thick (about 2 pounds)
Chopped fresh cilantro, if desired

Heat oven to 350°. Spray 10-inch nonstick skillet with nonstick cooking spray. Cook onion, garlic and chilis in skillet over medium heat, stirring frequently, until onion is tender; reduce heat. Stir in remaining ingredients except fish steaks. Simmer uncovered over low heat 5 minutes, stirring occasionally.

Arrange fish in ungreased rectangular baking dish, 11 × 7 × 1 1/2 inches. Spoon tomato mixture over fish. Bake uncovered 25 to 30 minutes or until fish flakes easily with fork. Sprinkle with cilantro.

1 SERVING: Calories 245 (Calories from Fat 30); Fat 3g (Saturated 1g); Cholesterol 120mg; Sodium 370mg; Carbohydrate 11g (Dietary Fiber 2g); Protein 45g.

Fish and Fennel Rice

4 servings

The anise flavor of fennel is a perfect complement to tarragon and spinach.

1 pound sole or other lean fish fillets
1 cup chopped fennel (about 1/2 bulb)
1/4 cup chopped onion (about 1 small)
2 tablespoons water
2 cups chicken broth
1 cup uncooked regular long-grain rice
1 cup shredded spinach (about
    1 1/2 ounces)
Paprika
1 tablespoon chopped fresh or 1 teaspoon
    dried tarragon
Lemon wedges

Cut fish fillets into 4 serving pieces. Cook fennel and onion in water in 10-inch nonstick skillet over medium heat about 4 minutes, stirring occasionally, until crisp-tender. Stir in broth, rice and spinach. Heat to boiling; reduce heat. Cover and simmer 10 minutes.

Place fish on rice mixture. Cover and simmer 8 to 10 minutes longer or until fish flakes easily with fork and liquid is absorbed. Sprinkle fish with paprika and tarragon. Serve with lemon wedges.

1 SERVING: Calories 345 (Calories from Fat 65); Fat 7g (Saturated 2g); Cholesterol 60mg; Sodium 460mg; Carbohydrate 42g (Dietary Fiber 1g); Protein 27g.

Fish and Fennel Rice

Salsa Cod

4 servings

Cilantro, a southwestern favorite, is also known as fresh coriander, Mexican parsley and Chinese parsley. While cilantro resembles flat-leaf parsley, its flavor is more intense.

1 pound cod, orange roughy or other
    medium-fat fish fillets (about
    1/2 inch thick)
1 cup chopped tomato (about 1 large)
1/2 cup chopped green bell pepper
    (about 1 small)
1/4 cup chopped onion (about 1 small)
2 tablespoons finely chopped fresh cilantro
    or parsley
1/4 teaspoon salt
1/4 cup dry white wine or chicken broth

If fish fillets are large, cut into 4 serving pieces. Spray 10-inch nonstick skillet with nonstick cooking spray. Heat over medium heat. Arrange fish in single layer in skillet. Cook uncovered 4 to 6 minutes, turning once, until fish flakes easily with fork. Remove fish to warm platter; keep warm.

Cook remaining ingredients except wine in skillet over medium heat 3 to 5 minutes, stirring frequently, until bell pepper and onion are crisp-tender. Stir in wine. Heat until hot. Spoon tomato mixture over fish.

1 SERVING: Calories 135 (Calories from Fat 20); Fat 2g (Saturated 1g); Cholesterol 40mg; Sodium 210mg; Carbohydrate 6g (Dietary Fiber 1g); Protein 24g.

Easy Fish and Vegetable Packets

4 servings

4 frozen lean fish fillets (about 1 pound)
1 package (16 ounces) frozen broccoli,
    cauliflower and carrots
1 tablespoon snipped fresh or 1 teaspoon
    dried dill weed
1/2 teaspoon salt
1/4 teaspoon pepper
4 tablespoons dry white wine

Heat oven to 450°. Place each frozen fish fillet on 12-inch square of aluminum foil. Top each fish fillet with one-fourth of the vegetables; sprinkle with dill weed, salt and pepper. Pour 1 tablespoon wine over each. Fold up sides of foil to make tent; fold top edges over to seal. Fold in sides, making a packet; fold to seal. Place packets on cookie sheet. Bake about 40 minutes or until vegetables are crisp-tender and fish flakes easily with fork.

1 SERVING: Calories 140 (Calories from Fat 20); Fat 2g (Saturated 1g); Cholesterol 40mg; Sodium 380mg; Carbohydrate 7g (Dietary Fiber 1g); Protein 25g.

Well Schooled Fish

If you like fish, you'll be interested to learn there are three classifications: lean, medium-fat and fatty. Fish is naturally rich in high-quality protein yet low in fat, saturated fat, cholesterol and calories. Percentages of fat in individual fish vary with the season, stage of maturity, locale, species and diet. One type of fish can be substituted for another of the same classification when preparing recipes.

Lean fish contain less than 2.5 percent fat and are mild flavored, with tender white or pale flesh. Lean fish are best steamed, poached, microwaved or fried. Examples: bass (sea or striped), burbot (freshwater cod), cod, cusk, flounder, grouper, haddock, halibut, lingcod, mackerel (king), mahi mahi (dolphinfish), monkfish, orange roughy, perch (ocean), pike (northern), pollock, red snapper, rockfish, scrod, smelt, sole, tilefish, tuna (skipjack and yellowfin) and whiting.

Medium-fat fish, with 2.5 to 5 percent fat content, are suitable for all cooking methods. Examples: anchovy, bluefish, catfish, croaker, mullet, porgy, redfish, salmon (pink), shark, swordfish, trout (rainbow and sea), tuna (bluefin), turbot and whitefish.

Fatty fish have a fat content greater than 5 percent and generally have a firmer texture, more pronounced flavor and deeper color. Fatty fish are best broiled, grilled, baked or microwaved. Examples: butterfish, carp, eel, herring, mackerel (Atlantic, Pacific and Spanish), pompano, sablefish, salmon (chinook, coho and sockeye), sardine, shad and trout (lake).

Italian Baked Bluefish

4 servings

The blue-red flesh of bluefish lightens with cooking. For a less "fishy" flavor, remove the dark fatty stripe down the side of the fillet. Halibut or ocean perch can be substituted in this recipe with fine results.

**1 pound bluefish or other medium-fat
    fish fillets**
1/4 cup dry red wine
2 tablespoons chopped ripe olives
1 tablespoon capers
**4 anchovy fillets, drained and finely
    chopped**
2 cloves garlic, crushed
**1 can (28 ounces) Italian plum tomatoes,
    drained and chopped**

Heat oven to 350°. Cut fish fillets into 4 serving pieces. Place in ungreased square baking dish, 8×8×2 inches. Mix remaining ingredients; pour over fish. Bake uncovered about 40 minutes or until fish flakes easily with fork.

1 SERVING: Calories 170 (Calories from Fat 45); Fat 5g (Saturated 1g); Cholesterol 65mg; Sodium 310mg; Carbohydrate 7g (Dietary Fiber 1g); Protein 25g.

Microwave Directions: Decrease wine to 2 tablespoons. Cut fish fillets into 4 serving pieces. Arrange fish, thickest parts to outside edges, in square microwavable dish, 8×8×2 inches. Mix remaining ingredients; pour over fish. Cover loosely and microwave on High 9 to 11 minutes, rotating dish 1/4 turn every 4 minutes, until fish flakes easily with fork.

Peking Fish

4 servings

The low-fat technique of braise-deglazing is basically stir-frying using very little cooking oil. Use a small amount of water or broth to prevent sticking and ensure that food browns attractively.

1/2 cup plus 2 tablespoons water
1/4 cup hoisin sauce
2 cloves garlic, finely chopped
2 tablespoons grated gingerroot
2 tablespoons soy sauce
1 tablespoon seasoned rice vinegar
3 teaspoons cornstarch
1 pound halibut, monkfish or sea bass fillets,
      1 inch thick
2 teaspoons dry sherry or water
1 teaspoon chili oil
1 pound broccoli, cut into flowerets and
      2×1/2-inch pieces (4 cups)
3 small carrots, roll-cut
1 medium yellow or red bell pepper,
      cut into 3/4-inch pieces
1 small red onion, cut into wedges

Mix 1/2 cup of the water, the hoisin sauce, garlic, gingerroot, soy sauce, vinegar and 2 teaspoons of the cornstarch. Cut fish into 3/4-inch pieces. Mix remaining 1 teaspoon cornstarch and the sherry in medium glass or plastic bowl. Stir in fish until coated.

Spray nonstick wok or 12-inch skillet with nonstick cooking spray; heat over medium-high heat until cooking spray starts to bubble. Add 1/2 teaspoon of the chili oil; rotate wok to coat sides. Add fish; stir-fry about 2 1/2 minutes or until fish flakes easily with fork. Remove fish from wok.

Add remaining 1/2 teaspoon chili oil to wok. Add broccoli, carrots, bell pepper, onion and remaining 2 tablespoons water. Cover and cook 5 to 7 minutes, stirring frequently, until vegetables are crisp-tender (add water if necessary to prevent sticking). Stir in hoisin sauce mixture; cook and stir until thickened. Stir in fish; heat through.

1 SERVING: Calories 185 (Calories from Fat 35); Fat 4g (Saturated 1g); Cholesterol 60mg; Sodium 650mg; Carbohydrate 21g (Dietary Fiber 5g); Protein 27g.

HEALTHY HINT

Here are some mild fish that are available at your seafood counter: cod, flounder, grouper, haddock, halibut, orange roughy, red snapper, sea trout and sole.

Catfish with Pesto

4 servings

Add warm bread, steamed broccoli and fresh straw-berries for dessert to complete the meal.

4 catfish, orange roughy or red snapper fillets (1 1/2 pounds)
1/4 cup pesto
20 strips roasted bell pepper (from 12-ounce jar)

Heat oven to 425°. If fish fillets are large, cut into 4 serving pieces. Place fish in greased square baking dish, 8×8×2 inches. Spread pesto evenly over each piece of fish. Top each piece with 5 roasted pepper strips. Cover and bake about 18 minutes or until fish flakes easily with fork.

1 SERVING: Calories 250 (Calories from Fat 110); Fat 12g (Saturated 3g); Cholesterol 95mg; Sodium 200mg; Carbohydrate 2g (Dietary Fiber 0g); Protein 34g.

Crispy Baked Catfish

4 servings

1/4 cup yellow cornmeal
1/4 cup dry bread crumbs
1 teaspoon chili powder
1/4 teaspoon paprika
1/2 teaspoon garlic salt
1/4 teaspoon pepper
1/4 cup reduced-fat French dressing
1 pound catfish fillets, cut into 4 pieces

Heat oven to 450°. Spray broiler pan rack with nonstick cooking spray. Mix cornmeal, bread crumbs, chili powder, paprika, garlic salt and pepper. Lightly brush dressing on fish fillets, coating all sides of fish. Coat fish with cornmeal mixture. Place fish on rack in broiler pan. Bake uncovered about 15 minutes or until fish flakes easily with fork.

1 SERVING: Calories 205 (Calories from Fat 45); Fat 5g (Saturated 1g); Cholesterol 70mg; Sodium 440mg; Carbohydrate 15g (Dietary Fiber 1g); Protein 26g.

Crispy Baked Catfish

Lemon-Curry Cod

4 servings

1 pound cod, halibut or red snapper fillets
1 tablespoon coconut, if desired
2 tablespoons reduced-fat mayonnaise
   or salad dressing
2 tablespoons honey
1 tablespoon lemon juice
1 tablespoon Dijon mustard
1 teaspoon curry powder
1/2 teaspoon salt

Set oven control to broil. Spray broiler pan rack with nonstick cooking spray. Place fish on rack in broiler pan. Mix remaining ingredients; spread evenly over fish. Broil with tops 4 to 6 inches from heat 5 to 8 minutes or until fish flakes easily with fork.

1 SERVING: Calories 165 (Calories from Fat 35); Fat 4g (Saturated 1g); Cholesterol 60mg; Sodium 480mg; Carbohydrate 10g (Dietary Fiber 0g); Protein 22g.

Cod with Tomato-Olive Sauce

4 servings

When buying frozen fish, look for packages that are well wrapped and free from ice crystals. Frozen fish should be thawed in the refrigerator or in the microwave. This is delicious served with chunks of crusty bread to sop up all of the flavorful juices. Serve with chopped fresh parsley for a bit of color.

1 pound cod fillets
1 tablespoon olive or vegetable oil
1 large onion, chopped (1 cup)
1 can (14 1/2 ounces) diced tomatoes with
   roasted garlic, onion and oregano
1 can (4 1/4 ounces) sliced ripe olives,
   drained
1/4 teaspoon salt
1/4 teaspoon pepper
2 tablespoons lemon juice

If fish fillets are large, cut into 4 serving pieces. Heat oil in 10-inch nonstick skillet over medium-high heat. Cook onion in oil 2 to 3 minutes, stirring occasionally, until crisp-tender. Stir in tomatoes, olives, salt and pepper; heat to boiling. Arrange fish fillets in single layer in tomato mixture. Sprinkle with lemon juice; reduce heat to medium-high. Cover and cook 8 to 10 minutes or until fish flakes easily with fork.

1 SERVING: Calories 185 (Calories from Fat 55); Fat 6g (Saturated 1g); Cholesterol 60mg; Sodium 640mg; Carbohydrate 12g (Dietary Fiber 2g); Protein 23g.

Broiled Cod with Sun-Dried Tomatoes

4 servings

Chewy, sweet and intensely favored, sun-dried tomatoes can be found packed in oil or packed dry in cellophane bags. They add a rich flavor to dishes that you can't get with fresh tomatoes.

1 pound cod or other firm lean fish fillets, about 3/4 inch thick
8 sun-dried tomato halves (not oil-packed)
1/4 cup mayonnaise or salad dressing
2 tablespoons chopped fresh parsley
1/8 teaspoon pepper

Set oven control to broil. Grease rack of broiler pan. Place fish on rack in broiler pan. Broil with tops 4 inches from heat 8 minutes. Soak tomato halves in 1 cup very hot water about 5 minutes or until softened; drain and finely chop. Mix with remaining ingredients; spread on fish. Broil 1 to 2 minutes longer or until topping is light brown and fish flakes easily with fork.

1 SERVING: Calories 205 (Calories from Fat 110); Fat 12g (Saturated 2g); Cholesterol 70mg; Sodium 240mg; Carbohydrate 2g (Dietary Fiber 0g); Protein 22g.

Halibut-Asparagus Stir-fry

4 servings

1 pound fresh asparagus, cut into 1-inch pieces, or 1 package (10 ounces) frozen asparagus cuts, thawed and drained
1 pound halibut or other lean fish steaks, cut into 1-inch pieces
1 medium onion, thinly sliced
3 cloves garlic, finely chopped
1 teaspoon finely chopped gingerroot
1 cup sliced mushrooms (3 ounces) or 1 jar (4 1/2 ounces) sliced mushrooms, drained
2 tablespoons reduced-sodium soy sauce
1 tablespoon lemon juice
1 medium tomato, cut into thin wedges

Spray nonstick wok or 10-inch nonstick skillet with nonstick cooking spray. Heat over medium-high heat until hot. Add asparagus; stir-fry 2 minutes. Add fish, onion, garlic and gingerroot; stir-fry 2 to 3 minutes or until fish flakes with fork. Carefully stir in remaining ingredients. Cook until mixture is heated through and fish flakes easily with fork. Serve with additional reduced-sodium soy sauce if desired.

1 SERVING: Calories 135 (Calories from Fat 20); Fat 2g (Saturated 0g); Cholesterol 50mg; Sodium 380mg; Carbohydrate 10g (Dietary Fiber 2g); Protein 21g.

Halibut with Braised Vegetables

6 servings

2 cups finely chopped onions (about 2 large)
1/2 cup tomato juice
1/2 cup apple juice
2 cloves garlic, finely chopped
1 cup chopped red or green bell pepper
    (about 1 medium)
1 cup cooked fresh, frozen (thawed)
    or canned (drained) whole kernel
    corn (about 2 medium ears)
1/2 cup sliced green onions
    (about 5 medium)
2 tablespoons lime juice
1 tablespoon Dijon mustard
1/4 teaspoon salt
1/4 teaspoon celery seed
1/4 teaspoon pepper
1 1/2 pounds halibut or other lean fish
    fillets, cut into 6 serving pieces

Heat onions, tomato juice, apple juice and garlic to boiling in 2-quart saucepan; reduce heat to medium. Cook uncovered about 10 minutes, stirring occasionally, until most of the liquid has evaporated. Stir in remaining ingredients except fish. Cook uncovered 6 to 8 minutes or until corn is tender. Cover and remove from heat.

Set oven control to broil. Spray broiler pan rack with nonstick cooking spray. Place fish on rack in broiler pan. Broil with tops about 4 inches from heat about 10 minutes or until fish flakes easily with fork. Serve with vegetables.

1 SERVING: Calories 175 (Calories from Fat 20); Fat 2g (Saturated 1g); Cholesterol 60mg; Sodium 290mg; Carbohydrate 16g (Dietary Fiber 3g); Protein 23g.

Doneness Tests for Fish

For food safety reasons, we recommend cooking fish to an internal temperature of 160°. If you do not own a meat thermometer, these guidelines will help you determine when fish is done:

- The fish separates easily into flakes but not to the point of falling apart.

- If a bone is present, the flesh separates from the bone, and the tone is no longer pink.

- The flesh has turned from translucent to opaque (usually white, depending on the kind of fish), and the juices are milky white.

Halibut with Braised Vegetables

Sweet-and-Sour Halibut with Lemon Rice

6 servings

This takeoff on sweet-and-sour pork is so delicious, it's hard to believe it's low in fat too. We've substituted fish for the pork and used nonstick cooking spray instead of oil.

1/4 cup cider vinegar
2 tablespoons chopped green onions
1 tablespoon tomato paste
2 teaspoons packed brown sugar
2 teaspoons finely chopped gingerroot
2 teaspoons reduced-sodium soy sauce
1/2 teaspoon ground anise
1/2 teaspoon salt
1/8 to 1/4 teaspoon ground red pepper
   (cayenne)
1 1/2 pounds halibut or whitefish fillets,
   cut into 1 1/2-inch pieces
1 can (8 ounces) crushed pineapple in juice,
   undrained
Lemon Rice (right)

Mix all ingredients except Lemon Rice in large glass or plastic bowl. Cover and refrigerate 2 hours. Heat oven to 375°. Spray rectangular baking dish, 13 × 9 × 2 inches, with nonstick cooking spray. Place fish mixture in dish. Bake uncovered 12 to 15 minutes, stirring once, until fish flakes easily with fork. Serve over Lemon Rice.

LEMON RICE

1/2 cup uncooked regular long-grain rice
1 cup water
1 tablespoon grated lemon peel
1 teaspoon chicken bouillon granules
4 to 6 drops red pepper sauce

Heat all ingredients to boiling, stirring once or twice. Cover and simmer 14 minutes. (Do not lift cover or stir.) Remove from heat. Let stand covered 10 minutes.

1 SERVING: Calories 200 (Calories from Fat 20); Fat 2g (Saturated 1g); Cholesterol 60mg; Sodium 570mg; Carbohydrate 24g (Dietary Fiber 1g); Protein 23g.

Fish Choices

Fin fish and shellfish are generally lower in fat than meats and poultry. Shellfish are higher than fin fish in cholesterol (shrimp are highest).

Choose water-packed when buying canned tuna, salmon and sardines, to limit overall fat intake.

Imitation crabmeat has less cholesterol, but more sodium, than real crabmeat. Balance sodium intake when enjoying this product.

Oven-Steamed Halibut with Garlic and Lemon

6 servings

Place the packets directly on the plates and serve— the aroma released when the foil is opened is wonderful. The fish is nice with potatoes, rice or pasta.

1 1/2 pounds halibut or whitefish fillets,
    cut into 6 serving pieces
2 cloves garlic, finely chopped
1/2 teaspoon salt
1/4 teaspoon pepper
1/3 cup white wine or apple juice
1 1/2 cups julienne strips carrots
    (about 3 medium)
12 slices lemon, 1/8 inch thick
    (about 2 medium)

Heat oven to 375°. Spray six 12-inch-square pieces of aluminum foil with nonstick cooking spray. Place 1 fish fillet in center of each piece of foil. Sprinkle fish with garlic, salt and pepper. Pour wine over fish. Place 1/4 cup carrots on each fillet. Top with 2 lemon slices. Wrap foil around fish; seal. Bake about 10 minutes or until fish flakes easily with fork.

1 SERVING: Calories 110 (Calories from Fat 10); Fat 1g (Saturated 0g); Cholesterol 60mg; Sodium 280mg; Carbohydrate 4g (Dietary Fiber 1g); Protein 22g.

Broiled Sesame Halibut Kabobs

4 servings

1 pound halibut or sea bass steaks or fillets,
    1 inch thick
1 medium zucchini, cut into 1/4-inch slices
1 medium yellow summer squash, cut into
    1/4-inch slices
1/4 teaspoon sugar
1 clove garlic, finely chopped
2 tablespoons soy sauce
1 teaspoon grated gingerroot
1 teaspoon sesame oil
1 tablespoon sesame seed

Cut fish into 3/4- to 1-inch pieces. Thread fish, zucchini and squash alternately on each of eight 8-inch skewers.* Set oven control to broil. Spray broiler pan rack with nonstick cooking spray. Mix sugar, garlic, soy sauce, gingerroot and sesame oil. Brush generously on all sides of kabobs. Sprinkle sesame seed over kabobs.

Place kabobs on rack in broiler pan. Broil with tops 4 inches from heat about 3 minutes; turn. Broil about 2 minutes longer or until fish flakes easily with fork.

1 SERVING: Calories 140 (Calories from Fat 35); Fat 4g (Saturated 1g); Cholesterol 60mg; Sodium 610mg; Carbohydrate 4g (Dietary Fiber 1g); Protein 23g.

*If using wooden bamboo skewers, soak in water for 30 minutes before using to prevent burning.

Parmesan-Basil Perch

4 servings

1 pound ocean perch or other lean fish
    fillets, cut into 4 serving pieces
2 tablespoons dry bread crumbs
1 tablespoon grated Parmesan cheese
1 tablespoon chopped fresh or 1 teaspoon
    dried basil leaves
1/2 teaspoon paprika
Dash of pepper
1 tablespoon margarine, melted
2 tablespoons chopped fresh parsley

Move oven rack to position slightly above middle of oven. Heat oven to 500°. Spray rectangular pan, 13 × 9 × 2 inches, with nonstick cooking spray. Mix ingredients except fish, margarine and parsley. Brush one side of fish with margarine; dip into crumb mixture. Place fish, coated sides up, in pan. Baked uncovered about 10 minutes or until fish flakes easily with fork. Sprinkle with parsley.

1 SERVING: Calories 135 (Calories from Fat 45); Fat 5g (Saturated 1g); Cholesterol 55mg; Sodium 160mg; Carbohydrate 3g (Dietary Fiber 0g); Protein 20g.

Orange Roughy with Red Peppers

4 servings

This dish also is delicious prepared with mahi mahi or red snapper.

1 pound orange roughy or other lean
    fish fillets
1 teaspoon olive or vegetable oil
1 small onion, cut into thin slices
2 medium red or green bell peppers,
    cut into julienne strips
1 tablespoon chopped fresh or 1 teaspoon
    dried thyme leaves
1/4 teaspoon pepper

If fish fillets are large, cut into 4 serving pieces. Heat oil in 10-inch nonstick skillet. Layer onion and bell peppers in skillet; sprinkle with half of the thyme and pepper. Layer fish on bell peppers, sprinkle with remaining thyme and pepper. Cover and cook over low heat 15 minutes. Uncover and cook 10 to 15 minutes longer or until fish flakes easily with fork.

1 SERVING: Calories 110 (Calories from Fat 20); Fat 2g (Saturated 1g); Cholesterol 55mg; Sodium 85mg; Carbohydrate 4g (Dietary Fiber 1g); Protein 20g.

Orange Roughy with Red Peppers

Zippy Red Snapper and Zucchini

4 servings

Lots of flavor and only 2 grams of fat per serving. Plus, using the microwave makes this meal a snap to prepare.

1 pound red snapper or other lean fish fillets, cut into 4 serving pieces
Tomato Chili Sauce (right)
2 tablespoons grated Parmesan cheese
2 small zucchini, cut into 1/4-inch slices (3 cups)
1/4 teaspoon garlic salt
1/4 cup coarsely shredded carrot

Arrange fish, thickest parts to outside edge, in microwavable pie plate, 9 × 1 1/4 inches. Cover with plastic wrap, folding back one side to vent. Microwave on High 3 minutes; drain.

Prepare Tomato Chili Sauce. Spread 1 tablespoon of the sauce over each piece of fish. Sprinkle 1 tablespoon of the cheese over fish. Place zucchini slices on fish. Sprinkle with garlic salt and remaining cheese. Re-cover and microwave on High 3 to 4 minutes or until fish flakes easily with fork. Top with carrot. Serve with remaining sauce.

TOMATO CHILI SAUCE

1 cup chili sauce
2 teaspoons prepared horseradish
2 teaspoons lemon juice
1/4 teaspoon Worcestershire sauce
1/8 teaspoon salt

Mix all ingredients in 2-cup microwavable measure. Microwave uncovered on High 1 to 2 minutes or until hot. Stir before serving.

1 SERVING: Calories 180 (Calories from Fat 20); Fat 2g (Saturated 1g); Cholesterol 60mg; Sodium 1,000mg; Carbohydrate 19g (Dietary Fiber 2g); Protein 24g.

Skinning Fillets of Fish

Insert a fork into the flesh at the thick end of an uncooked fillet without piercing the skin. Hold fillet under very hot running water for 45 to 60 seconds. Test the skin—it should peel off easily. If not, continue to hold under water for 15 to 30 seconds.

Zippy Red Snapper and Zucchini

Red Snapper Teriyaki

4 servings

Sugar snap peas are a cross between Chinese pea pods and garden peas. If you can't find them, you can use Chinese pea pods or 1-inch pieces of asparagus instead.

1 tablespoon vegetable oil
1 pound red snapper or other lean fish
    fillets, cut into 1-inch pieces
3 cups sugar snap peas
1 medium red bell pepper, cut into
    1/4-inch strips
1/2 cup teriyaki baste and glaze

Heat wok or 12-inch skillet until very hot. Add oil; rotate wok to coat sides. Add fish; stir-fry 2 minutes. Add peas and bell pepper; stir-fry 2 to 3 minutes or until vegetables are crisp-tender. Stir in teriyaki baste and glaze; cook and stir 30 seconds.

1 SERVING: Calories 175 (Calories from Fat 45); Fat 5g (Saturated 1g); Cholesterol 50mg; Sodium 1,460mg; Carbohydrate 11g (Dietary Fiber 2g); Protein 23g.

Steamed Red Snapper and Carrots

4 servings

Instead of using oil to cook the carrots and fish, we use chicken broth. The result? Lots of flavor, less fat.

1/2 cup reduced-sodium chicken broth
2 tablespoons oyster sauce
2 tablespoons rice wine vinegar or cider
    vinegar
1 pound baby-cut carrots (3 cups)
1 pound red snapper or other lean fish
    fillets, cut into 4 pieces
4 green onions, cut into 1-inch pieces
2 cups shredded napa (Chinese) cabbage
    (8 ounces), if desired

Mix broth, oyster sauce and vinegar in 12-inch skillet. Add carrots. Heat to boiling; reduce heat. Cover and simmer 5 minutes. Add fish. Heat to boiling; reduce heat to medium. Cover and simmer 10 to 15 minutes or until fish flakes easily with fork. Stir in onions. Cover and cook 2 minutes. Serve over cabbage.

1 SERVING: Calories 130 (Calories from Fat 10); Fat 1g (Saturated 0g); Cholesterol 50mg; Sodium 510mg; Carbohydrate 13g (Dietary Fiber 4g); Protein 21g.

Sizzling Swordfish Fajitas

6 servings

Fresh Spicy Salsa (right)
2 tablespoons lime juice
1 teaspoon vegetable oil
1/2 teaspoon coarsely ground pepper
1 pound swordfish or other medium-fat
    fish steaks
6 flour tortillas (8 inches in diameter),
    warmed
1 1/2 cups shredded lettuce
    (1/2 small head)
1 small red bell pepper, finely chopped
    (1/2 cup)

Prepare Fresh Spicy Salsa. Set oven control to broil. Spray rack of broiler pan with nonstick cooking spray. Mix lime juice, oil and pepper; brush on fish. Place fish on rack in broiler pan. Broil with tops about 4 inches from heat 5 minutes; turn. Broil 5 to 10 minutes longer or until fish flakes easily with fork.

Break fish into bite-size pieces. Spoon 1/3 cup fish onto center of each tortilla. Top with lettuce, bell pepper and salsa. Fold one end of each tortilla up about 1 inch over filling; fold right and left sides over folded end, overlapping. Fold down remaining end.

FRESH SPICY SALSA

2 medium tomatoes, finely chopped
    (1 1/2 cups)
2 cloves garlic, finely chopped
1 small jalapeño chili, finely chopped
1/2 cup sliced green onions (5 medium)
2 tablespoons chopped fresh cilantro
2 tablespoons lime juice
1/2 teaspoon ground cumin

Mix all ingredients.

1 SERVING: Calories 230 (Calories from Fat 45); Fat 5g (Saturated 1.5g); Cholesterol 40mg; Sodium 250mg; Carbohydrate 30g (Dietary Fiber 1g); Protein 18g.

Crustless Tuna Quiche

6 servings

2 cans (6 ounces each) tuna in water, drained
1 cup shredded Swiss cheese (4 ounces)
1 medium onion, chopped (1/2 cup)
2 tablespoons all-purpose flour
2 eggs
2 egg whites
1 cup skim milk
3/4 teaspoon salt
1/8 teaspoon red pepper sauce

Heat oven to 350°. Spray pie plate, 9×1 1/4 inches, with nonstick cooking spray. Toss tuna, cheese, onion and flour; spread in pie plate. Beat eggs and egg whites slightly in small bowl; beat in remaining ingredients. Pour egg mixture over tuna mixture. Bake uncovered 35 to 40 minutes or until knife inserted in center comes out clean. Let stand 10 minutes before cutting.

1 SERVING: Calories 185 (Calories from Fat 65); Fat 7g (Saturated 4g); Cholesterol 105mg; Sodium 580mg; Carbohydrate 6g (Dietary Fiber 0g); Protein 24g.

Tropical Fruit, Rice and Tuna Salad

4 servings

1 1/2 cups cold cooked brown or white rice
1/2 cup vanilla low-fat yogurt
1 can (8 ounces) pineapple tidbits in juice, drained and 1 teaspoon juice reserved
2 kiwifruit, peeled and sliced
1 medium mango, peeled and chopped (about 1 cup)
1 can (6 1/8 ounces) white tuna in water, drained and flaked
1 tablespoon coconut, toasted

Mix rice, yogurt and reserved pineapple juice in medium bowl. Cover and refrigerate 1 to 2 hours to blend flavors. Cut kiwifruit slices into fourths. Gently stir kiwifruit, pineapple, mango and tuna into rice mixture. Sprinkle with coconut.

1 SERVING: Calories 240 (Calories from Fat 20); Fat 2g (Saturated 1g); Cholesterol 15mg; Sodium 170mg; Carbohydrate 45g (Dietary Fiber 4g); Protein 15g.

Buying Whole Fish

Look for these characteristics when buying fresh fish:

Eyes: Clear, bright and not sunken

Flesh: Firm and elastic to the touch

Gills: Reddish pink, not brown

Skin: Shiny, taut and bright in color

Tropical Fruit, Rice and Tuna Salad

Fishing for Nutrition

Fish and seafood aren't really "brain foods," as they were once called, but they do offer many great-tasting nutritional benefits. These healthful food choices are richer in high-quality protein and lower in fat and saturated fat than many other entrée options. Meals that include fish or seafood products can fit easily within the daily dietary guidelines of no more than 30 percent of total calories from fat.

Many varieties of seafood are low in cholesterol as well. This may sound surprising when for years we've been told to avoid seafood because of its supposed high cholesterol content. Better research methods have shown us that mollusks, such as clams, oysters and scallops, actually have less cholesterol than beef! Shrimp, lobster and crab contain more cholesterol than mollusks, but that just means we should eat them less often.

Seafood also has the bonus of omega-3 oils. Omega-3 refers to the unique structure of fatty acids—the building blocks of fat—found in all animals and plants. Scientific studies suggest these oils may help reduce the risk of heart disease. That's good news for fish lovers, but researchers just aren't sure how fish oils may promote healthier hearts. Much research is still underway to try to better understand the big picture. Good sources of omega-3 are crab, mackerel, salmon, shrimp, trout and tuna.

Eat fish at least once each week!

Salmon with Mint Couscous

6 servings

Mint Sauce (below)
1 1/2 pounds salmon or other medium-fat fish fillets, cut into 6 serving pieces
1 teaspoon grated lemon peel
1/2 teaspoon salt
1/4 teaspoon pepper
3 cups hot cooked couscous
2 tablespoons finely chopped fresh or 2 teaspoons dried mint leaves

Prepare Mint Sauce. Sprinkle fish fillets with lemon peel, salt and pepper. Set oven control to broil. Spray broiler pan rack with nonstick cooking spray. Place fish on rack in broiler pan. Broil with tops about 4 inches from heat 5 to 6 minutes or until fish flakes easily with fork. Mix couscous and mint. Serve fish over couscous with Mint Sauce.

MINT SAUCE

3/4 cup plain nonfat yogurt
1 tablespoon finely chopped fresh or 1 teaspoon dried mint leaves
1 tablespoon cholesterol-free reduced-calorie mayonnaise or salad dressing
1 teaspoon grated orange peel
1 clove garlic, finely chopped (about 1/2 teaspoon)

Mix all ingredients.

1 SERVING: Calories 265 (Calories from Fat 55); Fat 8g (Saturated 2g); Cholesterol 45mg; Sodium 470mg; Carbohydrate 24g (Dietary Fiber 1g); Protein 30g.

Salmon with Mint Couscous

Calypso Shrimp

4 servings

The citrus-spiked bean salsa is the perfect counterpoint to the marinated shrimp.

Bean Salsa (right)
1/2 teaspoon grated orange peel
1 tablespoon orange juice
1 tablespoon vegetable oil
1 1/2 teaspoons chopped fresh or
    1/2 teaspoon dried thyme leaves
1 clove garlic, finely chopped
3/4 pound raw medium shrimp, peeled
    and deveined

Prepare Bean Salsa; set aside. Mix remaining ingredients except shrimp in medium bowl. Stir in shrimp. Spray 10-inch nonstick skillet with nonstick cooking spray; heat over medium-high heat. Cook shrimp mixture in skillet, turning shrimp once, until pink. Divide salsa among 4 serving plates. Arrange shrimp on salsa.

BEAN SALSA

1 can (15 ounces) black beans, rinsed
    and drained
1 medium mango, peeled and chopped
    (about 1 cup)
1 small red bell pepper, chopped
    (about 1/2 cup)
1/4 cup sliced green onions (2 to 3 medium)
2 tablespoons orange juice
1 tablespoon red wine vinegar
1/2 teaspoon grated orange peel

Mix all ingredients.

1 SERVING: Calories 235 (Calories from Fat 45); Fat 5g (Saturated 1g); Cholesterol 80mg; Sodium 350mg; Carbohydrate 39g (Dietary Fiber 9g); Protein 18g.

Calypso Shrimp

Cajun Seafood and Noodles

6 servings

If frozen shrimp and crab are not readily available, canned shrimp and crab are just as delicious.

6 ounces uncooked medium noodles
    (about 3 cups)
1 tablespoon vegetable oil
3/4 cup chopped green bell pepper
    (about 1 medium)
1/2 cup chopped onion (about 1 medium)
2 tablespoons chopped fresh parsley
1/8 teaspoon ground red pepper (cayenne)
1/8 teaspoon pepper
2 cloves garlic, finely chopped
1 tablespoon all-purpose flour
1 can (16 ounces) whole tomatoes,
    undrained
1 package (10 ounces) frozen cut okra,
    thawed
1 package (6 ounces) frozen cooked small
    shrimp, thawed and drained
1 package (6 ounces) frozen crabmeat,
    thawed, drained and cartilage removed

Cook noodles as directed on package; drain. Heat oil in 10-inch nonstick skillet over medium heat. Cook bell pepper, onion, parsley, red pepper, pepper and garlic in oil 3 minutes, stirring frequently. Stir in flour and tomatoes; break up tomatoes. Cook uncovered, stirring frequently, until mixture thickens and boils. Stir in okra, shrimp and crabmeat. Cook uncovered 5 minutes, stirring occasionally. Serve over noodles.

1 SERVING: Calories 225 (Calories from Fat 45); Fat 5g (Saturated 2g); Cholesterol 85mg; Sodium 240mg; Carbohydrate 31g (Dietary Fiber 1g); Protein 15g.

Cajun Seafood and Noodles

What Is Surimi?

Surimi is imitation crabmeat made from pollock (a fish similar to cod), artificial and natural flavors, starches and stiffeners. Before being frozen, it is often dyed pink and shaped to resemble crab legs or lump crabmeat. Calorie-wise, surimi is similar to other lean fish, about 25 calories per ounce. It does, however, contain almost twice the amount of sodium. Surimi can be used in most recipes that call for canned or frozen lump crabmeat. Try it in pasta salads and stir-fries.

Grilling

Honey Mustard Pork Chops (page 252)

(continued on next page)

Zesty Lime Steak

8 servings

Round steak is among the leanest beef cuts. "Select" is the leanest grade of beef, with less fat than either "choice" beef or "prime" beef.

2 pounds beef boneless top round steak, about 1 inch thick
1/2 teaspoon grated lime peel
1/3 cup lime juice
1/4 cup tomato juice
1 tablespoon chopped fresh cilantro or parsley
2 teaspoons vegetable oil
1/4 teaspoon salt
1/8 teaspoon red pepper sauce
2 cloves garlic, finely chopped

Pierce beef with fork several times on both sides. Mix remaining ingredients in shallow nonmetal dish or heavy-duty resealable plastic bag. Add beef; turn to coat with marinade. Cover dish or seal bag and refrigerate at least 8 hours, but no longer than 24 hours, turning beef occasionally.

Heat coals or gas grill. Remove beef from marinade; discard marinade. Cover and grill beef 4 to 5 inches from medium heat 25 to 30 minutes for medium doneness (160°), turning once. Cut beef across grain into thin slices.

1 SERVING: Calories 180 (Calories from Fat 80); Fat 9g (Saturated 3g); Cholesterol 65mg; Sodium 150mg; Carbohydrate 1g (Dietary Fiber 0g); Protein 24g.

Safe Sauces and Marinades

If you want to serve a leftover marinade or brushing sauce with the grilled meat, heat it to boiling, then boil for 1 minute, stirring constantly. Boiling will destroy any bacteria that may have been transferred on the brush from the raw meat to the marinade. Otherwise, discard any marinade or sauce that has been in contact with raw meat.

Peppercorn Steaks with Brandied Cream Sauce

6 servings

3 tablespoons cracked black pepper
6 beef boneless sirloin steaks, about
    3/4 inch thick
1 tablespoon margarine or butter
1/4 cup finely chopped shallots or
    green onions
1/4 cup brandy or beef broth
1/2 cup beef broth
1/2 cup sour cream

Heat coals or gas grill. Press pepper onto both sides of beef. Cover and grill beef 4 to 6 inches from medium heat 10 to 15 minutes for medium doneness, turning once.

Melt margarine in 1-quart saucepan over medium heat. Cook shallots in margarine about 2 minutes, stirring occasionally, until tender. Stir in brandy and broth. Cook over medium-high heat about 5 minutes, stirring occasionally, until mixture is slightly reduced. Stir in sour cream. Serve with beef.

1 SERVING: Calories 175 (Calories from Fat 80); Fat 9g (Saturated 4g); Cholesterol 65mg; Sodium 160mg; Carbohydrate 2g (Dietary Fiber 0g); Protein 21g.

Spicy Grilled Sirloin

6 servings

1 1/2 pounds beef boneless top sirloin
    steak, about 1 inch thick
1/4 cup soy sauce
2 tablespoons lemon juice
1 tablespoon vegetable oil
1 teaspoon ground cumin
1 teaspoon chili powder
1 clove garlic, finely chopped

Pierce beef with fork several times on both sides. Mix remaining ingredients in shallow nonmetal dish or heavy-duty resealable plastic bag. Add beef, turning to coat with marinade. Cover dish or seal bag and refrigerate, turning beef occasionally, at least 6 hours but no longer than 24 hours.

Heat coals or gas grill. Remove beef from marinade; discard marinade. Cover and grill beef 4 to 6 inches from medium heat 15 to 18 minutes for medium doneness, turning once. Cut beef cross grain into 1/2-inch slices.

1 SERVING: Calories 145 (Calories from Fat 55); Fat 6g (Saturated 2g); Cholesterol 55mg; Sodium 730mg; Carbohydrate 2g (Dietary Fiber 0g); Protein 21g.

HEALTHY HINT

If your grill does not have a cover and a recipe recommends using one, shape two sheets of heavy-duty aluminum foil into a dome shape the same size as the grill rack (form the foil over bent coat hangers to easily retain the shape).

Spicy Grilled Sirloin

Grilling Know-How

Grilled foods are now enjoyed all year long! Besides following the manufacturer's directions for use, care and cleaning of your grill, use the tips that follow to grill foods to perfection.

HEATING THE GRILL

- For charcoal grills, light coals at least 30 minutes before cooking begins to ensure the proper temperature is reached. Most coals take 30 to 45 minutes to reach the proper temperature.

- When are the coals ready? In the daylight, the coals should be completely covered with light gray ash. After dark, the coals will glow red.

- For gas grills, follow the manufacturer's directions or heat 5 to 10 minutes before cooking.

Direct Heat: In this method, food is cooked directly over the heat.

Indirect Heat: This is the preferred method for longer-cooking foods, such as whole poultry and whole turkey breasts. In this method, food is cooked away from the heat. When using coals, arrange them around the edge of the firebox, and place a drip pan under the grilling area. If using a dual-burner gas grill, heat only one side, and place food under the burner that is not lit. For single-burner gas grills, place food in a foil tray or on several layers of aluminum foil, and use low heat.

Teriyaki Beef Kabobs

6 servings

Teriyaki sauce comes in two forms. The baste-and-glaze type is thick and clings well to meats, poultry and seafood during cooking; the marinade type is thinner, and foods absorb the flavor best during marinating.

1 1/2 pounds beef boneless top sirloin
   steak, cut into 1-inch cubes
1 cup teriyaki baste and glaze
1 medium bell pepper, cut into 1-inch pieces
18 medium mushrooms
2 tablespoons vegetable oil
1/4 cup sesame seed, toasted

Place beef in shallow nonmetal dish or heavy-duty resealable plastic bag. Pour teriyaki baste over beef. Cover dish or seal bag and refrigerate, stirring beef occasionally, at least 4 hours but no longer than 24 hours.

Heat coals or gas grill. Remove beef from teriyaki baste; discard baste. Thread beef, bell pepper and mushrooms alternately on each of six 15-inch metal skewers, leaving space between each item. Brush bell pepper and mushrooms with oil. Sprinkle kabobs with sesame seed. Cover and grill kabobs 4 to 6 inches from medium heat 15 to 20 minutes, turning frequently.

1 SERVING: Calories 200 (Calories from Fat 90); Fat 10g (Saturated 2g); Cholesterol 55mg; Sodium 650mg; Carbohydrate 6g (Dietary Fiber 1g); Protein 23g.

Teriyaki Beef Kabobs

Sassy Southwestern Pork Chops

4 servings

**4 lean pork loin or rib chops, about 1/4 inch
thick (about 1 1/4 pounds)**
1 tablespoon reduced-sodium chicken broth
1 tablespoon lime juice
1/2 teaspoon chili powder
1 clove garlic, crushed
Cilantro-Mint Salsa (right)
Salt and pepper to taste

Place pork in shallow glass or plastic dish or
heavy-duty resealable plastic bag. Mix broth,
lime juice, chili powder and garlic; rub on
both sides of pork, using back of spoon.
Cover dish or seal bag and refrigerate at least
1 hour but no longer than 24 hours.

Prepare Cilantro-Mint Salsa. Heat coals or
gas grill. Place pork on grill; sprinkle with salt
and pepper. Cover and grill 4 to 5 inches
from medium heat 8 to 11 minutes, turning
frequently, for medium doneness (160°).
Serve with salsa.

CILANTRO-MINT SALSA

1 large tomato, seeded and chopped (1 cup)
1 jalapeño chili, seeded and finely chopped
1 tablespoon chopped fresh cilantro
**1 tablespoon chopped fresh or 1 teaspoon
dried mint leaves**
1 tablespoon chopped onion
1/2 teaspoon lime juice

Mix all ingredients in glass or plastic bowl.
Cover and let stand at least 1 hour before
serving.

1 SERVING: Calories 175 (Calories from Fat 70); Fat 8g
(Saturated 3g); Cholesterol 65mg; Sodium 55mg;
Carbohydrate 4g (Dietary Fiber 1g); Protein 23g.

Rub It In!

Rubs are mixtures of dry seasonings
rubbed completely over meat, using
one's fingers, before grilling. They give
grilled foods a delicious, complex flavor.
They're a healthy alternative to sauces or
oily marinades, as they contain no fat at
all. Unlike marinades, rubs do not contain liquids. They provide more surface
flavor than do marinades, which tend to
melt more with the flavor of the meat.
Rubs can be applied to foods just before
grilling, or for more flavor, cover and
refrigerate rubbed meats for 1 hour.

Caribbean Jerk Pork Chops

6 servings

1/4 cup water
1/3 cup lemon juice
1/3 cup chopped onion
1 tablespoon packed brown sugar
1 tablespoon chopped green onion
1 tablespoon canola or vegetable oil
3/4 teaspoon salt
3/4 teaspoon ground allspice
3/4 teaspoon ground cinnamon
3/4 teaspoon pepper
1/2 teaspoon ground thyme
1/4 teaspoon ground red pepper (cayenne)
6 lean pork loin or rib chops, about 5/8 inch
    thick (about 2 1/4 pounds)

Place all ingredients except pork in blender. Cover and blend until smooth. Reserve 1/2 cup of the marinade; cover and refrigerate for basting. Trim excess fat from pork. Place pork in shallow nonmetal dish or heavy-duty resealable plastic bag. Pour remaining marinade over pork. Cover dish or seal bag and refrigerate at least 12 hours but no longer than 24 hours.

Heat coals or gas grill. Remove pork from marinade; discard marinade. Cover and grill pork 4 to 5 inches from medium heat 8 to 11 minutes, turning frequently and brushing with reserved marinade, for medium doneness (160°) or until pork is slightly pink when cut near bone. Discard any remaining basting marinade.

1 SERVING: Calories 200 (Calories from Fat 90); Fat 10g (Saturated 3g); Cholesterol 65mg; Sodium 330mg; Carbohydrate 5g (Dietary Fiber 0g); Protein 23g.

Chicken-Vegetable Kabobs

6 servings

No matter what the spelling—kabob or kebab— everyone likes them! Include an assortment of vegetables so that guests can choose their favorites.

1/3 cup olive or vegetable oil
1 tablespoon chopped fresh or 1 teaspoon
    dried basil leaves
1 1/2 teaspoons snipped fresh or
    1/2 teaspoon dried dill weed
2 cloves garlic, finely chopped
1 pound skinless boneless chicken breast
    halves, cut into strips
Assorted bite-size pieces fresh vegetables
    (carrots,* zucchini, yellow squash, peeled
    red pearl onions, small red potatoes,*
    ears of corn cut into 1 1/2-inch chunks*)

Mix oil, basil, dill weed and garlic in medium glass or plastic dish. Add chicken; stir to coat with marinade. Cover dish or seal bag and refrigerate 1 to 2 hours. Remove chicken from marinade; reserve marinade.

Heat coals or gas grill. Thread chicken and vegetables alternately on each of six 15-inch metal skewers, leaving space between each. Cover and grill kabobs 4 to 5 inches from medium coals 10 to 15 minutes, turning and brushing 2 or 3 times with marinade, until chicken is no longer pink in center.

1 SERVING: Calories 265 (Calories from Fat 110); Fat 12g (Saturated 2g); Cholesterol 40mg; Sodium 50mg; Carbohydrate 23g (Dietary Fiber 3g); Protein 19g.

Partially cook before grilling to ensure doneness. Place carrots, potatoes, corn and 2 tablespoons water in microwavable dish. Cover and microwave on High 3 to 6 minutes.

Chicken-Vegetable Kabobs

Honey-Glazed Chicken

6 servings

1/2 cup honey
2 tablespoons reduced-sodium chicken broth
2 tablespoons mustard
1/2 teaspoon grated lemon peel
2 tablespoons lemon juice
1/4 teaspoon salt
3- to 3 1/2-pound cut-up broiler-fryer
    chicken, skin removed

Heat coals or gas grill. Mix all ingredients except chicken. Cover and grill chicken, bone sides down, 5 to 6 inches from medium heat 15 to 30 minutes. Turn chicken. Cover and grill 20 to 40 minutes longer, turning and brushing 2 or 3 times with honey mixture, until juice of chicken is no longer pink when centers of thickest pieces are cut. Discard any remaining honey mixture.

1 SERVING: Calories 255 (Calories from Fat 55); Fat 6g (Saturated 2g); Cholesterol 75mg; Sodium 240mg; Carbohydrate 24g (Dietary Fiber 0g); Protein 26g.

Spicy Peach Chicken

4 servings

1 jar (12 ounces) peach preserves
1 tablespoon orange juice concentrate
1 teaspoon grated gingerroot
1 teaspoon ground cinnamon
1/2 teaspoon ground nutmeg
1/4 teaspoon salt
4 skinless boneless chicken breast halves
    (about 1 pound)

Mix all ingredients except chicken in shallow nonmetal dish or heavy-duty resealable plastic bag. Add chicken, turning to coat with marinade. Cover dish or seal bag and refrigerate 2 to 4 hours, turning chicken occasionally.

Heat coals or gas grill. Remove chicken from marinade; reserve marinade. Place chicken on grill; brush with half of the marinade. Cover and grill 5 to 6 inches from medium heat 15 to 20 minutes, turning once and brushing with remaining marinade, until juice of chicken is no longer pink when centers of thickest pieces are cut.

If desired, heat remaining marinade to boiling. Boil 1 minute. Serve with chicken.

1 SERVING: Calories 370 (Calories from Fat 35); Fat 4g (Saturated 1g); Cholesterol 65mg; Sodium 240mg; Carbohydrate 57g (Dietary Fiber 1g); Protein 27g.

Spicy Peach Chicken

Chicken with Peppers and Artichokes

4 servings

1 jar (6 ounces) marinated artichoke hearts
1/3 cup white wine or white wine vinegar
4 skinless boneless chicken breast halves
   (1 pound)
2 medium bell peppers, each cut lengthwise
   into fourths
4 medium green onions, sliced (1/2 cup)
1/4 teaspoon pepper

Drain marinade from artichoke hearts; reserve marinade. Mix marinade and wine in shallow nonmetal dish or heavy-duty resealable plastic bag. Add chicken and peppers, turning to coat with marinade. Cover dish or seal bag and refrigerate at least 8 hours but no longer than 24 hours.

Brush grill rack with vegetable oil. Heat coals or gas grill for direct heat. Remove chicken and peppers from marinade; reserve marinade. Cover and grill chicken 4 to 6 inches from medium heat 5 minutes. Turn chicken; add peppers to grill. Cover and grill 10 to 15 minutes longer or until peppers are tender and juice of chicken is no longer pink when centers of thickest pieces are cut.

Strain marinade. Mix marinade, artichoke hearts, green onions and pepper. Heat to boiling; boil and stir 1 minute. Serve artichoke sauce with chicken and peppers.

1 SERVING: Calories 175 (Calories from Fat 45); Fat 5g (Saturated 2g); Cholesterol 65mg; Sodium 200mg; Carbohydrate 8g (Dietary Fiber 3g); Protein 28g.

Apple-Stuffed Chicken Breasts

4 servings

To add a savory kick to this sweetened chicken, add 1 teaspoon chopped fresh sage leaves to the cinnamon-sugar mixture.

4 skinless boneless chicken breast halves
   (about 1 pound)
2 tablespoons sugar
1/4 teaspoon ground cinnamon
2 medium tart cooking apples, peeled
   and cut into thin slices
1 cup apple cider
1 tablespoon cornstarch

Heat coals or gas grill. Place chicken breast halves between 2 pieces of waxed paper. Pound chicken to 1/8-inch thickness. Mix sugar and cinnamon. Coat apple slices with sugar mixture. Divide apple slices among chicken breast halves. Fold chicken around apples; secure with toothpicks.

Cover and grill chicken 4 to 6 inches from medium heat 20 to 25 minutes, turning once, until juice is no longer pink when centers of thickest pieces are cut. Remove toothpicks.

Mix apple cider and cornstarch in 1-quart saucepan. Cook over medium heat, stirring constantly, until thickened and bubbly. Spoon over chicken.

1 SERVING: Calories 235 (Calories from Fat 35); Fat 4g (Saturated 1g); Cholesterol 65mg; Sodium 65mg; Carbohydrate 25g (Dietary Fiber 1g); Protein 26g.

Apple-Stuffed Chicken Breasts

Ginger-Lime-Marinated Swordfish Steaks

6 servings

Any firm fish, such as tuna or halibut, can be used in this recipe.

1 1/2 pounds swordfish steaks, 3/4 to 1 inch thick
1/4 cup lime juice
2 tablespoons olive or vegetable oil
1 teaspoon finely chopped gingerroot
1/4 teaspoon salt
Dash of ground red pepper (cayenne)
1 clove garlic, crushed
Lime wedges, if desired

If fish steaks are large, cut into 6 serving pieces. Mix remaining ingredients except lime wedges in shallow nonmetal dish or heavy-duty resealable plastic bag. Add fish, turning to coat with marinade. Cover dish or seal bag and refrigerate at least 30 minutes but no longer than 2 hours.

Heat coals or gas grill. Remove fish from marinade; reserve marinade. Cover and grill fish 4 to 6 inches from medium heat 15 to 20 minutes, brushing 2 or 3 times with marinade and turning once, until fish flakes easily with fork. Discard any remaining marinade. Serve fish with lime wedges.

1 SERVING: Calories 170 (Calories from Fat 90); Fat 10g (Saturated 2g); Cholesterol 60mg; Sodium 150mg; Carbohydrate 1g (Dietary Fiber 0g); Protein 19g.

Strawberry Margarita Swordfish

6 servings

1/2 cup nonalcoholic margarita mix
3 tablespoons lime juice
1 clove garlic, crushed
1 1/2 pounds swordfish, tuna or marlin steaks, 1/2 to 1 inch thick
1/2 teaspoon coarse salt
3 cups quartered strawberries
1/2 cup coarsely broken fat-free pretzels

Mix margarita mix, lime juice and garlic in shallow glass or plastic dish. Add fish, turning to coat with marinade. Cover and refrigerate at least 1 hour but no longer than 24 hours.

Heat coals or gas grill. Remove fish from marinade; reserve marinade. Place fish on grill. Brush with marinade; sprinkle with 1/4 teaspoon of the salt. Cover and grill about 4 inches from medium heat 10 minutes, brushing 1 or 2 times with marinade. Turn fish. Brush with remaining marinade; sprinkle with remaining 1/4 teaspoon salt. Cover and grill 5 to 10 minutes longer or until fish flakes easily with fork. Spoon strawberries and pretzels over fish.

1 SERVING: Calories 185 (Calories from Fat 55); Fat 6g (Saturated 2g); Cholesterol 60mg; Sodium 360mg; Carbohydrate 14g (Dietary Fiber 2g); Protein 20g.

Strawberry Margarita Swordfish

Provençal Fish Kabobs

6 servings

1/2 cup red wine vinegar
1 tablespoon vegetable oil
2 teaspoons chopped fresh or 1/2 teaspoon
    dried tarragon leaves
2 teaspoons chopped fresh or 1/2 teaspoon
    dried thyme leaves
1 pound tuna or swordfish steaks, cut into
    2-inch pieces
1 small eggplant (1 pound)
2 cups cherry tomatoes
1/2 pound medium whole mushrooms
6 large cloves garlic, peeled

Mix vinegar, oil, tarragon and thyme in shallow nonmetal dish or heavy-duty resealable plastic bag. Add fish, stirring to coat with marinade. Cover dish or seal bag and refrigerate 20 minutes.

Brush grill with vegetable oil. Heat coals or gas heat for direct heat. Remove fish from marinade; reserve marinade. Cut eggplant into 1-inch slices; cut slices into fourths. Thread fish, eggplant, tomatoes and mushrooms alternately on each of six 15-inch skewers, leaving space between each. Thread 1 clove garlic on end of each skewer.

Cover and grill kabobs 5 to 6 inches from medium heat 12 to 15 minutes, turning and brushing 2 to 3 times with marinade, until fish flakes easily with fork. Discard any remaining marinade.

1 SERVING: Calories 170 (Calories from Fat 65); Fat 7g (Saturated 2g); Cholesterol 30mg; Sodium 40mg; Carbohydrate 11g (Dietary Fiber 3g); Protein 19g.

Salmon with Cucumber Relish

6 servings

Cucumber Relish (below)
1 large salmon fillet (about 2 pounds)
2 tablespoons olive or vegetable oil
1/4 to 1/2 teaspoon dried dill weed
1/2 teaspoon salt
1/4 teaspoon pepper

Prepare Cucumber Relish. Heat coals or gas grill for direct heat. Place fish on 24-inch piece of heavy-duty aluminum foil. Brush fish with oil. Sprinkle with dill weed, salt and pepper. Wrap foil securely around fish.

Cover and grill fish 4 inches from medium heat 20 to 30 minutes or until fish flakes easily with fork. Serve relish with fish.

CUCUMBER RELISH

1 medium cucumber, seeded and coarsely
    chopped (1 1/4 cups)
2 tablespoons chopped onion
2 tablespoons white vinegar
2 tablespoons water
1 teaspoon sugar
1/2 teaspoon salt
2 tablespoons chopped fresh parsley

Mix all ingredients in nonmetal bowl. Cover and refrigerate at least 1 hour but no longer than 8 hours. Drain relish.

1 SERVING: Calories 255 (Calories from Fat 115); Fat 13g (Saturated 3g); Cholesterol 100mg; Sodium 480mg; Carbohydrate 2g (Dietary Fiber 0g); Protein 32g.

Salmon with Cucumber Relish

Ginger-Lime Tuna Steaks

6 servings

Ginger-Lime Marinade (below)
**1 1/2 pounds tuna, swordfish or halibut
steaks, 3/4 to 1 inch thick**
Lime wedges, if desired

Prepare Ginger-Lime Marinade. If fish steaks are large, cut into 6 serving pieces. Place in shallow nonmetal dish or heavy-duty resealable plastic bag. Add marinade; turn fish to coat with marinade. Cover dish or seal bag and refrigerate at least 1 hour but no longer than 24 hours.

Brush grill rack with vegetable oil. Heat coals or gas grill for direct heat. Remove fish from marinade; reserve marinade. Cover and grill fish about 4 inches from medium heat 15 to 20 minutes, brushing 2 or 3 times with marinade and turning once, until fish flakes easily with fork. Discard any remaining marinade. Serve fish with lime wedges.

GINGER-LIME MARINADE

1/4 cup lime juice
2 tablespoons olive or vegetable oil
1 teaspoon finely chopped gingerroot
1/4 teaspoon salt
Dash of ground red pepper (cayenne)
1 clove garlic, crushed

Mix all ingredients.

1 SERVING: Calories 200 (Calories from Fat 90); Fat 10g (Saturated 2g); Cholesterol 45mg; Sodium 140mg; Carbohydrate 1g (Dietary Fiber 0g); Protein 26g.

Tarragon Marlin Steaks with Vermouth

6 servings

**1/2 cup dry vermouth or 1/4 cup lemon
juice plus 1/4 cup water**
1/4 teaspoon aromatic bitters
4 large sprigs tarragon
**1 1/2 pounds marlin, tuna or opah steaks,
1 to 1 1/2 inches thick**
**1 1/2 teaspoons chopped fresh or
1/2 teaspoons dried tarragon leaves**

Mix vermouth and bitters in shallow nonmetal dish. Add 2 sprigs tarragon. Add fish, turning to coat with marinade. Top fish with remaining 2 sprigs tarragon. Cover and let stand, turning once, at least 15 minutes but no longer than 30 minutes.

Brush grill rack with vegetable oil. Heat coals or gas grill for direct heat. Drain fish; discard marinade but not the tarragon sprigs. Place all 4 tarragon sprigs directly on hot coals. Immediate cover and grill fish 4 inches from medium heat 10 to 15 minutes, turning once, until fish flakes easily with fork. Remove fish to platter. Sprinkle with chopped tarragon.

1 SERVING: Calories 160 (Calories from Fat 70); Fat 8g (Saturated 2g); Cholesterol 65mg; Sodium 60mg; Carbohydrate 0g (Dietary Fiber 0g); Protein 22g.

Spicy Shrimp with Creole Sauce

4 servings

These delicious shrimp can also be served as an appetizer. Use the Creole Sauce on the side for dipping. Make grilling the shrimp easier by using a grill screen to cook them in.

1 pound fresh or frozen raw large shrimp
   in shells
1/2 cup olive or vegetable oil
1/2 teaspoon poultry seasoning
1/2 teaspoon dried oregano leaves
   (do not substitute fresh)
1/2 teaspoon chili oil or crushed red pepper
1/4 teaspoon salt
1 clove garlic, finely chopped
Creole Sauce (right)
3 cups hot cooked rice

Peel shrimp. (If shrimp are frozen, do not thaw; peel in cold water.) Make a shallow cut lengthwise down back of each shrimp; wash out vein.

Mix remaining ingredients except Creole Sauce and rice in large nonmetal bowl. Add shrimp, stirring to coat with marinade. Cover and refrigerate at least 15 minutes but no longer than 1 hour.

Brush grill rack with vegetable oil. Heat coals or gas grill for direct heat. Prepare Creole Sauce; keep warm. Drain shrimp; discard marinade. Grill shrimp uncovered 4 inches from medium heat 4 to 6 minutes, turning once, until shrimp are pink and firm.

Serve shrimp and sauce over rice.

CREOLE SAUCE

1 tablespoon margarine or butter
1 small green bell pepper, diced (1/2 cup)
2 cloves garlic, finely chopped
1 can (14 1/2 ounces) stewed tomatoes,
   undrained
1 tablespoon chopped fresh or 1 teaspoon
   dried thyme leaves
1/8 teaspoon pepper
1/8 teaspoon red pepper sauce
2 large bay leaves

Melt margarine in 1 1/2-quart saucepan over medium heat. Cook bell pepper and garlic in margarine, stirring occasionally, until bell pepper is crisp-tender. Stir in remaining ingredients, breaking up tomatoes. Heat to boiling; reduce heat to low. Simmer uncovered 5 to 10 minutes, stirring occasionally, until thickened. Discard bay leaves. Serve warm.

1 SERVING: Calories 310 (Calories from Fat 100); Fat 11g (Saturated 2g); Cholesterol 105mg; Sodium 330mg; Carbohydrate 39g (Dietary Fiber 2g); Protein 16g.

Get Fit with Fish

Fresh fish is a boon to anyone who is eating healthy. With the growing industry of farm-raised fish, buying fresh fish is much easier than ever before. Fish has lots of nutrients and is naturally low in calories. What's better, grilling fish adds lots of flavor without added calories. Try seasoning fish with fresh lemon, cocktail sauce or horseradish, rather than butter or tartar sauce.

Honey-Thyme Grilled Shrimp

6 servings

These shrimp swim in a sophisticated marinade, then leap on the grill as a no-fuss kabob. This champion comes from the Marvelous Marinade Recipe Contest, sponsored by Zip-Loc® Bags, Dow Brands.

Roasted Garlic Marinade (right)
2 pounds fresh or frozen raw large shrimp
   in shells
1 medium red bell pepper, cut into 1-inch
   pieces and blanched
1 medium yellow bell pepper, cut into
   1-inch pieces and blanched
1 medium red onion, cut into fourths and
   separated into chunks

Prepare Roasted Garlic Marinade. Peel shrimp. (If shrimp are frozen, do not thaw; peel in cold water.) Make a shallow cut lengthwise down back of each shrimp; wash out vein.

Pour 1/2 cup of the marinade into small resealable plastic bag; seal bag and refrigerate until serving. Pour remaining marinade into heavy-duty resealable plastic bag. Add shrimp, bell peppers and onion, turning to coat with marinade. Seal bag and refrigerate at least 2 hours but no longer than 24 hours.

Brush grill rack with vegetable oil. Heat coals or gas grill for direct heat. Remove shrimp and vegetables from marinade; drain well. Discard marinade. Thread shrimp and vegetables alternately on each of six 15-inch metal skewers, leaving space between each. Grill kabobs uncovered 4 to 6 inches from hot heat 7 to 10 minutes, turning once, until shrimp are pink and firm.

Place kabobs on serving tray. Cut a tiny corner from small plastic bag of reserve marinade, using scissors. Drizzle marinade over shrimp and vegetables.

ROASTED GARLIC MARINADE

1 medium bulb garlic
1/3 cup olive or vegetable oil
2/3 cup orange juice
1/4 cup spicy honey mustard
3 tablespoons honey
3/4 teaspoon dried thyme leaves, crushed

Heat oven to 375°F. Cut one-third off top of unpeeled garlic bulb, exposing cloves. Place garlic in small baking dish; drizzle with oil. Cover tightly and bake 45 minutes; cool. Squeeze garlic pulp from papery skin. Place garlic and remaining ingredients in blender. Cover and blend on high speed until smooth.

1 SERVING: Calories 135 (Calories from Fat 45); Fat 5g (Saturated 1g); Cholesterol 140mg; Sodium 200mg; Carbohydrate 7g (Dietary Fiber 1g); Protein 16g.

Herbed Seafood

4 servings

For a special touch, grill the seafood in natural baking shells, which are found at some supermarkets or kitchen specialty stores. Spray each shell with nonstick cooking spray before filling, then enclose each in a 12-inch square of aluminum foil. Cover and grill 5 to 7 minutes.

1/2 pound fresh or frozen raw large shrimp in shells
1/2 pound bay or sea scallops
1/2 pound orange roughy fillets, cut into 1-inch pieces
2 tablespoons chopped fresh or 2 teaspoons dried marjoram leaves
1/2 teaspoon grated lemon peel
1/8 teaspoon white pepper
3 tablespoons margarine or butter, melted
2 tablespoons lemon juice
4 cups hot cooked pasta or rice

Heat coals or gas grill for direct heat. If shrimp, scallops or fish are frozen, do not thaw; rinse in cold water. Peel shrimp. Make a shallow cut lengthwise down back of each shrimp; wash out vein. If using sea scallops, cut each in half.

Spray 18-inch square piece of heavy-duty aluminum foil with nonstick cooking spray. Arrange shrimp, scallops and fish on foil, placing shrimp on top. Sprinkle with marjoram, lemon peel and pepper. Drizzle with margarine and lemon juice. Bring corners of foil up to center and seal loosely.

Cover and grill foil packet 4 inches from medium heat 8 to 10 minutes or until scallops are white, fish flakes easily with fork and shrimp are pink and firm.

Serve seafood mixture over pasta.

1 SERVING: Calories 370 (Calories from Fat 100); Fat 11g (Saturated 3g); Cholesterol 130mg; Sodium 390mg; Carbohydrate 32g (Dietary Fiber 1g); Protein 37g.

Top It with Tomatoes

A thick, flavorful tomato sauce or cut-up fresh tomatoes seasoned with vinegar make a great topping for grilled chicken, fish or lean meats, and is low in calories. Try this easy topping the next time you fire up the grill.

Fresh Herb Vegetable Grill

4 servings

1 large bell pepper, cut lengthwise into fourths
2 medium zucchini, cut lengthwise in half
8 small new red potatoes, cut into fourths
1/3 cup plus 2 tablespoons reduced-fat Italian dressing
3 tablespoons chopped mixed fresh herbs (such as basil, cilantro, dill weed, rosemary, thyme)
4 ears unhusked corn
8 to 12 fresh herb leaves, if desired

Place bell pepper, zucchini, potatoes, 1/3 cup of the dressing and the chopped herbs in large resealable heavy-duty plastic bag. Shake sealed bag to evenly distribute dressing. Let stand at least 30 minutes but no longer than 1 hour.

Heat coals or gas grill. Carefully pull back husks from corn but do not detach. Remove silk. Brush corn lightly with remaining 2 tablespoons dressing. Place 2 or 3 herb leaves on corn. Pull husk back up around corn and tie security at tip with fine wire or heavy kitchen string. Remove vegetables from marinade; reserve marinade.

Cover and grill corn and potatoes about 4 inches from medium heat 10 minutes. Add zucchini and bell pepper to grill. Cover and grill 10 to 20 minutes, turning frequently and brushing with marinade, until vegetables are tender. (Remove vegetables from grill as they become done; keep warm.)

1 SERVING: Calories 310 (Calories from Fat 25); Fat 3g (Saturated 1g); Cholesterol 2mg; Sodium 150mg; Carbohydrate 71g (Dietary Fiber 8g); Protein 8g.

Fresh Herb Vegetable Grill

Veggie Grilling Guide

Hooray for roasted vegetables! Vegetables are loaded with vitamins and nutrients and are very low in fat—or fat-free. Roasting allows the sugars naturally present in vegetables to caramelize, which sweetens them, and the veggies pick up that great grilled flavor, making them a favorite on the dinner table. Instead of brushing on oil to roast the vegetables, spray them lightly with olive oil cooking spray. You'll save calories and fat but still have great taste.

Heat coals or gas grill. Grill vegetables 4 to 5 inches from medium heat. Use the chart below for approximate grilling times:

10 MINUTES

Carrots, small whole, partially cooked*

Cherry tomatoes, whole

Mushrooms, whole

Onions, cut into 1/2-inch slices

Potatoes, cut into 1-inch wedges, partially cooked*

15 MINUTES

Bell peppers, cut into 1-inch strips

Eggplant, cut into 3/4-inch slices

Green beans, whole

Pattypan squash, whole

Zucchini, cut into 3/4-inch pieces

20 MINUTES

Asparagus spears, whole

Broccoli spears, cut lengthwise in half

Cauliflowerets, but lengthwise in half

Corn on the cob, husked and wrapped in aluminum foil if desired

*Before grilling, cook in boiling water 5 to 10 minutes or just until tender.

Grilled Thai Marinated Summer Squash

4 servings

1 medium zucchini, cut lengthwise in half
1 medium yellow summer squash, cut
**   lengthwise in half**
1/4 cup reduced-sodium chicken broth
1 tablespoon lime juice
1/2 teaspoon chopped fresh or
**   1/8 teaspoon dried mint leaves**
1/2 teaspoon chopped fresh or
**   1/8 teaspoon dried basil leaves**
1/2 teaspoon finely chopped gingerroot
1/2 teaspoon finely chopped jalapeño chili
1 teaspoon reduced-sodium soy sauce

Place zucchini and squash in square baking dish 8×8×2 inches. Mix remaining ingredients; pour over vegetables. Cover and let stand at least 1 hour but no longer than 2 hours.

Heat coals or gas grill. Remove vegetables from marinade; reserve marinade. Cover and grill vegetables 4 inches from medium heat 10 to 15 minutes, turning and brushing 2 or 3 times with marinade, until golden brown and tender.

Cut each crosswise into 4 pieces. Toss with any remaining marinade.

1 SERVING: Calories 10 (Calories from Fat 0); Fat 0g (Saturated 0g); Cholesterol 0mg; Sodium 80mg; Carbohydrate 3g (Dietary Fiber 1g); Protein 1g.

Skewered Ratatouille

6 servings

Sprinkling eggplant with salt and letting it stand 30 minutes eliminates the bitter taste often found in eggplant.

1 small eggplant (about 3/4 pound)
3/4 teaspoon salt
2 small zucchini (about 1/2 pound)
1 medium green bell pepper
1 small onion
1/3 cup Italian dressing
1 cup spaghetti sauce or Italian tomato
**   sauce, heated**

Cut eggplant into 1-inch chunks. Place eggplant in colander over bowl or sink. Sprinkle with salt. Let drain 30 minutes. Rinse and pat dry.

Brush grill rack with vegetable oil. Heat coals or gas grill for direct heat. Cut zucchini, bell pepper and onion into 1-inch chunks. Thread eggplant, zucchini, bell pepper and onion alternately on each of six 10-inch metal skewers, leaving space between each. Brush with dressing. Cover and grill kabobs 4 to 6 inches from medium heat 15 to 20 minutes, turning and brushing twice with dressing, until vegetables are crisp-tender.

Heat spaghetti sauce in small pan or can with label removed during last 10 minutes of grilling, stirring occasionally. Serve kabobs with spaghetti sauce.

1 SERVING: Calories 120 (Calories from Fat 70); Fat 9g (Saturated 1g); Cholesterol 0mg; Sodium 670mg; Carbohydrate 13g (Dietary Fiber 3g); Protein 2g.

Meatless

Vegetarian Chili (page 288)

(continued on next page)

Hearty Bean and Pasta Stew

4 servings

Running late? For a quick and tasty meal, this stew can be prepared in about 20 minutes.

3/4 cup uncooked pasta shells
1/4 cup chopped green bell pepper
1 tablespoon chopped fresh or 1 teaspoon
    dried basil leaves
1 teaspoon Worcestershire sauce
1 large tomato, coarsely chopped (1 cup)
1 small onion, chopped (1/4 cup)
1 clove garlic, finely chopped
1 can (15 to 16 ounces) kidney beans,
    drained
1 can (14 1/2 ounces) ready-to-serve
    vegetable or chicken broth
1 can (8 ounces) garbanzo beans, drained

Mix all ingredients in 2-quart saucepan. Heat to boiling, stirring occasionally; reduce heat. Cover and simmer about 15 minutes, stirring occasionally, until pasta is tender.

1 SERVING: Calories 200 (Calories from Fat 20); Fat 2g (Saturated 0g); Cholesterol 0mg; Sodium 720mg; Carbohydrate 40g (Dietary Fiber 6g); Protein 11g.

Does Pasta Make You Fat?

First we hear how good pasta is for you; then, headlines and television news stories tell us that pasta makes you fat. The claim is that pasta boosts insulin levels and causes weight gain. So what is the truth about pasta? The truth is, there's no need to avoid eating pasta.

After eating, blood sugar (glucose) levels rise in our bodies, causing insulin, a component necessary to break down carbohydrates, to be released into the bloodstream. Insulin helps body cells take in and store glucose as energy. In insulin-resistant people, the cells are not as sensitive to insulin, so the body continues to make more, which eventually can result in diabetes. It isn't the insulin resistance that causes weight gain, but rather, obesity causes insulin resistance, which may increase risk for other diseases, such as high blood pressure, heart disease and diabetes.

Pasta is not a big problem for people who are insulin resistant, since it raises blood sugar only moderately. Experts in nutrition still recommend a diet low in fat and rich in carbohydrates. Your best bet is to eat less fat, count calories (any extra calories are stored as fat), choose foods high in fiber, such as whole grains, legumes and vegetables, and stay active, as exercise tones muscles and balances calorie intake.

Vegetarian Chili

4 servings

(photograph on page 284)

2 teaspoons vegetable oil
1 large onion, chopped (1 cup)
1 small green bell pepper, chopped (1/2 cup)
1 medium zucchini, cut into 1×1/2×1/4-inch
    sticks (2 cups)
2 cloves garlic, chopped
2 cans (15 to 16 ounces each) pinto beans,
    rinsed and drained
2 cans (14 1/2 ounces each) salsa tomatoes
    with diced green chilis, undrained
2 teaspoons chili powder
1/4 cup sour cream, if desired
Chili powder, if desired

Heat oil in 4-quart nonstick saucepan over medium-high heat. Cook onion, bell pepper, zucchini and garlic in oil, stirring frequently, until onion is tender. Stir in beans, tomatoes and 2 teaspoons chili powder; reduce heat. Cover and simmer 20 minutes. Serve with dollop of sour cream; sprinkle with chili powder.

1 SERVING: Calories 280 (Calories from Fat 35); Fat 4g (Saturated 1g); Cholesterol 0mg; Sodium 790mg; Carbohydrate 63g (Dietary Fiber 20g); Protein 18g.

HEALTHY HINT

Enjoy a bowl of creamy vegetable soup with lots of flavor but not lots of fat. Instead of adding cream to the soup, puree a portion or all of the cooked vegetables with some of the cooking liquid, then stir the pureed mixture into the remaining soup.

Squash and Bean Chili Stew

6 servings

2 tablespoons vegetable oil
1/4 cup chopped onion
1 clove garlic, finely chopped
1 large red bell pepper, cut into
    2×1/2-inch strips
2 medium poblano or Anaheim chilis,
    seeded and cut into 2×1/2-inch strips
1 jalapeño chili, seeded and chopped
1 cup cubed Hubbard or acorn squash
    (1/2 pound)
2 cans (14 1/2 ounces each) reduced-sodium
    chicken broth
1/2 teaspoon salt
1/2 teaspoon pepper
1/2 teaspoon ground coriander
1 cup thinly sliced zucchini
1 cup thinly sliced yellow summer squash
1 can (15 1/4 ounces) whole kernel corn,
    drained
1 can (15 to 16 ounces) pinto beans, drained

Heat oil in Dutch oven over medium heat. Cook onion and garlic in oil, stirring occasionally, until onion is tender. Stir in bell pepper and poblano and jalapeño chilis. Cook 15 minutes. Stir in Hubbard squash, broth, salt, pepper and coriander. Heat to boiling; reduce heat. Cover and simmer about 15 minutes or until squash is tender. Stir in remaining ingredients. Simmer uncovered about 10 minutes, stirring occasionally, until zucchini is tender.

1 SERVING: Calories 210 (Calories from Fat 55); Fat 6g (Saturated 1g); Cholesterol 0mg; Sodium 400mg; Carbohydrate 36g (Dietary Fiber 8g); Protein 11g.

Squash and Bean Chili Stew

Three-Bean Chili

5 servings

1 large onion, chopped (1 cup)
2 cloves garlic, crushed
1 can (14 1/2 ounces) ready-to-serve
   vegetable or chicken broth
2 large tomatoes, seeded and cubed (2 cups)
2 tablespoons chopped fresh cilantro
1 tablespoon chopped fresh or 1 teaspoon
   dried oregano leaves
2 teaspoons chili powder
1 teaspoon ground cumin
1 can (15 to 16 ounces) kidney beans,
   undrained
1 can (15 to 16 ounces) garbanzo beans,
   undrained
1 can (15 ounces) spicy chili beans,
   undrained

Cook onion and garlic in 1/4 cup of the broth in nonstick Dutch oven over medium heat about 5 minutes, stirring occasionally, until onion is crisp-tender. Stir in remaining broth and remaining ingredients except beans. Heat to boiling; reduce heat. Cover and simmer 30 minutes, stirring occasionally. Stir in beans. Heat to boiling; reduce heat. Simmer uncovered about 20 minutes, stirring occasionally, until desired consistency.

1 SERVING: Calories 245 (Calories from Fat); Fat 3g (Saturated g); Cholesterol 0mg; Sodium 740mg; Carbohydrate 53g (Dietary Fiber g); Protein 17g.

Mexican Polenta Pie

6 servings

1/4 cup cornmeal
2 cups water
1/4 teaspoon salt
1 egg, slightly beaten
1 can (15 to 16 ounces) chili beans, drained
3/4 cup shredded Monterey Jack cheese
   with jalapeño peppers (3 ounces)
1/3 cup crushed corn or tortilla chips

Heat oven to 375°. Grease pie plate, 9 × 1 1/4 inches. Mix cornmeal, water and salt in 2-quart saucepan. Heat to boiling, stirring constantly; reduce heat to medium. Cook about 6 minutes, stirring frequently, until mixture is very thick; remove from heat. Quickly stir in egg. Let stand 5 minutes.

Spread cornmeal mixture in pie plate. Bake uncovered 15 minutes. Spread beans over cornmeal mixture. Sprinkle with cheese and corn chips. Bake uncovered about 20 minutes or until center is set. Let stand 5 minutes before cutting.

1 SERVING: Calories 185 (Calories from Fat 65); Fat 7g (Saturated 3g); Cholesterol 50mg; Sodium 470mg; Carbohydrate 25g (Dietary Fiber 3g); Protein 8g.

Mexican Polenta Pie

Beans Are Healthy!

Not only do beans taste good, they also are incredibly good for you.

VITAMINS AND MINERALS: Most beans are rich in folic acid, a vitamin believed to help reduce the incidence of birth defects and heart disease. Beans are a good source of vitamin B6, niacin and thiamin, too. A one-cup serving of beans provides about 20 to 30 percent of the daily value of iron, plus some zinc, calcium and magnesium.

PROTEIN: One cup of cooked beans has the same amount of protein as two ounces of meat. Unlike other foods high in protein, such as meat, beans contain little or no fat. Less than 1 percent of the calories in beans comes from fat. In contrast, 60 to 85 percent of the calories in meat comes from fat.

FIBER: Beans are full of fiber. A diet high in fiber has been shown to help lower blood cholesterol levels and reduce the risk of colon cancer and possibly breast cancer. Fiber can relieve constipation as well. Increasing fiber can be tricky. It's best to start slowly so your body can adjust to the complex sugars, called oligosaccharides, that are found in beans. It's the inability of the body to digest oligosaccharides that may cause gas in some people.

Bean Breakdown

Bean (1 cup cooked)	Fiber (grams)	Protein (grams)	Iron (% Daily Value)	Folic Acid
Black	7	15	20	64
Great Northern	6	15	21	45
Kidney	6	15	29	57
Pinquitos (Pink)	7	15	22	71
Pinto	7	14	25	74
Red	11	11	29	33

Bean-Cheese Pie

8 servings

3/4 cup all-purpose flour
1 cup shredded Cheddar cheese (4 ounces)
1 1/2 teaspoons baking powder
1/2 teaspoon salt
1/3 cup milk
1 egg, slightly beaten
1 can (15 1/2 ounces) garbanzo beans, drained
1 can (15 ounces) kidney beans, drained
1 can (8 ounces) tomato sauce
1/2 cup chopped green bell pepper
   (about 1 small)
1/4 cup chopped onion (about 1 small)
2 teaspoons chili powder
2 teaspoons fresh or 1/2 teaspoon dried
   oregano leaves
1/4 teaspoon garlic powder

Heat oven to 375°. Spray pie plate, 10 × 1 1/2 inches, with nonstick cooking spray. Mix flour, 1/2 cup of the cheese, the baking powder and salt in medium bowl. Stir in milk and egg until blended. Spread over bottom and up sides of pie plate.

Mix remaining ingredients except 1/2 cup cheese. Spoon into pie plate; sprinkle with remaining cheese. Bake uncovered about 25 minutes or until edge is puffy and light brown. Let stand 10 minutes before cutting.

1 SERVING: Calories 315 (Calories from Fat 100); Fat 11g (Saturated 5g); Cholesterol 50mg; Sodium 730mg; Carbohydrate 40g (Dietary Fiber 4g); Protein 18g.

Spicy Garbanzos

4 servings

Mustard seeds, available in both white and brown varieties, add unexpected flavor and crunch to food.

1 tablespoon vegetable oil
1 teaspoon mustard seed
1 large onion, chopped (1 cup)
1/2 cup vegetable or chicken broth
2 tablespoons tomato paste
1/2 teaspoon salt
1/4 teaspoon ground cinnamon
1/8 teaspoon ground cloves
2 cans (15 to 16 ounces each) garbanzo
   beans, rinsed and drained
2 tablespoons chopped parsley, if desired

Heat oil in 2-quart saucepan over medium-high heat. Cook mustard seed and onion in oil, stirring occasionally, until onion is tender. Stir in remaining ingredients. Cook about 5 minutes, stirring occasionally, until beans are hot. Sprinkle with parsley.

1 SERVING: Calories 270 (Calories from Fat 70); Fat 8g (Saturated 1g); Cholesterol 0mg; Sodium 830mg; Carbohydrate 45g (Dietary Fiber 9g); Protein 14g.

Garden Phyllo Quiches

4 servings

Serve these individual quiches with lemon–poppy seed muffins and fresh strawberries.

1 package (10 ounces) frozen chopped
    spinach, thawed and squeezed to drain
1 cup sliced mushrooms (3 ounces)
1 cup milk
1/2 teaspoon ground mustard (dry)
1/4 teaspoon salt
1/8 teaspoon ground nutmeg
2 eggs
4 frozen (thawed) phyllo sheets
2 teaspoons margarine or butter, melted
1/4 cup shredded mozzarella cheese (1 ounce)
1/4 cup alfalfa sprouts

Heat oven to 350°. Spray 10-inch skillet with nonstick cooking spray. Cook spinach and mushrooms in skillet over medium heat, stirring occasionally, until spinach is wilted and mushrooms are tender; remove from heat. Mix milk, mustard, salt, nutmeg and eggs; set aside.

Spray four 6-ounce custard cups with nonstick cooking spray. Place 1 phyllo sheet on flat surface; lightly brush with margarine. Top with remaining phyllo sheets, brushing each with margarine. Cut phyllo into fourths. Place 1 phyllo section in each custard cup. Trim overhanging edge of phyllo 1 inch from rim of cup.

Divide spinach mixture evenly among cups. Pour about 1/3 cup egg mixture into each cup. Fold edges of phyllo toward center. Bake 15 to 20 minutes or until egg mixture is set. Sprinkle with cheese. Top with alfalfa sprouts. Serve immediately.

1 SERVING: Calories 185 (Calories from Fat 65); Fat 7g (Saturated 3g); Cholesterol 115mg; Sodium 370mg; Carbohydrate 20g (Dietary Fiber 1g); Protein 11g.

Spaghetti Torte

8 servings

For a new twist on spaghetti, try this simple torte. It's easy to cut and serve too!

1 package (16 ounces) spaghetti
1/2 cup grated Parmesan cheese
1/2 cup ricotta cheese
1 tablespoon Italian seasoning
4 egg whites or 1/2 cup fat-free
    cholesterol-free egg product
1/4 cup chopped fresh or 1 1/2 teaspoons
    dried basil leaves
2 medium tomatoes, coarsely chopped
4 slices (1 ounce each) provolone cheese,
    cut into fourths
Spaghetti sauce, if desired

Heat oven to 350°. Spray springform pan, 9×3 inches, with nonstick cooking spray. Cook and drain spaghetti as directed on package. Rinse with cold water; drain. Toss spaghetti, Parmesan cheese, ricotta cheese, Italian seasoning and egg whites until spaghetti is well coated.

Press half of the spaghetti mixture in bottom of pan. Sprinkle with half of the basil. Layer with half of the tomatoes and cheese slices. Press remaining spaghetti mixture on top. Sprinkle with remaining basil. Layer with remaining tomatoes and cheese slices.

Bake 30 minutes. Let stand 15 minutes. Remove sides of pan. Cut torte into wedges. Serve with spaghetti sauce.

1 SERVING: Calories 325 (Calories from Fat 70); Fat 8g (Saturated 5g); Cholesterol 20mg; Sodium 280mg; Carbohydrate 48g (Dietary Fiber 2g); Protein 17g.

Spaghetti Torte

Savory Zucchini Frittata

3 servings

6 eggs
1/4 cup water
3 tablespoons chopped parsley
2 tablespoons soft bread crumbs
1 teaspoon salt
1 clove garlic, finely chopped
1 tablespoon olive or vegetable oil
1 cup 1/4-inch zucchini slices
    (about 1 medium)
Flour
1 tablespoon grated Parmesan cheese

Beat eggs, water, parsley, bread crumbs, salt and garlic.

Heat oil in 8-inch nonstick ovenproof skillet over medium heat until hot. Coat zucchini lightly with flour; cook until golden, about 2 minutes on each side. Pour egg mixture over zucchini. Cook without stirring until eggs are thickened throughout but still moist, 3 to 5 minutes. Gently lift edge with fork so that uncooked portion can flow to bottom. Sprinkle with cheese.

Set oven control to broil. Broil omelet with top 5 inches from heat until golden brown, 3 to 4 minutes. Loosen edge with spatula; slip cheese side up onto serving plate.

1 SERVING: Calories 225 (Calories from Fat 135); Fat 15g (Saturated 4g); Cholesterol 425mg; Sodium 970mg; Carbohydrate 8g (Dietary Fiber 1g); Protein 15g.

Southwestern Frittata

6 servings

Serving corn bread will add a further touch of southwestern flavor to this festive quickie.

1/2 cup chopped onion (about 1 medium)
6 eggs
1/2 cup milk
1/2 teaspoon chili powder
1/4 teaspoon dried oregano leaves
1 can (11 ounces) whole kernel corn with
    red and green peppers, drained
1/4 cup shredded Cheddar cheese (1 ounce)
1/2 cup salsa

Spray 10-inch skillet with nonstick cooking spray. Cook onion in skillet over medium heat, stirring occasionally, until tender. Beat eggs, milk, chili powder and oregano until well mixed; pour over onion. Stir in corn. Cover and cook over medium-low heat 9 to 11 minutes or until eggs are set around edge and light brown on bottom. Sprinkle with cheese. Cut into wedges. Serve with salsa.

1 SERVING: Calories 145 (Calories from Fat 65); Fat 7g (Saturated 4g); Cholesterol 220mg; Sodium 430mg; Carbohydrate 12g (Dietary Fiber 1g); Protein 9g.

Southwestern Frittata

Spinach Frittata with Creole Sauce

4 servings

Corn muffins and cut-up fresh fruit make a delicious accompaniment to this frittata, which is inspired by the flavors of New Orleans.

Creole Sauce (right)
2 teaspoons margarine or butter
1 small onion, chopped (1/4 cup)
3 cups coarsely chopped spinach (4 ounces)
6 eggs or 1 1/2 cups fat-free cholesterol-free
    egg product
1/2 teaspoon chopped fresh or
    1/8 teaspoon dried thyme leaves
1/8 teaspoon salt
1/8 teaspoon pepper
2 tablespoons shredded mozzarella cheese

Prepare Creole Sauce; keep warm. Melt margarine in 10-inch nonstick skillet over medium heat. Cook onion in margarine 3 minutes, stirring occasionally. Add spinach; toss just until spinach is wilted. Reduce heat to medium-low.

Beat eggs, thyme, salt and pepper until blended; pour over spinach. Cover and cook 5 to 7 minutes or until eggs are set in center and light brown on bottom. Sprinkle with cheese. Cut into wedges. Serve with Creole Sauce.

CREOLE SAUCE

1 large tomato, coarsely chopped (1 cup)
1 small onion, chopped (1/4 cup)
2 tablespoons sliced celery
1/4 teaspoon paprika
1/8 teaspoon pepper
4 drops red pepper sauce

Heat all ingredients to boiling in 1-quart saucepan, stirring occasionally; reduce heat. Simmer uncovered about 5 minutes, stirring occasionally, until thickened.

1 SERVING: Calories 160 (Calories from Fat 90); Fat 10g (Saturated 3g); Cholesterol 320mg; Sodium 250mg; Carbohydrate 8g (Dietary Fiber 2g); Protein 12g.

Spinach Frittata with Creole Sauce

Baked Herb Omelet

6 servings

1 medium onion, chopped (1/2 cup)
1/2 cup shredded part-skim mozzarella cheese (2 ounces)
1 1/2 cups skim milk
1 cup fat-free cholesterol-free egg product or 2 eggs plus 3 egg whites
1/3 cup all-purpose flour
1/2 teaspoon baking powder
1/2 teaspoon dried basil leaves
1/2 teaspoon dried oregano leaves
1/4 teaspoon salt
3/4 cup salsa

Heat oven to 350°. Spray pie plate, 9×1 1/4 inches, with nonstick cooking spray. Sprinkle onion and cheese in bottom of pie plate. Place remaining ingredients except salsa in blender. Cover and blend on medium-high speed about 30 seconds or until smooth. Pour into pie plate.

Bake about 40 minutes or until knife inserted in center comes out clean. Let stand 5 minutes. Cut into wedges. Serve with salsa.

1 SERVING: Calories 100 (Calories from Fat 20); Fat 2g (Saturated 1g); Cholesterol 5mg; Sodium 470mg; Carbohydrate 13g (Dietary Fiber 2g); Protein 9g.

Savory Mushroom Strata

6 servings

This is a great dish to serve when company is coming. Make it the day before and pop it in the oven the next morning. No one will guess it's low in fat.

1 cup chopped mushrooms (4 ounces)
1 cup fat-free cottage cheese
1/4 cup chopped green onions (4 medium)
1 teaspoon chopped fresh or 1/2 teaspoon dried rosemary leaves
1 clove garlic, finely chopped
12 slices whole grain or white bread
1 1/2 cups skim milk
1 cup fat-free cholesterol-free egg product or 6 egg whites
1/4 cup shredded reduced-fat Havarti or Monterey Jack cheese

Spray square pan, 9×9×2 inches, with nonstick cooking spray. Mix mushrooms, cottage cheese, green onions, rosemary and garlic. Place 4 of the bread slices in pan. Spread with half the mushroom mixture. Beat milk and egg product; pour one-third of the milk mixture over bread in pan. Spread 4 of the bread slices with remaining mushroom mixture. Place bread, mushroom side up, in pan. Top with remaining 4 slices bread; press down gently if bread is higher than edge of dish. Pour remaining milk mixture over bread. Sprinkle with cheese. Cover and refrigerate at least 2 hours but no longer than 24 hours.

Heat oven to 325°. Bake uncovered 45 to 50 minutes or until mixture is set and top is golden brown. Let stand 10 minutes before cutting.

1 SERVING: Calories 220 (Calories from Fat 35); Fat 4g (Saturated 2g); Cholesterol 5mg; Sodium 540mg; Carbohydrate 33g (Dietary Fiber 4g); Protein 17g.

Spicy Five-Pepper Spoon Bread

4 servings

1 cup yellow cornmeal
2 cups milk
2 cups water
1/2 cup shredded Gruyère or Swiss cheese
    (2 ounces)
1 cup frozen whole kernel corn
1 cup chopped yellow bell pepper
    (about 1 medium)
1/2 cup chopped red bell pepper
    (about 1 small)
1/2 cup chopped green bell pepper
    (about 1 small)
1/2 cup chopped onion (about 1 medium)
1/2 teaspoon salt
1/4 teaspoon white pepper
1 can (4 ounces) chopped green chilis,
    drained
1 egg
3 egg whites
1 cup salsa

Heat oven to 400°. Grease 3-quart casserole. Mix cornmeal, milk and water in 2-quart saucepan. Cook, stirring constantly, until mixture thickens and boils; reduce heat. Stir in 1/4 cup of the cheese and the remaining ingredients except the 3 egg whites and salsa.

Beat egg whites on high speed until soft peaks form; fold into cornmeal mixture. Spoon into casserole (casserole will be full). Sprinkle with remaining cheese. Bake uncovered 35 to 40 minutes or until set and golden brown. Serve with salsa.

1 SERVING: Calories 335 (Calories from Fat 70); Fat 8g (Saturated 5g); Cholesterol 75mg; Sodium 1,380mg; Carbohydrate 53g (Dietary Fiber 5g); Protein 18g.

Heading Out of Town?

Pack some low-fat food to snack on in the car, so you won't have to stop as often or be tempted by fast food along the way. Here are some suggestions:

graham crackers

mini rice cakes

boxes of raisins

mini bagels

pretzels

eight-vegetable juice

dried cherries

apricots or prunes

low-fat granola bars

baby-cut carrots

fat-free cookies

fresh fruit (apples, pears or grapes)

Spaghetti with Broccoli and Mushrooms

8 servings

1 package (10 ounces) frozen chopped broccoli
1 jar (4 1/2 ounces) sliced mushrooms, drained
2 tablespoons reduced-fat margarine
1/2 teaspoon salt
1/8 teaspoon pepper
1 package (7 ounces) uncooked spaghetti
1/4 cup grated Parmesan cheese
1 tablespoon lemon juice

Cook broccoli as directed on package; drain. Stir in mushrooms, margarine, salt and pepper. Heat over low heat, stirring occasionally until mushrooms are hot, about 5 minutes. Cook spaghetti as directed on package; drain. Toss spaghetti, broccoli mixture, Parmesan cheese and lemon juice.

1 SERVING: Calories 125 (Calories from Fat 30); Fat 3g (Saturated 1g); Cholesterol 0mg; Sodium 210mg; Carbohydrate 21g (Dietary Fiber 2g); Protein 5g.

Pasta with Lemon and Herbs

6 servings

This is a wonderful, light dish that is ready in about 20 minutes!

6 ounces uncooked vermicelli
2 tablespoons chopped fresh basil
2 tablespoons chopped fresh parsley
1 tablespoon grated lemon peel
1/4 cup lemon juice
3 tablespoons olive or vegetable oil
1/2 teaspoon coarsely ground pepper
1 medium tomato, chopped
1/3 cup grated Parmesan cheese

Cook and drain vermicelli as directed on package. Toss vermicelli and remaining ingredients except cheese. Sprinkle with cheese.

1 SERVING: Calories 200 (Calories from Fat 80); Fat 9g (Saturated 2g); Cholesterol 5mg; Sodium 90mg; Carbohydrate 25g (Dietary Fiber 1g); Protein 6g.

Pasta with Lemon and Herbs

Rigatoni with Artichokes

6 servings

2 cups uncooked rigatoni pasta (6 ounces)
2 tablespoons margarine, butter or spread
1 1/2 cups soft bread crumbs (about
    2 1/2 slices bread)
1 tablespoon chopped fresh parsley
1 teaspoon olive or vegetable oil
2 cloves garlic, finely chopped
3/4 cup chicken broth
2 tablespoons finely chopped oil-packed
    sun-dried tomatoes, drained
1 teaspoon cornstarch
1/4 teaspoon salt
1/4 teaspoon crushed red pepper
1/4 teaspoon pepper
1 can (14 ounces) artichoke hearts, drained
1 tablespoon grated Romano or Parmesan
    cheese

Cook and drain pasta as directed on package. Melt margarine in 10-inch skillet over medium-high heat. Cook bread crumbs in margarine 5 to 6 minutes, stirring occasionally, until light brown. Stir in parsley. Remove bread crumbs from skillet; keep warm.

Heat oil in same skillet over medium-high heat. Cook garlic in oil, stirring frequently, until golden. Shake broth, tomatoes, cornstarch, salt, red pepper and pepper in tightly covered container. Gradually stir into garlic. Heat to boiling, stirring constantly. Boil and stir 1 minute. Stir in artichokes. Toss with pasta. Sprinkle with bread crumbs and cheese.

1 SERVING: Calories 210 (Calories from Fat 55); Fat 6g (Saturated 1g); Cholesterol 0mg; Sodium 380mg; Carbohydrate 35g (Dietary Fiber 3g); Protein 7g.

Winter Baked Pasta

6 servings

6 cups hot cooked tricolored wheel-shaped
    pasta
3 cups cooked broc-o-flower or broccoli
    flowerets (about 1 pound)
3 cups peeled and chopped cooked acorn,
    buttercup or butternut squash
1/2 cup chopped green onions
1/2 cup chopped celery
2 cups milk
1 cup part-skim or regular ricotta cheese
1 tablespoon cornstarch
1 teaspoon salt
1/2 teaspoon pepper
1/4 teaspoon ground nutmeg
1 clove garlic, finely chopped
1/2 cup soft bread crumbs
2 tablespoons grated fresh Parmesan cheese
2 tablespoons shredded Gouda cheese

Heat oven to 375°. Grease 3-quart casserole. Mix pasta, broc-o-flower, squash, green onions and celery. Mix milk, ricotta, cornstarch, salt, pepper and nutmeg. Pour over pasta, mix well. Spoon into casserole. Sprinkle with remaining ingredients. Bake uncovered about 35 minutes or until golden brown.

1 SERVING: Calories 390 (Calories from Fat 70); Fat 8g (Saturated 4g); Cholesterol 25mg; Sodium 800mg; Carbohydrate 67g (Dietary Fiber 7g); Protein 20g.

Zucchini Lasagna

8 servings

3 cups chunky spaghetti sauce
1 cup shredded zucchini (about 1 medium)
6 uncooked lasagna noodles
1 cup ricotta or small-curd creamed
    cottage cheese
1/4 cup grated Parmesan cheese
1 tablespoon chopped fresh or 1 teaspoon
    dried oregano leaves
2 cups shredded mozzarella cheese
    (8 ounces)

Heat oven to 350°. Mix spaghetti sauce and zucchini. Spread 1 cup mixture in ungreased rectangular baking dish, 11×7×1 1/2 inches. Top with 3 noodles. Mix ricotta cheese, Parmesan cheese and oregano; spread over noodles in dish. Spread with 1 cup of the spaghetti sauce mixture. Top with remaining noodles, sauce mixture and mozzarella cheese. Bake uncovered about 45 minutes or until hot and bubbly. Let stand 15 minutes before cutting.

1 SERVING: Calories 230 (Calories from Fat 110); Fat 12g (Saturated 4g); Cholesterol 35mg; Sodium 240mg; Carbohydrate 16g (Dietary Fiber 2g); Protein 15g.

Triple-Cheese Ravioli

4 servings

1 package (8 ounces) dried cheese-filled
    ravioli or tortellini
2 cups chopped tomatoes (about 2 large
    or 1 pound)
1/2 cup sliced mushrooms (about
    1 1/2 ounces)
1/4 cup chopped onion (about 1 small)
1/4 cup dry red wine or chicken broth
1 tablespoon chopped fresh or 1 teaspoon
    dried basil leaves
1/8 teaspoon salt
1/8 teaspoon pepper
1 clove garlic, finely chopped
1/2 cup part-skim ricotta cheese
2 tablespoons grated Parmesan cheese

Cook ravioli as directed on package; drain. Cook remaining ingredients except cheeses in 10-inch skillet over medium-high heat about 5 minutes, stirring frequently, until tomatoes are soft.

Heat oven to 325°. Place ravioli in ungreased square baking dish, 8×8×2 inches. Spread ricotta cheese over ravioli. Pour tomato sauce over top. Sprinkle with Parmesan cheese. Bake uncovered about 20 minutes or until hot.

1 SERVING: Calories 155 (Calories from Fat 35); Fat 4g (Saturated 2g); Cholesterol 30mg; Sodium 260mg; Carbohydrate 23g (Dietary Fiber 1g); Protein 8g.

Layered Eggplant Parmigiana

6 servings

2 cups water
1 cup uncooked bulgur
3/4 cup cholesterol-free egg product
    or 3 eggs
3/4 cup Italian-style dry bread crumbs
1/4 cup chopped fresh parsley
1/4 cup grated Parmesan cheese
1 tablespoon chopped fresh or 1 teaspoon
    dried basil leaves
1 tablespoon olive or vegetable oil
1 small eggplant (about 1 pound),
    thinly sliced
1 can (8 ounces) tomato sauce
1/2 cup shredded part-skim mozzarella
    cheese (2 ounces)

Heat water to boiling in 2-quart saucepan; remove from heat and stir in bulgur. Let stand uncovered 30 to 60 minutes or until liquid is absorbed. Mix bulgur, egg product, bread crumbs, parsley, Parmesan cheese and basil.

Heat oil in 10-inch skillet over low heat. Place half of the eggplant slices in skillet; top with bulgur mixture. Arrange remaining eggplant slices over bulgur; top with tomato sauce. Cover and cook 30 to 35 minutes or until eggplant is tender. Sprinkle with mozzarella cheese.

1 SERVING: Calories 260 (Calories from Fat 55); Fat 6g (Saturated 2g); Cholesterol 10mg; Sodium 500mg; Carbohydrate 46g (Dietary Fiber 9g); Protein 14g.

Garbanzo Bean Sandwiches

4 servings (2 sandwiches each)

Walnuts and garbanzo beans are a delicious duo in these hearty pita sandwiches.

1 can (15 to 16 ounces) garbanzo beans,
    rinsed and drained
1/2 cup water
2 tablespoons chopped fresh parsley
2 tablespoons chopped walnuts
1 tablespoon finely chopped onion
1 clove garlic, finely chopped
4 whole wheat pita breads (6 inches
    in diameter)
Lettuce leaves
1 medium tomato, seeded and chopped
1/2 medium cucumber, sliced and quartered
1/2 cup reduced-fat cucumber-ranch
    dressing

Place beans, water, parsley, walnuts, onion and garlic in food processor or blender. Cover and process until smooth. Cut each pita bread in half to form 2 pockets; line with lettuce leaves. Spoon 2 tablespoons bean spread into each pita half. Add tomato, cucumber and dressing.

1 SERVING: Calories 380 (Calories from Fat 90); Fat 10g (Saturated 2g); Cholesterol 0mg; Sodium 1,040mg; Carbohydrate 66g (Dietary Fiber 11g); Protein 17g.

Garbanzo Bean Sandwiches

Vegetable Burritos

4 servings

Try this dish especially if you're trying to cut down on your meat consumption. The beans take the place of meat and provide fiber along with protein.

1 teaspoon vegetable oil
1 large onion, finely chopped (1 cup)
1 medium green bell pepper, finely chopped (1 cup)
1 cup rinsed and drained canned kidney beans
2 teaspoons salt-free herb seasoning
2 tablespoons tomato sauce
4 flour tortillas (8 to 10 inches in diameter)
1 large tomato, finely chopped (1 cup)
1/2 cup shredded mozzarella cheese (2 ounces)
1 cup plain nonfat yogurt
1 cup alfalfa sprouts

Heat oven to 350°. Heat oil in 8-inch skillet over medium heat. Cook onion and bell pepper in oil about 5 minutes, stirring frequently, until tender.

Place beans, herb seasoning and tomato sauce in blender or food processor. Cover and blend on medium speed about 20 seconds or until smooth. Spread each tortilla with one-fourth of the bean mixture. Top with onion mixture, tomato, cheese, yogurt and sprouts.

Roll up tortillas, secure with toothpicks. Place in ungreased rectangular pan, 13 × 9 × 2 inches. Bake 10 to 12 minutes or until heated through and cheese is melted.

1 SERVING: Calories 290 (Calories from Fat 65); Fat 7g (Saturated 3g); Cholesterol 10mg; Sodium 380mg; Carbohydrate 47g (Dietary Fiber 6g); Protein 16g.

Caponata Pockets

6 servings

2 teaspoons olive or vegetable oil
1 medium onion, chopped (1/2 cup)
2 cloves garlic, crushed
1 1/2 large eggplants, peeled and chopped (7 cups)
1 medium tomato, chopped (3/4 cup)
2 tablespoons chopped fresh or 2 teaspoons dried basil leaves
2 tablespoons red wine vinegar
1/4 teaspoon pepper
1/8 teaspoon salt
3 pita breads (6 inches in diameter), cut in half
Leaf lettuce
Fresh basil leaves, if desired
1 jar (7 ounces) roasted red bell peppers, drained and cut into strips

Heat oil in 10-inch nonstick skillet over medium heat. Cook onion and garlic in oil about 3 minutes, stirring occasionally, until onion is tender. Stir in eggplant and tomato. Cook uncovered 8 to 10 minutes, stirring frequently, until eggplant is very tender. Stir in chopped basil, vinegar, pepper and salt. Cover and refrigerate about 2 hours or until cool; drain if necessary.

Line each pita bread half with lettuce, whole basil leaves and red bell peppers. Fill with eggplant mixture.

1 SERVING: Calories 140 (Calories from Fat 20); Fat 2g (Saturated 0g); Cholesterol 0mg; Sodium 220mg; Carbohydrate 32g (Dietary Fiber 6g); Protein 5g.

Caponata Pockets

Five Reasons to Eat Meatless

1. Less fat. Grains, legumes and vegetables have only small amounts of fat, unless fat is added in the preparation.

2. No cholesterol. There's no cholesterol in plant foods.

3. More fiber. Complex carbohydrates such as grains, legumes, fruits and vegetables often are good sources of dietary fiber.

4. Healthful. A diet high in grains, legumes, fruits and vegetables and low in fat may help to decrease your chance of developing certain cancers and heart disease.

5. Inexpensive. Compared to many other foods, a meatless diet may cost less.

Roasted-Vegetable Pizza

8 servings

The vegetables for this recipe can easily be prepared ahead of time and refrigerated until you make the pizza.

1 medium bell pepper, cut lengthwise into eighths
1 medium zucchini, cut into 1/4-inch slices
1/2 small eggplant (1/2 pound), cut into 1/4-inch slices
1 package (8 ounces) fresh portobello mushrooms, cut into 1/2-inch slices
1 tablespoon roasted garlic-flavored or regular vegetable oil
1/2 teaspoon salt
1/4 teaspoon pepper
1 package (10 ounces) thin Italian bread shell or ready-to-serve pizza crust (12 to 14 inches in diameter)
1/2 cup shredded reduced-fat mozzarella cheese (2 ounces)

Heat oven to 400°. Spray jelly roll pan, 15 1/2 × 10 1/2 × 1 inch, with nonstick cooking spray. Place bell pepper, zucchini, eggplant and mushrooms in single layer in pan. Brush with oil. Sprinkle with salt and pepper. Bake 25 to 30 minutes, turning vegetables once, until edges of vegetables are light brown.

Place bread shell on ungreased cookie sheet. Top with vegetables. Sprinkle with cheese. Bake 8 to 10 minutes or until cheese is melted.

1 SERVING: Calories 195 (Calories from Fat 55); Fat 6g (Saturated 1g); Cholesterol 0mg; Sodium 460mg; Carbohydrate 32g (Dietary Fiber 3g); Protein 6g.

Roasted-Vegetable Pizza

Vegetable Kung Pao

4 servings

1/2 cup partially defatted roasted peanuts
    or 1/4 cup dry-roasted peanuts
1 tablespoon cornstarch
1 teaspoon sugar
1 tablespoon cold water
1/2 cup fat-free reduced-sodium
    chicken broth
1 teaspoon chili puree with garlic
1 package (16 ounces) frozen broccoli,
    carrots, red peppers with garbanzo
    and other beans

Spray nonstick wok or 12-inch skillet with nonstick cooking spray; heat over medium-high heat until cooking spray starts to bubble. Spread peanuts in single layer on paper towel; spray lightly with cooking spray about 2 seconds. Add to wok; stir-fry about 1 minute or until toasted. Immediately remove from wok; cool.

Mix cornstarch, sugar and cold water; set aside. Mix broth and chili puree in wok; heat to boiling. Stir in vegetables. Heat to boiling; reduce heat to medium-low. Cover and cook 5 minutes, stirring several times.

Move vegetables to side of wok. Stir cornstarch mixture into liquid in skillet. Cook and stir vegetables and sauce over high heat about 1 minute or until sauce is thickened. Stir in peanuts.

1 SERVING: Calories 150 (Calories from Fat 35); Fat 4g (Saturated 0g); Cholesterol 0mg; Sodium 300mg; Carbohydrate 19g (Dietary Fiber 0g); Protein 10g.

Bok Choy with Baked Tofu

4 servings

1 package (14 ounces) firm lite tofu
8 large stalks bok choy
2 tablespoons soy sauce
1 teaspoon sugar
1/2 teaspoon garlic powder
1 teaspoon vegetable oil
3 shallots, thinly sliced
1/4 teaspoon salt
2 tablespoons oyster sauce

Wrap tofu in kitchen towel; cover with plastic wrap. Place heavy weight on top; let stand 30 minutes to press out excess moisture.

Cut tofu into 1×1×1/4-inch pieces. Remove leaves from bok choy stems. Cut leaves into 2-inch pieces; cut stems into 1/4-inch diagonal slices. Mix soy sauce, sugar and garlic powder.

Heat oven to 425°. Line cookie sheet with aluminum foil. Place tofu on foil, brushing with soy sauce mixture. Bake 5 minutes. Spray tofu with cooking spray; bake about 2 minutes or until brown. Turn tofu over; bake 5 minutes longer.

Meanwhile, spray nonstick wok or 12-inch skillet with nonstick cooking spray; heat over medium-high heat until cooking spray starts to bubble. Add oil; rotate wok to coat sides. Add bok choy and shallots; stir-fry 1 minute. Add salt, tofu and oyster sauce; cover and cook 1 minute.

1 SERVING: Calories 100 (Calories from Fat 35); Fat 4g (Saturated 0g); Cholesterol 0mg; Sodium 1,140mg; Carbohydrate 8g (Dietary Fiber 4g); Protein 12g.

Bok Choy with Baked Tofu

Tex-Mex Rice and Bean Bake

6 servings

2 cups cooked brown or white rice
1/4 cup fat-free cholesterol-free egg product
   or 1 egg
1 1/2 cups picante sauce
1 cup shredded reduced-fat or regular
   Cheddar cheese (4 ounces)
1 can (15 to 16 ounces) pinto beans, drained
1/4 teaspoon chili powder

Heat oven to 350°. Spray square baking dish, 8×8×2 inches, with nonstick cooking spray. Mix rice, egg product, 1/2 cup of the picante sauce and 1/2 cup of the cheese; press in bottom of baking dish.

Mix beans and remaining 1 cup picante sauce; spoon over rice mixture. Sprinkle with remaining 1/2 cup cheese and the chili powder. Bake uncovered 30 to 35 minutes or until cheese is melted and bubbly. Let stand 5 minutes before serving.

1 SERVING: Calories 215 (Calories from Fat 45); Fat 5g (Saturated 2g); Cholesterol 10mg; Sodium 680mg; Carbohydrate 36g (Dietary Fiber 7g); Protein 14g.

Fill Up on Fiber

Check out the fiber in these beans, grains and vegetables.

	Fiber (g) per 1/2 cup serving, cooked
Baked beans	6.5
Lentils	5.0
Peas, green	4.5
Garbanzo beans	4.5
Bulgur wheat	4.0
Acorn squash	3.5
Brussels sprouts	3.5
Broccoli	3.0
Brown rice	1.5
Spinach	1.5
Couscous	1.0

Indian Lentils and Rice

6 servings

8 medium green onions, chopped (1/2 cup)
1 tablespoon finely chopped gingerroot
1/8 teaspoon crushed red pepper
2 cloves garlic, finely chopped
5 1/4 cups vegetable broth*
1 1/2 cups dried lentils, sorted and rinsed
1 teaspoon ground turmeric
1/2 teaspoon salt
1 large tomato, chopped (1 cup)
1/4 cup shredded coconut
2 tablespoons chopped fresh or 2 teaspoons
    dried mint leaves
3 cups hot cooked rice
1 1/2 cups plain nonfat yogurt

Spray 3-quart saucepan with nonstick cooking spray. Cook green onions, gingerroot, red pepper and garlic in saucepan over medium heat 3 to 5 minutes, stirring occasionally, until onions are tender. Stir in 5 cups of the broth, the lentils, turmeric and salt. Heat to boiling; reduce heat.

Cover and simmer about 25 to 30 minutes, adding remaining stock if needed, until lentils are tender. Stir in tomato, coconut and mint. Serve over rice with yogurt.

1 SERVING: Calories 335 (Calories from Fat 35); Fat 4g (Saturated 2g); Cholesterol 0mg; Sodium 920mg; Carbohydrate 61g (Dietary Fiber 9g); Protein 23g.

5 1/4 cups water and 2 tablespoons vegetable bouillon granules can be substituted for the vegetable broth.

Chili Baked Potatoes

4 servings

4 large baking potatoes
1 can (15 to 16 ounces) chili beans,
    undrained
1/4 cup grated Parmesan cheese
Salt and pepper to taste
Cottage Cheese Topping (below)
Chopped bell pepper, if desired

Heat oven to 375°. Pierce potatoes with fork. Bake potatoes 1 1/4 to 1 1/2 hours (or microwave on High 12 to 14 minutes) until tender. Cool just until easy to handle.

Heat chili beans in 2-quart saucepan over medium heat until hot. Split open potatoes; top with beans. Sprinkle with cheese, salt and pepper. Serve with Cottage Cheese Topping. Sprinkle with bell pepper.

COTTAGE CHEESE TOPPING

1 1/2 cups cottage cheese
1 to 2 tablespoons milk
1 tablespoon lemon juice

Place all ingredients in blender. Cover and blend on medium-high speed, stopping blender occasionally to scrape sides, until smooth. Add additional milk if necessary to achieve desired creaminess.

1 SERVING: Calories 290 (Calories from Fat 55); Fat 6g (Saturated 4g); Cholesterol 15mg; Sodium 1,330mg; Carbohydrate 46g (Dietary Fiber 6g); Protein 19g.

Breads and Sides

Zucchini-Apricot Bread (page 341)

(continued on next page)

Easy Multigrain Bread

1 loaf (20 slices)

Using multigrain hot cereal is a shortcut to keeping several different flours on hand for breadmaking.

1 package active dry yeast
1 1/4 cups warm water (105° to 115°)
2 cups all-purpose flour
2 tablespoons honey
2 tablespoons margarine, softened
1 teaspoon salt
1 cup whole wheat flour
1/2 cup uncooked mixed grain
     hot cereal (dry)

Dissolve yeast in warm water in large bowl. Add all-purpose flour, honey, margarine and salt. Beat on low speed 30 seconds, scraping bowl constantly. Beat on medium speed 2 minutes, scraping bowl occasionally (or beat 300 vigorous strokes by hand). Stir in whole wheat flour and cereal until well blended. Scrape batter from side of bowl.

Cover and let rise in warm place 40 to 45 minutes or until almost double. Spray loaf pan, 9×5×3 or 1 1/2×4 1/2×2 1/2 inches, with nonstick cooking spray. Stir down batter by beating about 25 strokes. Spread batter in pan. Smooth and pat batter, using floured hands. Cover and let rise in warm place about 30 minutes or until double. (Batter is ready if indentation remains when touched with floured finger.)

Heat oven to 375°. Bake 35 to 40 minutes or until loaf sounds hollow when tapped. Remove loaf from pan; cool on wire rack.

1 SLICE: Calories 80 (Calories from Fat 10); Fat 1g (Saturated 0g); Cholesterol 0mg; Sodium 125mg; Carbohydrate 15g (Dietary Fiber 1g); Protein 2g.

Tomato Pesto Batter Bread

1 loaf (16 slices)

3 cups all-purpose or bread flour
2 tablespoons sugar
1 1/2 teaspoons salt
1/3 cup pesto
1 package regular or quick active dry yeast
1 cup very warm water (120° to 130°)
1/2 cup coarsely chopped sun-dried
     tomatoes (not oil-packed)
Butter or margarine, softened

Mix 1 1/2 cups of the flour, the sugar, salt, pesto and yeast in large bowl. Add water. Beat with electric mixer on low speed 1 minute, scraping bowl frequently. Beat on medium speed 2 minutes, scraping bowl occasionally. Stir in tomatoes and remaining flour until smooth (batter will be very stiff). Scrape batter from side of bowl.

Cover and let rise in warm place about 30 minutes or until double. (Batter is ready if indentation remains when touched with floured finger.) Grease 2-quart casserole. Stir down batter by beating about 25 strokes. Spread evenly in casserole. Round top of loaf by patting with floured hands. Cover and let rise in warm place about 40 minutes or until double.

Move oven rack to low position so that top of casserole will be in center of oven. Heat oven to 375°. Bake 40 to 45 minutes or until loaf is brown and sounds hollow when tapped. Immediately remove loaf from casserole to wire rack. Brush top of loaf with butter; cool.

1 SLICE: Calories 130 (Calories from Fat 35); Fat 4g (Saturated 1g); Cholesterol 5mg; Sodium 280mg; Carbohydrate 21g (Dietary Fiber 1g); Protein 3g.

Tomato Pesto Batter Bread

Fluffy Corn Bread

8 servings

1 egg, separated
1 egg white
1/4 teaspoon cream of tartar
2/3 cup all-purpose flour
1/3 cup yellow cornmeal
2/3 cup skim milk
1 tablespoon vegetable oil
1 1/2 teaspoons baking powder
1 1/2 teaspoons chopped fresh cilantro
1/4 teaspoon salt
1/4 teaspoon ground cumin
Whole cilantro leaves, if desired
Additional cornmeal to sprinkle on top

Heat oven to 425°. Spray round pan, 8 × 1 1/2 inches, with nonstick cooking spray. Beat the 2 egg whites and the cream of tartar in medium bowl with electric mixer on high speed until stiff but not dry.

Mix egg yolk, flour, cornmeal, milk, oil, baking powder, cilantro, salt and cumin in medium bowl; beat vigorously 30 seconds. Fold cornmeal mixture into egg whites. Pour into pan.

Place cilantro leaves on batter. Sprinkle with additional cornmeal. Bake 15 to 20 minutes or until golden brown. Cut into wedges. Serve warm.

1 SERVING: Calories 95 (Calories from Fat 25); Fat 3g (Saturated 1g); Cholesterol 25mg; Sodium 180mg; Carbohydrate 14g (Dietary Fiber 0g); Protein 3g.

Irish Yogurt Bread

8 servings

1 3/4 cups all-purpose flour
1/2 cup currants or raisins
1 1/2 teaspoons baking powder
1/4 teaspoon baking soda
1/4 teaspoon salt
1 cup lemon, orange or plain low-fat yogurt
2 tablespoons vegetable oil

Heat oven to 375°. Spray round pan, 9 × 1 1/2 inches, with nonstick cooking spray. Mix flour, currants, baking powder, baking soda and salt in medium bowl. Mix yogurt and oil; stir into flour mixture just until flour is moistened. Spread dough in pan.

Bake 20 to 25 minutes or until toothpick inserted in center comes out clean. Serve warm or cool.

1 SERVING: Calories 170 (Calories from Fat 35); Fat 4g (Saturated 1g); Cholesterol 2mg; Sodium 220mg; Carbohydrate 30g (Dietary Fiber 1g); Protein 4g.

Low-Fat Spreads

For a healthful treat, top bread with low-fat spreads. For a sweet spread, try honey, maple syrup, preserves, thawed frozen reduced-fat whipped topping, fat-free yogurt with fruit pieces or fat-free cream cheese with fruit pieces added. For a savory spread, try mustard, ketchup, reduced-fat dressing, salsa, fat-free cottage cheese with fresh herbs added or chopped chutney.

Zucchini-Apricot Bread

1 loaf (24 slices)

(photograph on page 334)

1 medium zucchini, shredded (1 1/2 cups)
3/4 cup sugar
1/4 cup vegetable oil
3 egg whites or 1/2 cup fat-free
    cholesterol-free egg product
1 1/2 cups all-purpose flour
1 teaspoon ground cinnamon
2 teaspoons vanilla
3/4 teaspoon baking soda
1/2 teaspoon salt
1/4 teaspoon baking powder
1/4 teaspoon ground cloves
1/2 cup finely chopped dried apricots
Fat-free cream cheese, if desired

Heat oven to 350°. Spray loaf pan, 8 1/2 × 4 1/2 × 2 1/2 or 9 × 5 × 3 inches, with nonstick cooking spray. Mix zucchini, sugar, oil and egg whites in large bowl. Stir in remaining ingredients except apricots and cream cheese. Stir in apricots. Pour into pan.

Bake 1 hour to 1 hour 10 minutes or until toothpick inserted in center comes out clean. Cool 10 minutes. Loosen sides of loaf from pan; remove from pan. Cool completely on wire rack before slicing. Serve with cream cheese.

1 SLICE: Calories 80 (Calories from Fat 20); Fat 2g (Saturated 0g); Cholesterol 0mg; Sodium 95mg; Carbohydrate 14g (Dietary Fiber 0g); Protein 1g.

Pumpkin-Fruit Bread

1 loaf (24 slices)

1 cup canned pumpkin
2/3 cup packed brown sugar
3 tablespoons vegetable oil
1 teaspoon vanilla
3 egg whites or 1/2 cup cholesterol-free
    egg product
1 1/2 cups all-purpose flour
1/2 cup diced dried fruit and raisin mixture
2 teaspoons baking powder
3/4 teaspoon ground cinnamon
1/2 teaspoon salt
1/4 teaspoon ground cloves

Heat oven to 350°. Spray loaf pan, 9 × 5 × 3 or 8 1/2 × 4 1/2 × 2 1/2 inches, with nonstick cooking spray. Mix pumpkin, brown sugar, oil, vanilla and egg whites in large bowl. Stir in remaining ingredients just until moistened. Pour into pan.

Bake 50 to 60 minutes or until toothpick inserted in center comes out clean. Cool 5 minutes. Loosen sides of loaf from pan; remove from pan. Cool completely on wire rack before slicing. Store tightly wrapped in refrigerator up to 1 week.

1 SLICE: Calories 80 (Calories from Fat 20); Fat 2g (Saturated 0g); Cholesterol 0mg; Sodium 100mg; Carbohydrate 15g (Dietary Fiber 0g); Protein 1g.

Apple-Rhubarb Bread

2 loaves (24 slices each)

1 1/2 cups finely chopped rhubarb
 (1/2 pound)
1 1/2 cups chopped peeled or unpeeled
 apples (1 1/2 medium)
1 1/2 cups sugar
1/2 cup vegetable oil
1 teaspoon vanilla
4 eggs
3 cups all-purpose flour
1 cup chopped walnuts or pecans, if desired
3 1/2 teaspoons baking powder
1 teaspoon salt
1 teaspoon ground cinnamon

Move oven rack to low position so that tops of pans will be in center of oven. Heat oven to 350°. Grease bottoms only of 2 loaf pans, 8 1/2×4 1/2×2 1/2 or 9×5×3 inches. Mix rhubarb, apples, sugar, oil, vanilla and eggs in large bowl. Stir in remaining ingredients. Pour into pans.

Bake 50 to 60 minutes or until toothpick inserted in center comes out clean. Cool 10 minutes. Loosen sides of loaves from pans; remove from pans to wire rack. Cool completely before slicing.

1 SLICE: Calories 85 (Calories from Fat 25); Fat 3g (Saturated 1g); Cholesterol 20mg; Sodium 90mg; Carbohydrate 13g (Dietary Fiber 0g); Protein 1g.

Blueberry Corn Muffins

12 muffins

1 cup fresh or unthawed frozen blueberries
1 tablespoon all-purpose flour
1 cup plain nonfat yogurt
3 tablespoons vegetable oil
1 teaspoon vanilla
1 egg or 1/4 cup fat-free cholesterol-free
 egg product
1 cup whole wheat flour
1 cup cornmeal
1/4 cup sugar
3 teaspoons baking powder
1 teaspoon baking soda

Heat oven to 400°. Spray 12 medium muffin cups, 2 1/2×1 1/4 inches, with nonstick cooking spray, or line with paper baking cups. Toss blueberries and all-purpose flour; set aside. Beat yogurt, oil, vanilla and egg in large bowl. Stir in remaining ingredients just until moistened. Carefully stir in blueberries.

Divide batter evenly among muffin cups (cups will be about two-thirds full). Bake about 15 minutes or until golden. Immediately remove from pan to wire rack. Serve warm if desired.

1 MUFFIN: Calories 145 (Calories from Fat 35); Fat 4g (Saturated 1g); Cholesterol 20mg; Sodium 250mg; Carbohydrate 25g (Dietary Fiber 2g); Protein 4g.

Blueberry Corn Muffins

Basil Pepper Biscuits

about 10 biscuits

1/4 cup shortening
2 cups all-purpose or whole wheat flour
2 tablespoons chopped fresh or 2 teaspoons
   dried basil leaves
1 tablespoon sugar, if desired
3 teaspoons baking powder
1 teaspoon salt
1 teaspoon cracked black pepper
About 3/4 cup milk

Heat oven to 450°. Cut shortening into re-maining ingredients except milk in medium bowl with pastry blender or 2 knives until mix-ture resembles fine crumbs. Stir in just enough milk so dough leaves side of bowl and forms a ball. (Too much milk will make dough sticky; not enough will make biscuits dry.)

Turn dough onto lightly floured surface. Knead lightly 20 to 25 times. Roll or pat 1/2 inch thick. Cut with floured 2 1/2-inch biscuit cutter. Place on ungreased cookie sheet about 1 inch apart for crusty sides, touching for soft sides.

Bake 10 to 12 minutes or until golden brown. Immediately remove from cookie sheet. Serve warm.

1 BISCUIT: Calories 145 (Calories from Fat 55); Fat 6g (Saturated 2g); Cholesterol 2mg; Sodium 390mg; Carbohydrate 21g (Dietary Fiber 1g); Protein 3g.

Bulgur Biscuits

about 10 biscuits

1/4 cup shortening
1 cup all-purpose flour
1 cup whole wheat flour
3 teaspoons baking powder
1/2 teaspoon salt
1/2 cup cooked bulgur or brown rice
About 2/3 cup skim milk

Heat oven to 450°. Cut shortening into flours, baking powder and salt with pastry blender or 2 knives in large bowl until mixture resem-bles fine crumbs. Stir in bulgur. Stir in just enough milk so dough leaves side of bowl and forms a ball.

Turn dough onto lightly floured surface; gently roll in flour to coat. Knead lightly 10 times. Roll or pat 1/2 inch thick. Cut with floured 2 1/2-inch biscuit cutter. Place about 1 inch apart on ungreased cookie sheet.

Bake 12 to 14 minutes or until golden brown. Immediately remove from cookie sheet.

1 BISCUIT: Calories 140 (Calories from Fat 55); Fat 6g (Saturated 1g); Cholesterol 0mg; Sodium 280mg; Carbohydrate 21g (Dietary Fiber 2g); Protein 3g.

Bulgur Biscuits

Hearty Multigrain Biscuits

about 10 biscuits

You can expect these biscuits (and other breads made with whole grains) to be a little lower in volume than traditional biscuits.

1/4 cup shortening
3/4 cup whole wheat flour
1/2 cup all-purpose flour
1/2 cup stone-ground or degerminated
   cornmeal
3 teaspoons baking powder
1/2 teaspoon salt
1/2 cup quick-cooking or regular oats
About 3/4 cup skim milk

Heat oven to 450°. Cut shortening into whole wheat flour, all-purpose flour, cornmeal, baking powder and salt with pastry blender or 2 knives in large bowl until mixture resembles fine crumbs. Stir in oats. Stir in just enough milk so dough leaves side of bowl and forms a ball.

Turn dough onto lightly floured surface; gently roll in flour to coat. Knead lightly 10 times. Roll or pat 1/2 inch thick. Cut with 2 1/2-inch biscuit cutter. Place about 1 inch apart on ungreased cookie sheet. Brush with milk and sprinkle with oats if desired.

Bake 10 to 12 minutes or until golden brown. Immediately remove from cookie sheet. Serve hot.

1 BISCUIT: Calories 140 (Calories from Fat 55); Fat 6g (Saturated 1g); Cholesterol 0mg; Sodium 230mg; Carbohydrate 21g (Dietary Fiber 2g); Protein 3g.

Topping Tips

Many breads, eaten by themselves, are not high in fat. It's what we put on them that gets us into trouble. Toast is terrific with just a little jam or jelly. If you must have a spread, use reduced-calorie margarine.

- Pancakes really don't need margarine or butter at all. Just stack them up and enjoy with fresh fruit, preserves or a little syrup.

- Use chopped or pureed fruits and vegetables to add flavor and tenderness to breads while decreasing fats.

Onion Bagels

12 bagels

*Try your hand at making homemade bagels—
an activity your whole family will enjoy! The water
dip creates a crusty outside.*

2 packages regular active dry yeast
1 1/4 cups warm water (105° to 115°)
1 small onion, finely chopped (1/4 cup)
2 large shallots, finely chopped (1/4 cup)
1 teaspoon salt
1/8 teaspoon pepper
3 1/2 to 4 cups all-purpose flour
Stone-ground or degerminated cornmeal
Hot water

Dissolve yeast in warm water in large bowl.
Stir in onion, shallots, salt, pepper and
enough flour, 1 cup at a time, to make dough
easy to handle.

Turn dough onto lightly floured surface.
Knead about 10 minutes or until dough is
smooth and elastic. Spray large bowl with
nonstick cooking spray. Place dough in bowl,
and turn greased side up. Cover and let rise
in warm place about 30 minutes or until
almost double. (Dough is ready if indentation
remains when touched.)

Spray cookie sheet with nonstick cooking
spray; sprinkle with cornmeal. Punch down
dough. Divide dough into 12 equal pieces.
Shape each piece into a ball with floured
hands. Poke a hole into the center of each ball
and enlarge hole with thumb to 1 1/2 inches.
Place on cookie sheet. Cover and let rise in
warm place 15 minutes.

Heat oven to 400°. Carefully lift each
bagel off cookie sheet and dip into hot water.
Place back on cookie sheet; reshape hole if
necessary. Bake 25 to 30 minutes or until
golden brown. Remove from cookie sheet.
Cool on wire rack.

1 BAGEL: Calories 125 (Calories from Fat 0); Fat 0g
(Saturated 0g); Cholesterol 0mg; Sodium 180mg;
Carbohydrate 29g (Dietary Fiber 2g); Protein 4g.

Irish Soda Bread

1 loaf (16 slices)

There are many variations of this traditional Irish bread, but it is nearly always identified by the cross on top of the loaf.

3 tablespoons margarine, softened
2 1/2 cups all-purpose flour
2 tablespoons sugar
1 teaspoon baking soda
1 teaspoon baking powder
1/2 teaspoon salt
1/3 cup raisins, if desired
3/4 cup nonfat buttermilk

Heat oven to 375°. Grease cookie sheet. Cut margarine into flour, sugar, baking soda, baking powder and salt with pastry blender or 2 knives until mixture resembles fine crumbs. Stir in raisins and enough buttermilk to make a soft dough.

Turn dough onto lightly floured surface. Knead 1 to 2 minutes or until smooth. Shape into round loaf, about 6 1/2 inches in diameter. Place on cookie sheet. Cut an X about one-fourth of the way through loaf with floured knife.

Bake 35 to 45 minutes or until golden brown. Brush with margarine if desired. Remove from cookie sheet; cool on wire rack.

1 SLICE: Calories 95 (Calories from Fat 20); Fat 2g (Saturated 1g); Cholesterol 0mg; Sodium 210mg; Carbohydrate 17g (Dietary Fiber 0g); Protein 2g.

Herb Popovers

6 popovers

For variety, try substituting dried dill weed or crumbled rosemary leaves for the basil in this recipe.

1 egg
2 egg whites
1 cup all-purpose flour
1 cup skim milk
1/2 teaspoon dried basil leaves
1/4 teaspoon onion salt

Heat oven to 450°. Spray six 6-ounce custard cups with nonstick cooking spray. Place all ingredients in blender. Cover and blend on medium speed about 15 seconds, stopping blender to scrape sides if necessary, just until smooth. Fill custard cups about half full.

Bake 20 minutes. Reduce oven temperature to 350°. Bake 15 to 20 minutes longer or until deep golden brown. Immediately remove from cups. Serve hot.

1 POPOVER: Calories 105 (Calories from Fat 10); Fat 1g (Saturated 0g); Cholesterol 35mg; Sodium 140mg; Carbohydrate 18g (Dietary Fiber 0g); Protein 6g.

Stir-fried Asparagus with Sichuan Sauce

4 servings

2 teaspoons sesame seed
1 teaspoon sugar
1 teaspoon sesame oil
1 teaspoon chili puree with garlic
1 pound asparagus, cut into 2-inch
   diagonal pieces
1/4 cup fat-free reduced-sodium
   chicken broth

Heat nonstick wok or 12-inch skillet over medium-high heat until hot; reduce heat to medium-low. Add sesame seed; cook and stir about 2 minutes or until light brown. Remove sesame seed from wok. Mix sugar, sesame oil and chili puree.

   Cool wok slightly; wipe clean. Spray with nonstick cooking spray and heat over medium-high heat until cooking spray starts to bubble. Add asparagus; stir-fry 1 minute. Stir in broth; cover and cook 2 minutes. Add chili sauce mixture; stir-fry 1 minute. Stir in sesame seed.

1 SERVING: Calories 40 (Calories from Fat 20); Fat 2g (Saturated 0g); Cholesterol 0mg; Sodium 45mg; Carbohydrate 4g (Dietary Fiber 1g); Protein 2g.

Beets in Sweet Orange Sauce

4 servings

2 bunches beets (9 or 10 medium)
2 teaspoons olive or vegetable oil
1/2 cup reduced-sodium chicken broth
2 teaspoons grated orange peel
2/3 cup orange juice
1/4 cup packed brown sugar
6 tablespoons chopped fresh parsley
1 teaspoon chopped crystallized ginger
   or 1/2 teaspoon ground ginger

Heat oven to 400°. Cut beets into fourths. Place beets, oil and broth in ovenproof 3-quart saucepan. Cover and bake 30 to 45 minutes, stirring occasionally, until beets are tender. Remove from oven.

   Stir in orange peel, orange juice and brown sugar. Cook over medium-high heat 5 to 8 minutes, stirring frequently, until sauce is reduced and beets are coated with glaze. Stir in parsley and ginger.

1 SERVING: Calories 170 (Calories from Fat 25); Fat 3g (Saturated 0g); Cholesterol 0mg; Sodium 200mg; Carbohydrate 36g (Dietary Fiber 3g); Protein 3g.

Vitamin C–Packed Veggies

Vitamin C, also called ascorbic acid, may be helpful in reducing your risk of developing cancer. Eat lots of these C-rich favorites daily.

	Vitamin C (mg) per 1/2 cup serving
Green pepper	45
Broccoli	40
Parsley	40
Brussels sprouts	35
Sweet potato	30
Cauliflower	25
Spinach	15
Cabbage	10
Potato, with skin	10

Broccoli and Pasta in Dijon Sauce

4 servings

1 cup uncooked anelli (tiny rings) pasta (4 ounces)
1 package (10 ounces) frozen chopped broccoli
2 tablespoons reduced-fat sour cream
2 teaspoons Dijon mustard
1/4 teaspoon salt

Cook and drain pasta and broccoli as directed on packages. Toss pasta, broccoli and remaining ingredients. Serve warm.

1 SERVING: Calories 140 (Calories from Fat 10); Fat 1g (Saturated 0g); Cholesterol 2mg; Sodium 190mg; Carbohydrate 27g (Dietary Fiber 3g); Protein 6g.

Sweet-and-Sour Broccoli and Baby Corn

4 servings

A tasty sweet-and-sour sauce with minimal cooking makes this broccoli dish delicious without any added fat. Leftover canned broth can be frozen in ice cube trays; remove when frozen and seal in freezer bag; one cube is about 1 tablespoon of broth.

1 pound broccoli, cut into flowerets and
    1-inch pieces (4 cups)*
2 teaspoons cornstarch
2 teaspoons cold water
2 tablespoons fat-free reduced-sodium
    chicken broth
2 tablespoons honey
2 tablespoons lemon juice
1 tablespoon ketchup
1 teaspoon finely chopped garlic
1 teaspoon grated lemon peel
1/4 teaspoon salt
Dash of crushed red pepper, if desired
1 cup canned baby corn, rinsed and drained

Cut any broccoli stems more than 1 inch wide lengthwise in half. Place broccoli in boiling water; heat to boiling. Boil 1 minute; drain. Immediately rinse with cold water; drain. Mix cornstarch and cold water.

Heat broth, honey, lemon juice, ketchup, garlic, lemon peel and salt to boiling in non-stick wok or 12-inch skillet, stirring frequently. Stir in cornstarch mixture. Cook and stir about 1 minute or until thickened. Stir in red pepper. Add broccoli and corn; cook and stir about 30 seconds or until heated through.

1 SERVING: Calories 85 (Calories from Fat 0); Fat 0g (Saturated 0g); Cholesterol 0mg; Sodium 210mg; Carbohydrate 21g (Dietary Fiber 3g); Protein 3g.

*1 package (16 ounces) frozen broccoli cuts, thawed and drained, can be substituted for the fresh broccoli. Do not cook.

Vegetables with A+

Studies show that eating plenty of foods high in beta-carotene, a form of vitamin A, may help to reduce your risk of developing cancer.

	Beta-carotene (µg) per 1/2 cup serving, cooked
Sweet potato	16,660
Pumpkin	16,180
Carrots	11,470
Spinach	4,195
Acorn squash	2,610
Broccoli	1,040

Cream of Corn and Broccoli Casserole

4 servings

1 package (10 ounces) frozen broccoli flowerets
1 can (15 ounces) cream-style corn
1/4 cup fat-free cholesterol-free egg product or 2 egg whites, slightly beaten
1/3 cup chopped onion
1/4 teaspoon salt
Pepper to taste
2 slices white bread
1 teaspoon margarine

Heat oven to 350°. Spray 2-quart casserole with nonstick cooking spray. Cook broccoli as directed on package. Mix broccoli, corn, egg product, onion, salt and pepper; spoon into casserole.

Cut desired shapes from bread with small cookie cutters. Spread margarine on one side of bread cutouts; arrange margarine side up on broccoli mixture. Cover and bake about 45 minutes or until heated through.

1 SERVING: Calories 160 (Calories from Fat 27); Fat 3g (Saturated 1g); Cholesterol 0mg; Sodium 590mg; Carbohydrate 30g (Dietary Fiber 4g); Protein 7g.

Roasted Cauliflower and Mushrooms

6 servings

Balsamic vinegar is dark in color and has a pungent sweetness that results from being aged in wood barrels.

3 cups cauliflowerets (1 pound)
1 cup chopped mushrooms (4 ounces)
1/2 cup chopped red onion (1/2 medium)
1 tablespoon olive or vegetable oil
2 teaspoons lemon juice
2 teaspoons balsamic or cider vinegar
1/2 teaspoon salt
1/4 teaspoon pepper
2 cloves garlic, finely chopped
1/3 cup chopped green onions (4 medium)

Heat oven to 350°. Spray rectangular baking dish, $13 \times 9 \times 2$ inches, with nonstick cooking spray. Mix all ingredients except green onions. Spread evenly in baking dish.

Bake uncovered 40 to 45 minutes, stirring occasionally, until vegetables are tender and golden brown. Sprinkle with green onions.

1 SERVING: Calories 40 (Calories from Fat 20); Fat 2g (Saturated 0g); Cholesterol 0mg; Sodium 200mg; Carbohydrate 6g (Dietary Fiber 2g); Protein 2g.

Roasted Cauliflower and Mushrooms

Roasted Baby Carrots

6 servings

Roasting carrots makes them even sweeter because while they cook, more of the carrot starches turn into sugar. Another plus—carrots are very high in vitamin A.

4 teaspoons vegetable oil
1 tablespoon chopped fresh or 1 teaspoon dried thyme leaves
1/4 teaspoon garlic salt
1/8 teaspoon pepper
1 package (16 ounces) baby-cut carrots (6 cups)

Heat oven to 425°. Spray rectangular pan, 13×9×2 inches, with cooking spray. Mix all ingredients except carrots in large bowl; toss to coat. Spread carrots in pan.

Bake uncovered 35 to 40 minutes, stirring occasionally, until carrots are tender.

1 SERVING: Calories 70 (Calories from Fat 30); Fat 3g (Saturated 0g); Cholesterol 0mg; Sodium 80mg; Carbohydrate 12g (Dietary Fiber 3g); Protein 1g.

Ginger-Glazed Carrots

6 servings

8 medium carrots, cut into 1/4-inch slices (4 cups)
1/2 cup water
1/2 cup dry white wine or apple juice
2 teaspoons margarine
1 teaspoon ground ginger
1 tablespoon lemon juice
2 teaspoons packed brown sugar

Cook all ingredients except lemon juice and brown sugar in 10-inch skillet over medium heat 12 to 15 minutes, stirring occasionally, until liquid has evaporated. Reduce heat to medium-low. Stir in lemon juice and brown sugar. Cook 5 minutes, stirring occasionally, until carrots are glazed.

1 SERVING: Calories 50 (Calories from Fat 10); Fat 1g (Saturated 0g); Cholesterol 0mg; Sodium 50mg; Carbohydrate 12g (Dietary Fiber 3g); Protein 1g.

Antioxidants Abound

Antioxidant nutrients—vitamins A, C and E—are thought to help slow the aging process and reduce risk of cancer and heart disease, according to medical experts. Antioxidants can help bolster our immune system as well. Choose fruits and veggies with yellow-orange flesh for vitamin A, citrus for vitamin C and nuts or vegetable oil for vitamin E.

Ginger-Glazed Carrots

Baked Eggplant with Two Cheeses

4 servings

You'll never believe this dish, oozing with cheese, is low in fat!

1 medium eggplant (1 1/2 pounds)
1 can (14 1/2 ounces) stewed tomatoes,
    undrained
2 teaspoons sugar
1 teaspoon all-purpose flour
1/2 teaspoon salt
1/2 teaspoon garlic powder
1/2 teaspoon paprika
1/4 teaspoon dried oregano leaves
1/4 teaspoon pepper
2/3 cup shredded reduced-fat Swiss
    or mozzarella cheese
2 tablespoons grated Parmesan cheese

Heat oven to 350°. Spray rectangular baking dish, 11×7×1 1/2 inches, with nonstick cooking spray. Cut unpeeled eggplant into 1/2-inch slices. Place in 3-quart saucepan; cover with water (salted if desired). Heat to boiling; reduce heat. Cover and simmer 5 minutes; drain and pat dry.

Mix remaining ingredients except cheeses in 2-quart saucepan. Cook over medium-high heat about 5 minutes, stirring frequently, until slightly thickened.

Place eggplant in baking dish; top with tomato mixture and cheeses. Cover and bake 20 minutes. Uncover and bake about 10 minutes longer or until light brown.

1 SERVING: Calories 110 (Calories from Fat 25); Fat 3g (Saturated 2g); Cholesterol 5mg; Sodium 500mg; Carbohydrate 17g (Dietary Fiber 3g); Protein 7g.

Honey Green Beans with Cranberries

4 servings

1 1/2 pounds green beans
1 teaspoon grated orange peel
1/2 cup dried cranberries
2 tablespoons honey
Shredded orange peel, if desired

Heat beans and orange peel in 1 inch water to boiling in 2-quart saucepan. Boil uncovered 5 minutes; reduce heat. Cover and simmer 10 to 15 minutes or until beans are crisp-tender; drain. Toss beans, cranberries and honey. Garnish with orange peel.

1 SERVING: Calories 70 (Calories from Fat 0); Fat 0g (Saturated 0g); Cholesterol 0mg; Sodium 15mg; Carbohydrate 21g (Dietary Fiber 5g); Protein 2g.

Fitness Facts

Can you burn fat from specific areas of the body by exercising those areas?

Contrary to popular belief, there is no such thing as "spot reduction." When exercising, your body produces energy by metabolizing fat from all regions of the body, not just from the body parts involved. For example, doing sit-ups will not trim fat from your abdomen but will tone the muscles; aerobic exercise is needed to burn the fat.

Three-Pepper Stir-fry

4 servings

2 teaspoons grated gingerroot
2 cloves garlic, finely chopped
1/4 cup reduced-sodium chicken broth
1 medium red bell pepper, thinly sliced
1 medium yellow bell pepper, thinly sliced
1 medium orange or green bell pepper,
    thinly sliced
1 tablespoon hoisin sauce

Spray nonstick wok or 10-inch skillet with nonstick cooking spray; heat over medium-high heat. Add gingerroot and garlic; stir-fry 1 minute. Add broth; heat until boiling. Add bell peppers. Cook 5 to 8 minutes, stirring occasionally, until crisp-tender. Stir in hoisin sauce.

1 SERVING: Calories 20 (Calories from Fat 0); Fat 0g (Saturated 0g); Cholesterol 0mg; Sodium 30mg; Carbohydrate 5g (Dietary Fiber 1g); Protein 1g.

Ratatouille

8 servings

3 cups 1/2-inch cubes eggplant
    (about 1/2 pound)
1 cup 1/4-inch slices zucchini (1 small)
2 cloves garlic, chopped
1 small onion, sliced
1/2 medium green bell pepper,
    cut into strips
2 tablespoons chopped fresh parsley
1 tablespoon chopped fresh or 1/2 teaspoon
    dried basil leaves
2 tablespoons water
1/2 teaspoon salt
1/4 teaspoon pepper
2 medium tomatoes, cut into eighths

Cook all ingredients except tomatoes in 10-inch skillet over medium heat until vegetables are tender, about 10 minutes. Remove from heat; stir in tomatoes. Cover and let stand 2 to 3 minutes.

1 SERVING: Calories 25 (Calories from Fat 0); Fat 0g (Saturated 0g); Cholesterol 0mg; Sodium 140mg; Carbohydrate 5g (Dietary Fiber 2g); Protein 1g.

Microwave Directions: Omit water. Mix all ingredients in 2-quart microwavable casserole. Cover tightly and microwave on High 5 minutes; stir. Cover and microwave until vegetables are tender, 2 to 5 minutes longer.

Steamed Vegetables with Yogurt Sauce

8 servings

Drizzled with herb-yogurt sauce, these vegetables will be the star of your plate!

Yogurt Sauce (right)
3 cups cauliflowerets (1 pound)
2 medium zucchini, cut into 1-inch slices
1 medium red or green bell pepper,
    cut into 1/4-inch strips
1 lemon half

Prepare Yogurt Sauce. Place steamer basket in 1/2 inch water in saucepan or skillet (water should not touch bottom of basket). Place cauliflowerets, zucchini and bell pepper in basket. Cover tightly and heat to boiling; reduce heat. Steam about 6 minutes or until vegetables are crisp-tender Arrange vegetables on plate. Squeeze juice from lemon over vegetables. Serve with sauce.

YOGURT SAUCE

1 cup plain nonfat yogurt
2 tablespoons honey
1 teaspoon Dijon mustard
1/4 teaspoon salt
3/4 teaspoon chopped fresh or
    1/4 teaspoon dried basil leaves
3/4 teaspoon chopped fresh or
    1/4 teaspoon dried tarragon leaves
1 clove garlic, crushed
Dash of dried dill weed

Mix all ingredients. Cover and refrigerate at least 2 hours but no longer than 24 hours.

1 SERVING: Calories 40 (Calories from Fat 0); Fat 0g (Saturated 0g); Cholesterol 0mg; Sodium 110mg; Carbohydrate 8g (Dietary Fiber 1g); Protein 3g.

Microwave Directions: Prepare Yogurt Sauce as directed. Place cauliflowerets, zucchini, bell pepper, 1/4 cup water and 1/2 teaspoon salt in 2-quart microwavable casserole. Cover tightly and microwave on High 7 to 9 minutes, stirring after 4 minutes, until vegetables are crisp-tender; drain.

Steamed Vegetables with Yogurt Sauce

Sweet-and-Sour Veggies and Beans

4 servings

Using purchased sweet-and-sour sauce makes this recipe extra easy. Try serving it with grilled turkey burgers.

1/2 cup water
1 package (16 ounces) frozen broccoli, carrots, water chestnuts and red peppers
1 can (15 to 16 ounces) kidney beans, rinsed and drained
1/3 cup sweet-and-sour sauce
1 tablespoon sesame seed, toasted

Heat water to boiling in 12-inch nonstick skillet. Cook vegetables in water 4 to 6 minutes, stirring occasionally, until tender. Stir in beans and sweet-and-sour sauce; heat through, stirring occasionally. Sprinkle with sesame seed. Serve warm or cold.

1 SERVING: Calories 175 (Calories from Fat 20); Fat 2g (Saturated 0g); Cholesterol 0mg; Sodium 360mg; Carbohydrate 38g (Dietary Fiber 11g); Protein 12g.

HEALTHY HINT

Spray slices of French bread with butter- or olive oil-flavored nonstick cooking spray. Sprinkle bread with garlic powder and grated fat-free Parmesan cheese. Wrap in foil and heat in oven until warm.

Cajun Side Dish

6 servings

When selecting okra, look for fresh pods that are bright green in color, firm and less than 4 inches long.

1 tablespoon vegetable oil
2 1/2 cups sliced okra (about 8 ounces)
1 cup frozen whole kernel corn
1 large onion, chopped (about 1 cup)
1 medium green, red or yellow bell pepper, chopped (about 1 cup)
3 large tomatoes, seeded and chopped (about 3 cups)
1 can (15 to 16 ounces) black-eyed peas, rinsed and drained
2 teaspoons chopped fresh or 1/2 teaspoon dried thyme leaves
2 teaspoons chopped fresh or 1/2 teaspoon dried oregano leaves
1/2 teaspoon salt
1/2 teaspoon paprika
1/8 to 1/4 teaspoon ground red pepper (cayenne)

Heat oil in 12-inch nonstick skillet over medium-high heat. Cook okra, corn, onion and bell pepper in oil, stirring frequently, until crisp-tender. Stir in remaining ingredients. Cook about 5 minutes, stirring frequently, until hot.

1 SERVING: Calories 135 (Calories from Fat 25); Fat 3g (Saturated 1g); Cholesterol 0mg; Sodium 360mg; Carbohydrate 30g (Dietary Fiber 11g); Protein 8g.

Cajun Side Dish

Tossed Greens with Sesame and Oranges

4 servings

1 can (11 ounces) mandarin orange
    segments, drained and 2 tablespoons
    syrup or juice reserved
Orange-Sesame Dressing (right)
5 cups bite-size pieces lettuce
    (Bibb, romaine, red leaf)
1 cup sliced mushrooms (3 ounces)
1 cup bean sprouts
1/3 cup sliced red onion
2 teaspoons sesame seed, toasted*

Place orange segments in shallow glass or plastic dish. Pour Orange-Sesame Dressing over oranges. Cover and refrigerate at least 15 minutes.

    Toss lettuce, mushrooms, bean sprouts and onion in large salad bowl. Spoon oranges and dressing onto salad; toss lightly. Sprinkle with sesame seed before serving.

ORANGE-SESAME DRESSING

3 tablespoons seasoned rice vinegar
2 tablespoons reserved mandarin
    orange syrup
1 tablespoon honey
1 teaspoon sesame oil
Dash of ground cinnamon

Shake all ingredients in tightly covered container.

1 SERVING: Calories 110 (Calories from Fat 20); Fat 2g (Saturated 0g); Cholesterol 0mg; Sodium 10mg; Carbohydrate 21g (Dietary Fiber 2g); Protein 2g.

*To toast sesame seed, heat the seed in an ungreased skillet over medium heat about 2 minutes, stirring occasionally, until golden brown.

Best Salad Bar Choices

Salad bars offer so much variety and are a fast way to create a meal. With all of the tempting options, what should you choose if you want to lose?

- Pile on the plain veggies! Choose greens, cucumbers, tomatoes, carrots, celery, broccoli, cauliflower, mushrooms, sprouts, peppers, squash, water chestnuts, radishes and onions.

- Add a little protein. Choose chicken, turkey, ham, imitation crab, flaked tuna, kidney or garbanzo beans, and cottage cheese.

- Choose fresh fruit, such as pineapple, melon, bananas and apples.

- Avoid marinated or mayonnaise-based salads, cheeses, chopped egg and olives.

- Limit higher-fat toppings, such as croutons, shoestring potatoes, chow mein noodles, tortilla chips, sunflower seeds and bacon bits.

- Choose low-fat or fat-free salad dressing or vinegar or lemon juice.

Jicama-Spinach Salad with Lime-Yogurt Dressing

6 servings

The Lime-Yogurt Dressing is delightful on any tossed green salad. Try it on a salad of spinach, mandarin orange segments and slivered almonds.

Lime-Yogurt Dressing (below)
2 cups shredded spinach
1 cup finely chopped jicama
2 medium carrots, chopped (1 cup)
1 small red bell pepper, chopped (1/2 cup)
1/2 medium red onion, finely chopped
    (1/2 cup)
2 cups shredded lettuce

Prepare Lime-Yogurt Dressing in large glass or plastic bowl. Add remaining ingredients except lettuce; toss. Cover and refrigerate about 2 hours or until chilled. Serve on lettuce.

LIME-YOGURT DRESSING

3/4 cup plain nonfat yogurt
3 tablespoons chopped fresh parsley
2 tablespoons lime juice
2 tablespoons red wine vinegar
1/2 teaspoon grated lime peel
1/2 teaspoon salt
1/4 teaspoon pepper

Mix all ingredients with fork or wire whisk.

1 SERVING: Calories 50 (Calories from Fat 0); Fat 0g (Saturated 0g); Cholesterol 0mg; Sodium 230mg; Carbohydrate 10g (Dietary Fiber 2g); Protein 3g.

Lemon Greek Salad

4 servings

There is only 1 tablespoon of olive oil in this salad, so you may want to use one with a good olive flavor. As a rule of thumb, the darker the color of the oil, the stronger the olive flavor. Oils that are quite green in appearance usually have rich flavor.

1 medium unpeeled cucumber
2 cups bite-size pieces spinach
2 cups bite-size pieces Boston lettuce
1/4 cup crumbled feta cheese
2 tablespoons sliced green onions (with tops)
10 pitted ripe olives, sliced
1 medium tomato, cut into thin wedges
Lemon and Mustard Dressing (below)

Score cucumber by running tines of fork lengthwise down sides; slice. Toss cucumber slices and remaining ingredients with Lemon and Mustard Dressing.

LEMON AND MUSTARD DRESSING

2 tablespoons lemon juice
1 tablespoon olive or vegetable oil
1 teaspoon sugar
1 teaspoon Dijon mustard
1/8 teaspoon pepper

Shake all ingredients in tightly covered container.

1 SERVING: Calories 100 (Calories from Fat 65); Fat 7g (Saturated 2g); Cholesterol 10mg; Sodium 210mg; Carbohydrate 8g (Dietary Fiber 3g); Protein 4g.

HEALTHY HINT

Dress down! Cut down on the fat in your home-made salad vinaigrette. Replace one-quarter to one-half of the amount of oil with water.

Creamy Coleslaw

4 servings

It is hard to believe that coleslaw can be part of a lower-calorie menu. This one is as crunchy and creamy as delicatessen coleslaw.

1/3 cup plain nonfat yogurt
2 tablespoons Dijon mustard
1 tablespoon reduced-fat mayonnaise
    or salad dressing
2 teaspoons sugar
Freshly ground pepper
3 cups finely shredded red or green cabbage
1/2 cup shredded carrot (about 1 small)
3 tablespoons chopped red onion

Mix yogurt, mustard, mayonnaise, sugar and pepper in medium glass or plastic bowl or in heavy plastic bag. Stir in remaining ingredients until evenly coated. Cover and refrigerate at least 1 hour.

1 SERVING: Calories 50 (Calories from Fat 20); Fat 2g (Saturated 0g); Cholesterol 0mg; Sodium 155mg; Carbohydrate 7g (Dietary Fiber 3g); Protein 2g.

Garden Potato Salad

12 servings

Ordinary potato salad weighs in at about three times the calories of this version, made crunchy with added vegetables.

1 cup plain nonfat yogurt
1 tablespoon reduced-fat French dressing
2 teaspoons mustard
1/2 teaspoon celery seed
1/2 teaspoon salt
1/4 teaspoon pepper
2 cups diced cooked potatoes
1 cup sliced radishes
1 cup diced zucchini (about 1 medium)
1 cup thinly sliced celery (about 2 medium
    stalks)
1/2 cup shredded carrots (about 2 medium)
1/2 cup sliced green onions (with tops)
2 hard-cooked eggs, chopped

Mix yogurt, French dressing, mustard, celery seed, salt and pepper in medium glass or plastic bowl or in heavy plastic bag. Add remaining ingredients; toss until vegetables are evenly coated. Cover and refrigerate at least 3 hours.

1 SERVING: Calories 50 (Calories from Fat 10); Fat 1g (Saturated 0g); Cholesterol 45mg; Sodium 150mg; Carbohydrate 9g (Dietary Fiber 2g); Protein 3g.

Two-Potato Salad with Dill Dressing

4 servings

1/2 cup extra-creamy plain nonfat yogurt
  or 1/2 container (8-ounce size) plain
  nonfat yogurt
1 tablespoon fat-free mayonnaise or salad
  dressing
1 teaspoon chopped fresh or 1/2 teaspoon
  dried dill weed
1 teaspoon Dijon mustard
1/4 teaspoon salt
1 large white potato, cooked and cubed
  (2 cups)
1 large sweet potato, cooked and cubed
  (2 cups)
1 small stalk celery, chopped (1/3 cup)
2 medium green onions, chopped
  (2 tablespoons)
1/4 cup sliced radishes

Mix yogurt, mayonnaise, dill weed, mustard
and salt in large glass or plastic bowl. Add
remaining ingredients; toss. Cover and refrigerate about 4 hours or until chilled.

1 SERVING: Calories 90 (Calories from Fat 0); Fat 0g
(Saturated 0g); Cholesterol 0mg; Sodium 240mg;
Carbohydrate 22g (Dietary Fiber 2g); Protein 3g.

Macaroni with Marinated Tomatoes

6 servings

2 cups chopped tomatoes (about 2 medium)
2 green onions (with tops), chopped
2 cloves garlic, finely chopped
1/4 cup chopped fresh parsley
1/2 teaspoon salt
2 teaspoons chopped fresh or 1/2 teaspoon
  dried basil leaves
1/8 teaspoon coarsely cracked pepper
2 tablespoons olive or vegetable oil
1 package (7 ounces) uncooked pasta shells

Mix all ingredients except macaroni shells.
Cover and refrigerate at least 2 hours but no
longer than 24 hours. Prepare macaroni as
directed on package; drain. Immediately toss
with tomato mixture.

1 SERVING: Calories 175 (Calories from Fat 45); Fat 5g
(Saturated 0g); Cholesterol 0mg; Sodium 190mg;
Carbohydrate 28g (Dietary Fiber 1g); Protein 5g.

Macaroni with Marinated Tomatoes

Picnic Pasta Salad

12 servings

1 package (16 ounces) uncooked rotini pasta
1 can (8 ounces) tomato sauce
1 cup fat-free Italian dressing
1 tablespoon chopped fresh or 1 teaspoon
    dried basil leaves
1 tablespoon chopped fresh or 1 teaspoon
    dried oregano leaves
1 cup sliced mushrooms (3 ounces)
5 Roma (plum) tomatoes, coarsely chopped
    (1 1/2 cups)
1 large cucumber, coarsely chopped
    (about 1 1/2 cups)
1 medium red onion, chopped
1 can (2 1/4 ounces) sliced ripe olives,
    drained
Fresh basil leaves, if desired
Sliced tomatoes, if desired

Cook and drain pasta as directed on package. Rinse with cold water; drain. Mix tomato sauce, dressing, basil and oregano in large bowl. Add remaining ingredients; toss. Cover and refrigerate about 2 hours or until chilled. Garnish with basil and tomatoes.

1 SERVING: Calories 170 (Calories from Fat 20); Fat 3g (Saturated 0g); Cholesterol 0mg; Sodium 320mg; Carbohydrate 35g (Dietary Fiber 3g); Protein 6g.

Dressing Tips

If you like mayonnaise and salad dressing, but are confused by the choices available, here's an easy lesson:

- Regular mayonnaise or salad dressing contains 60 to 100 calories per tablespoon.

- Reduced-calorie, light or "lite" mayonnaise contains 20 to 50 calories per tablespoon.

- Regular cholesterol-free mayonnaise and salad dressing have 60 to 120 calories per tablespoon but do not contain cholesterol because the egg yolk has been omitted.

- Reduced-calorie, light or "lite" cholesterol-free mayonnaise contains 20 to 50 calories per tablespoon and also has no cholesterol.

- Vinaigrette-type bottled salad dressings are made from vegetable oils and are cholesterol-free but can contain 45 to 100 calories and 4 to 9 grams of fat per tablespoon. The total oil content has been cut in the reduced-calorie counterparts, which in many cases are oil-free. Recipes for salad dressings typically use 3 parts oil to 1 part vinegar. Try using 1 part oil to 1 part vinegar. Mild vinegars with flavorings such as balsamic or raspberry reduce tartness.

- Creamy bottled salad dressings vary widely in fat content, cholesterol and calorie counts. Many bottled dressings average 60 to 80 calories and 6 to 8 grams of fat per tablespoon, while the reduced-calorie versions are one-quarter to one-half that amount.

Bread Salad

6 servings

Making bread salad, or panzanella, *is a favorite way for Italian cooks to use up dried bread. It may turn into one of your favorites as well.*

6 slices day-old French or Italian bread,
    1 inch thick
2 medium tomatoes, chopped (1 1/2 cups)
1 medium cucumber, peeled and chopped
    (1 1/4 cups)
1 small onion, thinly sliced
1/3 cup fat-free red wine vinegar dressing
2 tablespoons chopped fresh or 2 teaspoons
    dried basil leaves
1/4 teaspoon pepper

Tear bread into 1-inch pieces. Mix bread and remaining ingredients in nonmetal bowl. Cover and refrigerate, stirring once, at least 1 hour to blend flavors and soften bread. Stir before serving.

1 SERVING: Calories 90 (Calories from Fat 10); Fat 1g (Saturated 0g); Cholesterol 0mg; Sodium 250mg; Carbohydrate 18g (Dietary Fiber 1g); Protein 3g.

HEALTHY HINT

For a delicious, fat-free homemade salad dressing, combine equal parts of melted seedless raspberry jam and raspberry vinegar. Not only is this great on salads, but it is wonderful as a basting sauce for grilled chicken too.

Mixed Vegetable Salad

8 servings

2 cups cauliflowerets
2 cups bite-size pieces broccoli flowerets
    and stems
1 package (10 ounces) frozen green peas
1/3 cup reduced-fat mayonnaise or
    salad dressing
1/4 cup plain nonfat yogurt
1 tablespoon lemon juice
1/4 teaspoon salt
1/4 teaspoon pepper
1 1/2 medium carrots, thinly sliced
    (3/4 cup)
2 cups cherry tomatoes, cut in half

Heat 1 inch water to boiling in 2-quart saucepan. Add cauliflowerets and broccoli. Heat to boiling; reduce heat. Cover and cook 5 minutes; drain. Rinse with cold water; drain. Rinse peas with cold water to separate; drain.

Mix mayonnaise, yogurt, lemon juice, salt and pepper in large glass or plastic bowl. Add cauliflowerets, broccoli, peas and carrots; toss. Cover and refrigerate at least 4 hours. Stir in tomatoes.

1 SERVING: Calories 90 (Calories from Fat 35); Fat 4g (Saturated 1g); Cholesterol 0mg; Sodium 170mg; Carbohydrate 11g (Dietary Fiber 3g); Protein 3g.

Greek Couscous Salad

7 servings

10 sun-dried tomato halves (not oil-packed)
1 1/2 cups cold cooked couscous
1 small unpeeled cucumber, seeded and
    coarsely chopped (about 3/4 cup)
2 tablespoons chopped fresh parsley
    or 2 teaspoons dried parsley flakes
1 tablespoon chopped fresh or 1 teaspoon
    dried basil leaves
2 ounces feta cheese, crumbled
    (about 1/3 cup)
1 tablespoon pine nuts, toasted
1 tablespoon olive or vegetable oil
1 tablespoon lemon juice
1 1/2 teaspoons chopped fresh or
    1/2 teaspoon dried oregano leaves
1/4 teaspoon salt
1/8 teaspoon coarsely ground pepper

Pour enough hot water over sun-dried tomatoes to cover. Let stand 10 to 15 minutes or until softened; drain and coarsely chop. Mix tomatoes, couscous, cucumber, parsley, basil, cheese and nuts in large bowl. Mix remaining ingredients. Pour over couscous mixture; toss. Cover and refrigerate 1 to 2 hours to blend flavors.

1 SERVING: Calories 105 (Calories from Fat 45); Fat 5g (Saturated 2g); Cholesterol 5mg; Sodium 260mg; Carbohydrate 13g (Dietary Fiber 1g); Protein 3g.

Vegetable-Kasha Salad

4 servings

1/2 cup uncooked roasted buckwheat
    kernels or groats (kasha)
1 egg white
1 cup boiling water
1/4 cup thinly sliced green onions
    (2 to 3 medium)
2 medium tomatoes, seeded and coarsely
    chopped (about 1 1/2 cups)
1 medium unpeeled cucumber, seeded and
    chopped (about 1 1/4 cups)
Balsamic Vinaigrette (below)

Mix buckwheat and egg white. Cook buckwheat mixture in 8-inch skillet over medium-high heat, stirring constantly, until kernels separate and dry. Transfer buckwheat to medium bowl. Pour boiling water over buckwheat; let stand 10 to 15 minutes or until water is absorbed.

Add green onions, tomatoes and cucumber to buckwheat. Pour Balsamic Vinaigrette over buckwheat mixture; toss. Cover and refrigerate 1 to 2 hours to blend flavors.

BALSAMIC VINAIGRETTE

1 tablespoon olive or vegetable oil
1 tablespoon balsamic or red wine vinegar
1 teaspoon sugar
1/4 teaspoon salt
1/8 teaspoon pepper
1 clove garlic, finely chopped

Shake all ingredients in tightly covered container.

1 SERVING: Calories 110 (Calories from Fat 35); Fat 4g (Saturated 1g); Cholesterol 0mg; Sodium 160mg; Carbohydrate 17g (Dietary Fiber 2g); Protein 3g.

Vegetable-Kasha Salad

Crunchy Lemon Rice

6 servings

1/2 cup uncooked regular long-grain rice
1 cup water
1 tablespoon chicken bouillon granules
4 to 6 drops red pepper sauce
1 can (8 ounces) water chestnuts, drained and chopped
1/3 cup sliced green onions
1 tablespoon finely shredded lemon peel

Heat rice, water, bouillon granules and pepper sauce to boiling in 2-quart saucepan, stirring once or twice; reduce heat. Cover and simmer 14 minutes (do not lift cover or stir); remove from heat. Stir in remaining ingredients. Cover and let stand 10 minutes. Fluff lightly with fork.

1 SERVING: Calories 80 (Calories from Fat 0); Fat 0g (Saturated 0g); Cholesterol 0mg; Sodium 640mg; Carbohydrate 19g (Dietary Fiber 1g); Protein 2g.

Creamy Rice-Fruit Salad

8 servings

Leftover cooked rice is just right for this easy salad.

1 kiwifruit, peeled and cut into 1/4-inch slices
1 cup lemon or orange low-fat yogurt
1 tablespoon honey
2 cups cold cooked wild or brown rice
1 cup strawberries, cut in half
1/2 cup seedless green grapes, cut in half
1 teaspoon chopped fresh or 1/4 teaspoon dried mint leaves
1 medium seedless orange, cut into 1-inch pieces (about 1 cup)

Cut kiwifruit into fourths. Mix yogurt and honey in medium bowl. Add kiwifruit and remaining ingredients; toss. Refrigerate remaining salad.

1 SERVING: Calories 115 (Calories from Fat 10); Fat 1g (Saturated 1g); Cholesterol 0mg; Sodium 170mg; Carbohydrate 25g (Dietary Fiber 1g); Protein 2g.

Creamy Rice-Fruit Salad

Millet Pilaf

6 servings

1 medium onion, thinly sliced
1 medium green bell pepper, chopped
    (about 1 cup)
1 cup uncooked millet
3 cups water
1 tablespoon low-sodium chicken bouillon
    granules
1/8 teaspoon ground ginger
1 medium unpeeled apple, coarsely chopped
    (about 1 cup)

Spray 10-inch nonstick skillet with nonstick cooking spray. Cook onion, bell pepper and millet in skillet about 5 minutes over medium heat, stirring occasionally, until onion is crisp-tender. Stir in water, bouillon granules and ginger. Heat to boiling; reduce heat. Cover and simmer about 15 to 20 minutes or until millet is tender. Stir in apple; heat through.

1 SERVING: Calories 155 (Calories from Fat 20); Fat 2g (Saturated 1g); Cholesterol 0mg; Sodium 5mg; Carbohydrate 32g (Dietary Fiber 2g); Protein 4g.

Layered Mixed Vegetable Salad

16 servings

8 cups bite-size pieces mixed salad greens
1 small red onion, thinly sliced and
    separated into rings
2 medium stalks celery, sliced (1 cup)
2 small zucchini, thinly sliced (3 cups)
1 cup shredded Cheddar cheese (4 ounces)
1 1/2 cups frozen green peas, thawed
    and drained
2 cups cherry tomatoes, cut in half
1 cup reduced-fat mayonnaise or
    salad dressing
1 tablespoon mustard
1/2 teaspoon prepared horseradish
Cherry tomatoes, parsley, watercress
    for garnish, if desired

Place about half of the salad greens in large glass bowl. Layer with onion, celery, zucchini, cheese, peas, remaining salad greens and the tomatoes. Mix mayonnaise or salad dressing, mustard and horseradish; spread over tomatoes, spreading to edge of bowl.

Cover and refrigerate at least 8 hours but no longer than 24 hours. Garnish with additional cherry tomatoes and parsley or watercress.

1 SERVING: Calories 60 (Calories from Fat 35); Fat 4g (Saturated 2g); Cholesterol 10mg; Sodium 200mg; Carbohydrate 5g (Dietary Fiber 2g); Protein 3g.

Sweet-and-Spicy Carrot Salad

6 servings

This Southwest-inspired salad is not your everyday carrot-raisin salad. Herb enthusiasts might enjoy using fresh pineapple mint in this dish.

4 medium carrots, shredded (2 1/2 cups)
3/4 cup finely chopped pineapple
1/3 cup plain nonfat yogurt
2 tablespoons chopped fresh mint
2 tablespoons lemon juice
1 teaspoon honey
1/2 teaspoon ground cinnamon
1/4 teaspoon ground cumin
3 cups bite-size pieces leaf lettuce
    (1/2 large head)

Mix all ingredients except lettuce in glass or plastic bowl. Cover and refrigerate about 2 hours or until chilled. Serve on lettuce.

1 SERVING: Calories 40 (Calories from Fat 0); Fat 0g (Saturated 0g); Cholesterol 0mg; Sodium 30mg; Carbohydrate 11g (Dietary Fiber 2g); Protein 1g.

Honey-Lime Fruit Salad

8 servings

Enjoy this refreshing salad with a variety of fresh fruit—kiwifruit, strawberries, pineapple, mangoes and papayas.

1/4 cup honey
1/4 cup frozen (thawed) limeade
    concentrate
4 teaspoons poppy seed, if desired
4 cups cut-up fresh fruit
1/2 cup slivered almonds, toasted

Mix honey, limeade concentrate and poppy seed in medium bowl. Carefully toss fruit and honey mixture. Sprinkle with almonds.

1 SERVING: Calories 130 (Calories from Fat 35); Fat 4g (Saturated 0g); Cholesterol 0mg; Sodium 5mg; Carbohydrate 24g (Dietary Fiber 2g); Protein 2g.

Easy Does It

Making gradual changes for a more healthful eating style will help pave the way to success. Start by substituting reduced- or low-fat products for regular products, mixing high-fiber cereals with regular ones, cutting back on meats and increasing pasta, grains, fruits and vegetables in your diet.

Desserts

Marble Cheesecake (page 409)

(continued on next page)

Upside-Down Apple Cake

9 servings

1 large peeled or unpeeled cooking apple, thinly sliced
1/4 cup packed brown sugar
1/2 teaspoon ground cinnamon
1 package (16 ounces) Betty Crocker Sweet Rewards® apple cinnamon muffin mix
3/4 cup water
2 egg whites or 1/4 cup fat-free cholesterol-free egg product

Heat oven to 375°. Spray square pan, $9 \times 9 \times 2$ inches, with nonstick cooking spray. Arrange apple slices in pan, overlapping slices if necessary. Mix brown sugar and cinnamon; sprinkle over apple slices.

Mix cake mix (dry), water and egg whites in medium bowl, using spoon, about 1 minute or until all mix is moistened. Pour batter over apple slices.

Bake 30 to 35 minutes or until toothpick inserted in center comes out clean. Cool 5 minutes. Loosen edges of cake from pan. Turn upside down onto heatproof serving plate. Serve warm.

1 SERVING: Calories 185 (Calories from Fat 0); Fat 0g (Saturated 0g); Cholesterol 0mg; Sodium 250mg; Carbohydrate 44g (Dietary Fiber 0g); Protein 2g.

Pineapple-Lemon Upside-Down Cake

8 servings

1 can (8 1/4 ounces) crushed pineapple in juice, drained and juice reserved
1 package (0.3 ounce) sugar-free lemon- or orange-flavored gelatin
2 eggs
1 egg white
3/4 cup sugar
1 teaspoon vanilla
3/4 cup all-purpose flour
1 teaspoon baking powder
1/4 teaspoon salt

Heat oven to 375°. Line round pan, $9 \times 1 \ 1/2$ inches, with waxed paper; spray with nonstick cooking spray. Spread pineapple evenly in pan; sprinkle with gelatin (dry).

Beat eggs and egg white in small bowl on high speed until very thick and lemon colored, about 5 minutes; pour into medium bowl. Gradually beat in sugar. Add enough water to reserved pineapple juice to measure 1/3 cup. Beat in pineapple juice and vanilla on low speed. Gradually add flour, baking powder and salt, beating just until batter is smooth. Pour into pan.

Bake until wooden toothpick inserted in center comes out clean, 25 to 30 minutes. Immediately loosen cake from edge of pan; invert pan on heatproof serving plate. Carefully remove waxed paper. Serve warm.

1 SERVING: Calories 160 (Calories from Fat 20); Fat 2g (Saturated 1g); Cholesterol 70mg; Sodium 170mg; Carbohydrate 33g (Dietary Fiber 0g); Protein 3g.

Sacher Cake Roll

10 servings

Sifted cocoa, rather than powdered sugar, is sprinkled on the towel before the cake is rolled, enhancing the deep chocolate flavor.

2 eggs
2 egg whites
3/4 cup sugar
1/3 cup water
1 teaspoon vanilla
3/4 cup all-purpose flour
3 tablespoons cocoa plus extra for sprinkling
1 teaspoon baking powder
1/4 teaspoon salt
1/2 cup apricot preserves or jam
Chocolate Glaze (right)

Heat oven to 375°. Line jelly roll pan, 15 1/2 × 10 1/2 × 1 inch, with aluminum foil or waxed paper; spray with nonstick cooking spray. Beat eggs and egg whites in small bowl on high speed until very thick and lemon colored, about 5 minutes. Pour into medium bowl. Gradually beat in sugar. Beat in water and vanilla on low speed. Gradually beat in flour, 3 tablespoons of the cocoa, the baking powder and salt just until batter is smooth. Pour into pan.

Bake until wooden toothpick inserted in center comes out clean, 12 to 15 minutes. Immediately loosen cake from edges of pan; invert on towel sprinkled with cocoa. Carefully remove foil. Trim off stiff edges of cake if necessary. While hot, carefully roll cake and towel from narrow end. Cool on wire rack at least 30 minutes.

Unroll cake; remove towel. Beat preserves with fork to soften; spread over top of cake. Roll up cake. Prepare Chocolate Glaze; immediately spread over cake roll.

CHOCOLATE GLAZE

1/3 cup powdered sugar
1 tablespoon cocoa
1 1/2 to 2 1/2 teaspoons hot water
1/4 teaspoon vanilla

Mix all ingredients until smooth and of desired consistency.

1 SERVING: Calories 180 (Calories from Fat 20); Fat 2g (Saturated 1g); Cholesterol 55mg; Sodium 125mg; Carbohydrate 38g (Dietary Fiber 0g); Protein 3g.

Raspberry Jelly Roll

10 servings

3 eggs
1 cup granulated sugar
1/3 cup water
1 teaspoon vanilla
3/4 cup all-purpose flour or 1 cup
   cake flour
1 teaspoon baking powder
1/4 teaspoon salt
Powdered sugar
About 2/3 cup raspberry jelly or jam

Heat oven to 375°. Line jelly roll pan, 15 1/2 × 10 1/2 × 1 inch, with cooking parchment paper, aluminum foil or waxed paper; generously grease foil or waxed paper. Beat eggs in small bowl with electric mixer on high speed about 5 minutes or until very thick and lemon colored. Pour eggs into medium bowl. Gradually beat in granulated sugar. Beat in water and vanilla on low speed. Gradually add flour, baking powder and salt, beating just until batter is smooth. Pour into pan, spreading to corners.

Bake 12 to 15 minutes or until toothpick inserted in center comes out clean. Immediately loosen cake from edges of pan and turn upside down onto towel generously sprinkled with powdered sugar. Carefully remove paper. Trim off stiff edges of cake if necessary. While hot, carefully roll cake and towel from narrow end. Cool on wire rack at least 30 minutes.

Unroll cake and remove towel. Beat jelly slightly with fork to soften; spread over cake. Roll up cake. Sprinkle with powdered sugar.

1 SERVING: Calories 190 (Calories from Fat 20); Fat 2g (Saturated 1g); Cholesterol 65mg; Sodium 130mg; Carbohydrate 40g (Dietary Fiber 0g); Protein 3g.

Delicious Desserts

Eat sugary desserts in moderation, but when it comes to fresh fruit, you can really go to town. Enjoy it chopped, pureed, cold, hot, with sauces or without. Always use ripe fruit for the most flavorful results.

When recipes call for such products as whipped cream, sour cream, cream cheese and ricotta cheese, use low-fat versions.

Angel food cake is a perfect dessert for the low-fat crowd. Try Chocolate-Orange Angel Food Cake on page 390.

Fresh fruit ices and sherbets can be made easily without any eggs or cream, a boon to fat watchers. Combine luscious complementary fruits for seemingly endless variety.

Chocolate-Orange Angel Food Cake

16 servings

1 1/2 cups powdered sugar
3/4 cup cake flour
1/4 cup cocoa
1 1/2 cups egg whites (about 12)
1 1/2 teaspoons cream of tartar
1 cup granulated sugar
1/4 teaspoon salt
3 cups orange sherbet, softened

Move oven rack to lowest position. Heat oven to 375°. Sift together powdered sugar, flour and cocoa. Beat egg whites and cream of tartar in large bowl on medium speed until foamy. Beat in granulated sugar, 2 tablespoons at a time, on high speed, adding salt with the last addition of sugar. Continue beating until stiff and glossy. Do not underbeat.

Sprinkle cocoa mixture, 1/4 cup at a time, over meringue, folding in just until cocoa mixture disappears. Spread batter in ungreased tube pan, 10×4 inches. Gently cut through batter with metal spatula.

Bake 30 to 35 minutes or until cracks feel dry and top springs back when touched lightly. Invert pan onto metal funnel or glass bottle about 2 hours or until cake is completely cool. Remove from pan.

Slice off top of cake about 1 inch down; set aside. Cut down into cake 1 inch from outer edge and 1 inch from edge of hole, leaving substantial "walls" on each side. Remove cake within cuts with curved knife or spoon, being careful to leave a base of cake 1 inch thick. Spoon sherbet into cake cavity; smooth up. Replace top of cake. Cover and freeze about 3 hours or until firm.

1 SERVING: Calories 175 (Calories from Fat 10); Fat 1g (Saturated 1g); Cholesterol 5mg; Sodium 85mg; Carbohydrate 39g (Dietary Fiber 0g); Protein 3g.

Chocolate-Orange Angel Food Cake

Nature's Sweet Treats

Fresh fruits are perfect for dessert. They have enough natural sweetness to satisfy everyone's sweet tooth.

Fruit (Serving size)	Calories
Apple (2 1/2 inch)	70
Banana (6 inch)	80
Cantaloupe (5 inch, 1/2)	60
Grapefruit (1/2 medium)	50
Grapes (1/2 cup)	50
Honeydew melon (5 inch, 1/4)	35
Orange (2 1/2 inch)	65
Pear (3 × 2 1/2 inch)	100
Pineapple (1/2 cup)	40

Chocolate-Cherry Cobbler

6 servings

3 tablespoons packed brown sugar
2 tablespoons cornstarch
1 can (16 ounces) pitted red tart cherries
    packed in water, undrained
1/4 teaspoon almond extract
6 drops red food color, if desired
2 tablespoons reduced-fat margarine
1/2 cup all-purpose flour
1 tablespoon plus 1 teaspoon cocoa
3/4 teaspoon baking powder
1/8 teaspoon salt
1/3 cup skim milk
1 teaspoon vanilla

Heat oven to 375°. Mix 2 tablespoons of the brown sugar and the cornstarch in 2-quart saucepan; stir in cherries. Cook over medium heat, stirring occasionally, until slightly thickened, 4 to 5 minutes. Stir in almond extract and food color. Pour into ungreased 1-quart casserole.

Cut margarine into flour, cocoa, remaining 1 tablespoon brown sugar, the baking powder and salt until mixture resembles fine crumbs. Stir in milk and vanilla. Drop dough by 6 spoonfuls onto hot cherry mixture.

Bake until topping is no longer doughy, 20 to 25 minutes. Serve warm.

1 SERVING: Calories 135 (Calories from Fat 30); Fat 3g (Saturated 0g); Cholesterol 0mg; Sodium 150mg; Carbohydrate 25g (Dietary Fiber 0g); Protein 2g.

Almond Apple Crisp

6 servings

1 tablespoon water
1 teaspoon almond extract
6 cups sliced unpeeled tart eating apples
    (about 4 medium)
1/2 cup coarsely crushed zwieback crumbs
2 tablespoons all-purpose flour
2 tablespoons sugar
2 tablespoons chopped almonds
1/2 teaspoon ground cinnamon
3 tablespoons reduced-fat margarine
Yogurt Topping (below)

Heat oven to 375°. Mix water and almond extract; toss with apples in 1 1/2-quart casserole sprayed with nonstick cooking spray. Mix remaining ingredients except Yogurt Topping until crumbly; sprinkle over apples.

Bake until top is golden brown and apples are tender, about 30 minutes. Serve warm with Yogurt Topping.

YOGURT TOPPING

1/2 cup plain nonfat yogurt
1/8 teaspoon almond extract
1 teaspoon sugar

Mix all ingredients.

1 SERVING: Calories 155 (Calories from Fat 65); Fat 7g (Saturated 1g); Cholesterol 0mg; Sodium 80mg; Carbohydrate 24g (Dietary Fiber 3g); Protein 2g.

Fat Substitutes for Baking

Because baking is a science in which exact ingredient combinations and amounts are critical, it is trickier to reduce fat, but it can be done. Fat contributes moistness and tenderness to baked goods, and when there is not enough, the results can be dry, tough, gummy or rubbery.

- Eggs and butter, margarine, oil or shortening are the primary sources of fat. Replacing whole eggs with fat-free cholesterol-free egg substitute or egg whites is easy. Replacing butter or margarine is more challenging. Applesauce, yogurt, pureed prunes and bananas as well as baby food all work, but none can be substituted for all of the fat in a recipe.

- Overall, applesauce and yogurt work the best in most recipes. They add the necessary moistness, don't alter the flavor as much as prunes and bananas do, and result in a good texture. The flavor of prune puree is especially good with chocolate, spice and carrot cakes. Banana puree works well in carrot and banana cake or muffins.

- Prune puree mixtures are now sold in the grocery store in the baking section; the label may state that it's a butter and oil or fat replacer (follow label directions for use).

- For best texture and flavor, we recommend replacing half of the fat (butter, margarine, shortening, oil) listed in a recipe with applesauce, yogurt, pureed prunes and bananas or baby food.

- Use fat-free cholesterol-free egg substitutes or 2 egg whites for each whole egg called for in a recipe.

Strawberry Margarita Pie

8 servings

Graham Cracker Shell (right)
2 envelopes unflavored gelatin
1/2 cup water
3 cups strawberries
1/3 cup sugar
1/4 cup tequila
1 tablespoon orange-flavored liqueur
1/2 package (2.8-ounce size) whipped
**   topping mix (1 envelope)**

Prepare Graham Cracker Shell. Sprinkle gelatin on water in 2-quart saucepan. Let stand 1 minute to soften. Place strawberries, sugar, tequila and liqueur in blender or food processor. Cover and blend on medium speed until smooth. Stir 1 cup strawberry mixture into gelatin mixture in saucepan.

Heat over low heat 3 to 5 minutes, stirring constantly, until gelatin is dissolved. Stir in remaining strawberry mixture. Place pan in bowl of ice and water, or refrigerate 30 to 40 minutes, stirring occasionally, just until mixture mounds slightly when dropped from spoon.

Prepare topping mix in large bowl as directed on package—except omit vanilla and substitute skim milk for the milk. Fold strawberry mixture into whipped topping. Spoon into pie shell. Sprinkle with reserved crumb mixture from shell. Refrigerate about 2 hours or until set.

GRAHAM CRACKER SHELL

1 1/4 cups graham cracker crumbs
2 tablespoons strawberry jelly
1 tablespoon vegetable oil

Spray pie plate, 9 × 1 1/4 inches, with non-stick cooking spray. Mix all ingredients. Reserve 2 tablespoons mixture for topping. Press remaining mixture firmly against bottom and side of pie plate.

1 SERVING: Calories 175 (Calories from Fat 45); Fat 5g (Saturated 2g); Cholesterol 0mg; Sodium 115mg; Carbohydrate 30g (Dietary Fiber 1g); Protein 3g.

Strawberry Margarita Pie

To Indulge or Not to Indulge

Eating something indulgent doesn't have to lead to guilt. Before you indulge:

- Ask yourself if something lower in fat would satisfy your craving (a fat-free muffin instead of a cupcake).

- Consider eating half of the amount you usually would eat (splitting a dessert or ordering a smaller portion).

- Eat the whole piece and thoroughly enjoy it; just commit to doing some additional exercise that day.

Streusel-Topped Pumpkin Pie

8 servings

Brown Sugar Topping (below)
1 can (12 ounces) evaporated skim milk
3 egg whites
1 can (16 ounces) pumpkin
1/2 cup sugar
1/2 cup all-purpose flour
1 1/2 teaspoons pumpkin pie spice
3/4 teaspoon baking powder
1/8 teaspoon salt
2 teaspoons grated orange peel

Heat oven to 350°. Prepare Brown Sugar Topping. Spray pie plate, 10×1 1/2 inches, with nonstick cooking spray. Place remaining ingredients in blender or food processor in order listed. Cover and blend until smooth. Pour into pie plate. Sprinkle with topping.

Bake 50 to 55 minutes or until knife inserted in center comes out clean. Cool 15 minutes. Refrigerate at least 4 hours or up to 24 hours.

BROWN SUGAR TOPPING

1/4 cup packed brown sugar
1/4 cup quick-cooking oats
1 tablespoon margarine or butter, softened

Mix all ingredients.

1 SERVING: Calories 180 (Calories from Fat 20); Fat 2g (Saturated 1g); Cholesterol 2mg; Sodium 150mg; Carbohydrate 36g (Dietary Fiber 1g); Protein 6g.

Streusel-Topped Pumpkin Pie

Rice Pudding

8 servings

2 egg whites
1 egg
2 cups cooked white rice
1/2 cup sugar
1/2 cup golden raisins
2 cups skim milk
1/2 teaspoon vanilla
1/4 teaspoon ground cardamom

Heat oven to 325°. Beat egg whites and egg in ungreased 1 1/2-quart casserole. Stir in remaining ingredients. Bake uncovered 50 to 60 minutes, stirring after 30 minutes, until knife inserted halfway between center and edge comes out clean. Serve warm or cold. Immediately refrigerate any remaining pudding.

1 SERVING: Calories 170 (Calories from Fat 10); Fat 1g (Saturated 0g); Cholesterol 30mg; Sodium 245mg; Carbohydrate 36g (Dietary Fiber 1g); Protein 5g.

Microwave Directions: Prepare as directed—except use 1 1/2-quart microwavable casserole and decrease skim milk to 1 1/2 cups. Elevate casserole on inverted microwave pie plate in microwave oven. Microwave uncovered on Medium 8 to 10 minutes, stirring every 3 minutes, just until creamy. (Pudding will continue to cook while standing.) Let stand uncovered on heatproof surface 10 minutes. Sprinkle with ground cinnamon if desired. Cover and refrigerate any remaining pudding.

Maple Custard

4 servings

1 3/4 cups skim milk
1 egg
2 egg whites
3 tablespoons sugar
1/2 teaspoon maple flavoring
Dash of salt
4 teaspoons maple-flavored syrup
2 cups cut-up fruit

Heat oven to 350°. Heat milk in 1-quart saucepan just to boiling. Remove from heat; cool. Beat egg, egg whites, sugar, maple flavoring and salt in small bowl. Gradually stir in milk. Pour into four 6-ounce custard cups. Drop 1 teaspoon maple-flavored syrup carefully onto center of mixture in each cup (syrup will sink to bottom).

Place cups in square pan, $9 \times 9 \times 2$ inches, on oven rack. Pour very hot water into pan to within 1/2 inch of tops of cups. Bake about 45 minutes or until knife inserted halfway between center comes out clean. Remove cups from water. Let stand 15 minutes. Unmold and serve warm with fruit. Or cover, refrigerate and unmold at serving time. Immediately refrigerate any remaining custard.

1 SERVING: Calories 170 (Calories from Fat 20); Fat 2g (Saturated 1g); Cholesterol 55mg; Sodium 180mg; Carbohydrate 32g (Dietary Fiber 1g); Protein 7g.

Maple Custard

Raspberry Bread Pudding

6 servings

Stale bread that is not quite totally dried out is best for this bread pudding. White, whole wheat or cinnamon-raisin bread all work equally well. If using cinnamon-raisin bread, omit raisins and cinnamon from recipe. Blueberries also make a nice substitution for the raspberries.

**4 cups 2-inch cubes day-old bread
    (5 to 7 slices)**
1 cup fresh raspberries
1/2 cup raisins
2 1/2 cups low-fat milk
1/2 cholesterol-free egg product
2 tablespoons packed brown sugar
1 teaspoon vanilla
1/2 teaspoon ground cinnamon
1/4 teaspoon ground nutmeg

Heat oven to 350°. Spray square baking dish, 8 × 8 × 2 inches, with nonstick cooking spray. Mix all ingredients; let stand 15 minutes. Spread mixture in baking dish. Place baking dish in rectangular pan, 13 × 9 × 2 inches, on oven rack. Pour boiling water into pan until 1 inch deep. Bake 25 to 30 minutes or until brown.

1 SERVING: Calories 185 (Calories from Fat 30); Fat 3g (Saturated 2g); Cholesterol 10mg; Sodium 200mg; Carbohydrate 33g (Dietary Fiber 1g); Protein 7g.

Peach Bread Pudding

4 servings

This pudding is a real treat for people trying to watch their fat grams. Each serving has only 2 grams of fat!

**2 cups cubed French bread (about four
    1/2-inch-thick slices)**
**2 medium peaches, peeled and chopped, or
    2 cups frozen (thawed) sliced peaches**
1 cup skim milk
**1/4 cup fat-free cholesterol-free egg
    product or 1 egg**
**1/4 cup peach or apricot spreadable fruit,
    melted**
2 tablespoons packed brown sugar
1/2 teaspoon vanilla
Peach or apricot spreadable fruit, if desired

Heat oven to 350°. Spray loaf pan, 9 × 5 × 3 or 8 1/2 × 4 1/2 × 2 1/2 inches, with nonstick cooking spray. Toss bread and peaches in pan. Beat milk, egg product, melted spreadable fruit, brown sugar and vanilla with wire whisk or fork in medium bowl until blended. Pour evenly over bread and peaches.

Place loaf pan in rectangular pan, 13 × 9 × 2 inches, on oven rack. Pour boiling water into rectangular pan until 1 inch deep. Bake 30 to 35 minutes or until knife inserted in center comes out clean. Spread additional spreadable fruit over top of bread pudding for glaze. Cool 10 minutes; cut into 4 pieces. Serve warm. Cover and refrigerate any remaining bread pudding.

1 SERVING: Calories 160 (Calories from Fat 20); Fat 2g (Saturated 1g); Cholesterol 5mg; Sodium 120mg; Carbohydrate 33g (Dietary Fiber 2g); Protein 5g.

Peach Bread Pudding

Raspberry Brûlée

8 servings

This dessert isn't just low-fat, it's easy! Crème brûlée, a restaurant favorite, can now be made quickly and deliciously at home.

1 cup raspberries
1/3 cup sugar
2 tablespoons cornstarch
1/4 teaspoon salt
2 cups nonfat half-and-half or skim milk
1/2 teaspoon vanilla
4 teaspoons packed brown sugar

Place raspberries evenly in bottom of four 10-ounce custard cups or ramekins. Mix sugar, cornstarch and salt in 2-quart saucepan. Stir in half-and-half. Heat to boiling over medium heat, stirring frequently. Stir in vanilla. Spoon over raspberries.

Set oven control to broil. Sprinkle 1 teaspoon brown sugar over mixture in each custard cup. Broil with tops 4 to 6 inches from heat 2 to 3 minutes or just until brown sugar is melted. Serve immediately. Cover and refrigerate any remaining desserts.

1 SERVING: Calories 180 (Calories from Fat 0); Fat 0g (Saturated 0g); Cholesterol 2mg; Sodium 210mg; Carbohydrate 43g (Dietary Fiber 2g); Protein 4g.

Oatmeal Raisin Cookies

about 3 dozen cookies

Who doesn't love oatmeal raisin cookies? This recipe uses unsweetened applesauce to replace some of the margarine and egg substitute in place of eggs.

2/3 cup granulated sugar
2/3 cup packed brown sugar
1/2 cup margarine or butter, softened
1/2 cup unsweetened applesauce
1/2 cup fat-free cholesterol-free egg product or 2 eggs
1 1/2 teaspoons ground cinnamon
1 teaspoon baking soda
1/2 teaspoon baking powder
1/2 teaspoon salt
1 1/2 teaspoons vanilla
3 cups quick-cooking or old-fashioned oats
1 cup all-purpose flour
2/3 cup raisins

Heat oven to 375°. Mix all ingredients except oats, flour and raisins in large bowl. Stir in oats, flour and raisins. Drop dough by rounded tablespoonfuls about 2 inches apart onto ungreased cookie sheet. Bake 9 to 11 minutes or until light brown. Immediately remove from cookie sheet. Cool on wire rack.

1 COOKIE: Calories 100 (Calories from Fat 30); Fat 3g (Saturated 1g); Cholesterol 0mg; Sodium 110mg; Carbohydrate 18g (Dietary Fiber 1g); Protein 2g.

Raspberry Brûlée

Orange Almond Biscotti

about 3 1/2 dozen cookies

1 cup sugar
1/2 cup margarine or butter, softened
1 tablespoon grated orange peel
2 eggs
3 1/2 cups all-purpose flour
1 teaspoon baking powder
1/2 teaspoon salt
1/3 cup slivered almonds, chopped

Heat oven to 350°. Beat sugar, margarine, orange peel and eggs in large bowl. Stir in flour, baking powder and salt. Stir in almonds. Shape half of the dough at a time into rectangle, 10 × 3 inches, on ungreased cookie sheet. Bake about 20 minutes or until toothpick inserted in center comes out clean. Cool on cookie sheet 15 minutes.

Cut crosswise into 1/2-inch slices. Place slices cut sides down on cookie sheet. Bake about 15 minutes or until crisp and light brown. Remove from cookie sheet. Cool on wire rack.

1 COOKIE: Calories 85 (Calories from Fat 25); Fat 3g (Saturated 1g); Cholesterol 10mg; Sodium 70mg; Carbohydrate 13g (Dietary Fiber 0g); Protein 1g.

Chocolate Kiss–Peanut Butter Cookies

about 3 dozen cookies

1 can (14 ounces) sweetened condensed milk
3/4 cup peanut butter
2 cups Bisquick Original baking mix
1 teaspoon vanilla
Sugar
About 36 foil-wrapped milk chocolate or milk and white chocolate kisses, unwrapped

Heat oven to 375°. Mix milk and peanut butter in large bowl until smooth. Stir in baking mix and vanilla. Shape dough into 1 1/4-inch balls. Roll in sugar. Place 2 inches apart on ungreased cookie sheet. Bake 8 to 10 minutes or until bottoms of cookies just begin to brown. Immediately press chocolate kiss into top of each cookie.

1 COOKIE: Calories 140 (Calories from Fat 55); Fat 6g (Saturated 3g); Cholesterol 5mg; Sodium 140mg; Carbohydrate 18g (Dietary Fiber 0g); Protein 3g.

HEALTHY HINT

Enjoy the many specially flavored teas and coffees, such as macadamia nut, hazelnut, cinnamon and chocolate mint. Many of these are available without any added fat or calories, and they make a delicious dessert.

Chocolate Kiss–Peanut Butter Cookies

Gingerbread with Orange Sauce

8 servings

1 cup all-purpose flour
1/4 cup molasses
1/4 cup hot water
2 tablespoons packed brown sugar
2 tablespoons shortening
1/2 teaspoon baking soda
1/2 teaspoon ground ginger
1/2 teaspoon ground cinnamon
1/8 teaspoon salt
1 egg white
Frozen (thawed) reduced-fat whipped topping, if desired
Orange Sauce (right)

Heat oven to 325°. Spray loaf pan, 8 1/2 × 4 1/2 × 2 1/2 inches, with nonstick cooking spray. Beat all ingredients except whipped topping and Orange Sauce in medium bowl with electric mixer on low speed 30 seconds, scraping bowl constantly. Beat on medium speed 3 minutes, scraping bowl occasionally. Pour into pan.

Bake 30 to 35 minutes or until toothpick inserted in center comes out clean. Cool 10 minutes; remove from pan. Serve warm or cool with whipped topping and Orange Sauce.

ORANGE SAUCE

3 tablespoons sugar
1 tablespoon cornstarch
1 cup water
1 tablespoon finely shredded orange peel
1 tablespoon orange juice

Mix sugar and cornstarch in 1-quart saucepan. Gradually stir in water. Cook over medium heat, stirring constantly, until mixture thickens and boils. Boil and stir 1 minute; remove from heat. Stir in orange peel and orange juice. Serve warm or cool.

1 SERVING: Calories 150 (Calories from Fat 25); Fat 3g (Saturated 1g); Cholesterol 0mg; Sodium 125mg; Carbohydrate 29g (Dietary Fiber 0g); Protein 2g.

Brown Sugar Strawberries

4 servings

(photograph on page 69)

A fabulous fat-free dessert that everyone will love!

2 cups fresh strawberries
1/3 cup plain nonfat yogurt
1/3 cup loosely packed brown sugar

Rinse and dry strawberries but do not hull. Place strawberries in serving bowl. Place yogurt and brown sugar in 2 separate bowls. To eat, dip strawberries into yogurt and then into brown sugar.

1 SERVING: Calories 95 (Calories from Fat 0); Fat 0g (Saturated 0g); Cholesterol 0mg; Sodium 25mg; Carbohydrate 24g (Dietary Fiber 1g); Protein 1g.

Gingerbread with Orange Sauce

Cheesecake with Strawberry Topping

12 servings

4 cups plain nonfat yogurt
4 chocolate wafers, crushed (about 1/4 cup)
1 package (8 ounces) reduced-fat cream cheese (Neufchâtel), softened
2/3 cup sugar
1/4 cup low-fat milk
2 tablespoons all-purpose flour
2 teaspoons vanilla
3 egg whites or 1/2 cup cholesterol-free egg product
Strawberry Topping (right)

Line 6-inch strainer with basket-style paper coffee filter or double thickness of cheesecloth. Place strainer over bowl. Spoon yogurt into strainer. Cover and refrigerate 12 hours, draining liquid from bowl occasionally.

Heat oven to 300°. Spray springform pan, 9 × 3 inches, with nonstick cooking spray. Sprinkle chocolate wafer crumbs on bottom of pan. Beat yogurt and cream cheese in medium bowl on medium speed until smooth. Add sugar, milk, flour, vanilla and egg whites. Beat on medium speed about 2 minutes or until smooth. Carefully spread batter over crumbs in pan.

Bake 1 hour. Turn off oven; leave cheesecake in oven 30 minutes. Remove from oven. Cool 15 minutes. Prepare Strawberry Topping; spread over cheesecake. Cover and refrigerate at least 3 hours. Run metal spatula along side of cake to loosen; remove side of pan. Refrigerate any remaining cheesecake.

STRAWBERRY TOPPING

1 package (10 ounces) frozen strawberries in light syrup, thawed, drained and syrup reserved
1/4 cup sugar
2 tablespoons cornstarch

Add enough water to reserved syrup to measure 1 1/4 cups. Mix sugar and cornstarch in 1 1/2-quart saucepan. Stir in juice mixture and strawberries. Heat to boiling over medium heat, stirring frequently. Boil and stir 1 minute; cool.

1 SERVING: Calories 185 (Calories from Fat 45); Fat 5g (Saturated 3g); Cholesterol 15mg; Sodium 170mg; Carbohydrate 28g (Dietary Fiber 1g); Protein 8g.

HEALTHY HINT

If you are planning to serve desserts to guests, prepare only enough for the number of people you plan to serve. That way, you won't be tempted to eat what's left over.

Marble Cheesecake

12 servings

(photograph on page 384)

2 cups Thick Yogurt (right)
4 chocolate wafers, crushed (1/4 cup)
1 package (8 ounces) reduced-fat cream
    cheese (Neufchâtel), softened
2/3 cup sugar
1/4 cup skim milk
2 tablespoons all-purpose flour
2 teaspoons vanilla
3 egg whites
1 tablespoon cocoa
1 teaspoon chocolate extract
3/4 cup raspberry preserves, if desired

Prepare Thick Yogurt. Heat oven to 300°. Spray springform pan, 9 × 3 inches, with nonstick cooking spray. Sprinkle chocolate wafer crumbs on bottom of pan.

Beat Thick Yogurt and cream cheese in medium bowl with electric mixer on medium speed until smooth. Add sugar, milk, flour, vanilla and egg whites. Beat on medium speed about 2 minutes or until smooth. Place 1 cup batter in small bowl. Beat in cocoa and chocolate extract until blended.

Carefully spread vanilla batter over crumbs in pan. Drop chocolate batter by spoonfuls onto vanilla batter. Swirl through batters with metal spatula, being careful not to touch bottom, for marbled design.

Bake 1 hour. Turn off oven; leave cheesecake in oven 30 minutes. Cool 15 minutes. Cover and refrigerate at least 3 hours. Heat preserves in 1-quart saucepan over medium-low heat, stirring occasionally, until warm. Serve with cheesecake.

THICK YOGURT

4 cups plain nonfat yogurt (without gelatin)

Line 6-inch strainer with basket-style paper coffee filter or double thickness of cheesecloth. Place strainer over bowl. Spoon yogurt into strainer. Cover strainer and bowl and refrigerate at least 12 hours, draining liquid from bowl occasionally.

1 SERVING: Calories 180 (Calories from Fat 55); Fat 6g (Saturated 4g); Cholesterol 20mg; Sodium 150mg; Carbohydrate 27g (Dietary Fiber 1g); Protein 6g.

Poached Raspberry Pears

6 servings

Bosc pears are perfect here, as they hold up well to cooking; firm Anjous can also be used. Apricot spreadable fruit would make a nice flavor and color variation in place of the raspberry.

1/2 cup seedless raspberry spreadable fruit
1 cup apple juice
2 teaspoons grated lemon peel
2 tablespoons lemon juice
3 firm Bosc pears, peeled and cut into
     fourths

Mix all ingredients except pears in 10-inch skillet. Add pears. Heat to boiling; reduce heat to medium-low. Simmer uncovered 30 minutes, spooning juice mixture over pears and turning every 10 minutes, until pears are tender. Serve warm or chilled.

1 SERVING: Calories 110 (Calories from Fat 0); Fat 0g (Saturated 0g); Cholesterol 0mg; Sodium 5mg; Carbohydrate 28g (Dietary Fiber 3g); Protein 0g.

Double Orange Delight

4 servings

Arranging the fruit over the yogurt sauce gives this dessert a very elegant look. The oranges can be peeled easily by hand, while peeling with a knife will give a more finished look.

1/2 cup plain nonfat yogurt
1 tablespoon frozen (partially thawed)
     orange juice concentrate
2 large oranges, peeled and sectioned
2 tablespoons semisweet chocolate chips
1 teaspoon shortening

Mix yogurt and orange juice concentrate. Spoon 2 tablespoons yogurt mixture onto each of 4 dessert plates. Arrange orange sections on yogurt mixture.

Heat chocolate chips and shortening over low heat, stirring constantly, until chocolate is melted. Carefully drizzle chocolate in thin lines over oranges.

1 SERVING: Calories 105 (Calories from Fat 30); Fat 3g (Saturated 2g); Cholesterol 0mg; Sodium 25mg; Carbohydrate 18g (Dietary Fiber 2g); Protein 3g.

Yogurt Sauce Magic

Low-fat yogurt makes great low-cal dessert sauces. Mixed with softened frozen yogurt, it's a thick sauce to serve with warm, puddinglike desserts. Heated slowly with a little powdered sugar and some crushed peppermint candies until smooth, it's a pink peppermint sauce to serve with chocolate desserts. Stirred with a splash of almond or hazelnut liqueur, it's a sauce to drizzle over fruit.

Raspberry Marbled Brownies

4 dozen bars

Cream Cheese Filling (right)
1 cup (2 sticks) margarine or butter
4 ounces unsweetened chocolate
2 cups sugar
2 teaspoons vanilla
4 eggs
1 1/2 cups all-purpose flour
1/2 teaspoon salt
1 cup coarsely chopped nuts, if desired
1/3 cup raspberry jam or preserves

Heat oven to 350°. Grease square pan, 9 × 9 × 2 inches. Prepare Cream Cheese Filling. Melt margarine and chocolate over low heat, stirring occasionally; cool.

Beat chocolate mixture, sugar, vanilla and eggs in medium bowl with electric mixer on medium speed 1 minute, scraping bowl occasionally. Beat in flour and salt on low speed 30 seconds, scraping bowl occasionally. Beat on medium speed 1 minute. Stir in nuts.

Spread half of the batter in pan. Spread with filling. Gently spread remaining batter over filling. Drop jam by scant teaspoonfuls randomly over batter. Gently swirl through batter, filling and jam with spoon in an over-and-under motion for marbled design.

Bake 55 to 65 minutes or until toothpick inserted in center comes out clean; cool. Cut into about 1 1/2 × 1-inch bars.

CREAM CHEESE FILLING

1 package (8 ounces) cream cheese, softened
1/4 cup sugar
1 teaspoon ground cinnamon
1 1/2 teaspoons vanilla
1 egg

Beat all ingredients in small bowl with electric mixer on medium speed 2 minutes, scraping bowl occasionally.

1 BAR: Calories 125 (Calories from Fat 65); Fat 7g (Saturated 3g); Cholesterol 30mg; Sodium 90mg; Carbohydrate 15g (Dietary Fiber 0g); Protein 1g.

HEALTHY HINT

Use nuts in low-fat baking in reduced amounts. Cut the amount of nuts in half, and place them on the top of the batter. The nuts will toast nicely as they bake, releasing more flavor.

Chocolate-Glazed Brownies

16 brownies

1 cup sugar
1/3 cup margarine, softened
1 teaspoon vanilla
3 egg whites
2/3 cup all-purpose flour
1/2 cup cocoa
1/2 teaspoon baking powder
1/4 teaspoon salt
Chocolate Glaze (below)

Heat oven to 350°. Spray square pan, 8 × 8 × 2 inches, with nonstick cooking spray. Mix sugar, margarine, vanilla and egg whites in medium bowl. Stir in remaining ingredients except Chocolate Glaze. Spread in pan.

Bake 20 to 25 minutes or until toothpick inserted in center comes out clean; cool. Prepare Chocolate Glaze. Spread glaze evenly over brownies. Cut into about 2-inch squares.

CHOCOLATE GLAZE

2/3 cups powdered sugar
2 tablespoons cocoa
1/4 teaspoon vanilla
3 to 4 teaspoons hot water

Mix all ingredients.

1 BROWNIE: Calories 135 (Calories from Fat 35); Fat 4g (Saturated 1g); Cholesterol 0mg; Sodium 100mg; Carbohydrate 70g (Dietary Fiber 0g); Protein 2g.

Amaretto Brownies

39 brownies

2/3 cup blanched whole almonds, toasted
1 package (8 ounces) semisweet baking chocolate
1/3 cup butter or margarine
1 1/4 cups all-purpose flour
1 cup sugar
2 tablespoons amaretto
1 teaspoon baking powder
1/2 teaspoon salt
2 eggs
Amaretto Frosting (below)

Heat oven to 350°. Grease rectangular pan, 13 × 9 × 2 inches. Place 1/3 cup of the almonds in food processor. Cover and process, using quick on-and-off motions, until almonds are ground; set aside. Chop remaining 1/3 cup almonds; reserve.

Melt chocolate and butter in 3-quart saucepan over low heat, stirring frequently; remove from heat. Stir in ground almonds and remaining ingredients except Amaretto Frosting. Spread in pan.

Bake 22 to 27 minutes or until toothpick inserted in center comes out clean. Cool completely. Prepare Amaretto Frosting. Spread on brownies. Sprinkle with reserved chopped almonds. Cut into about 3 × 1-inch bars.

AMARETTO FROSTING

2 cups powdered sugar
3 tablespoons butter or margarine, softened
1 tablespoon amaretto
1 to 2 tablespoons milk

Mix all ingredients until smooth.

1 BROWNIE: Calories 130 (Calories from Fat 55); Fat 6g (Saturated 3g); Cholesterol 20mg; Sodium 65mg; Carbohydrate 19g (Dietary Fiber 1g); Protein 1g.

Glazed Lemon Bars

2 dozen bars

1 cup Bisquick Original baking mix
2 tablespoons powdered sugar
2 tablespoons firm margarine or butter
3/4 cup granulated sugar
1/4 cup flaked coconut, if desired
1 tablespoon Bisquick Original baking mix
2 eggs
2 teaspoons grated lemon peel
2 tablespoons lemon juice
Lemon Glaze (below)

Heat oven to 350°. Mix 1 cup of the baking mix and the powdered sugar. Cut in margarine until crumbly. Press in ungreased square pan, 8 × 8 × 2 inches. Bake about 10 minutes or until light brown.

Mix remaining ingredients except Lemon Glaze. Pour over baked layer. Bake about 25 minutes or until set and golden brown. Loosen edges from sides of pan while warm. Prepare glaze. Spread evenly over baked layer; cool completely. Cut into 2 × 1 1/4-inch bars.

LEMON GLAZE

1/2 cup powdered sugar
1 tablespoon lemon juice

Mix ingredients until smooth and spreading consistency.

1 BAR: Calories 75 (Calories from Fat 20); Fat 2g (Saturated 1g); Cholesterol 20mg; Sodium 90mg; Carbohydrate 13g (Dietary Fiber 0g); Protein 1g.

Toffee Bars

32 bars

1 cup butter or margarine, softened
1 cup packed brown sugar
1 teaspoon vanilla
1 egg yolk
2 cups all-purpose flour
1/4 teaspoon salt
2/3 cup milk chocolate chips
1/2 cup chopped nuts

Heat oven to 350°. Mix butter, brown sugar, vanilla and egg yolk in large bowl. Stir in flour and salt. Press dough in ungreased rectangular pan, 13 × 9 × 2 inches.

Bake 25 to 30 minutes or until very light brown (crust will be soft). Immediately sprinkle chocolate chips over hot crust. Let stand about 5 minutes or until soft; spread evenly. Sprinkle with nuts. Cool 30 minutes in pan on wire rack. Cut into 2 × 1 1/2-inch bars while warm.

1 BAR: Calories 135 (Calories from Fat 70); Fat 8g (Saturated 5g); Cholesterol 20mg; Sodium 60mg; Carbohydrate 15g (Dietary Fiber 0g); Protein 1g.

Cardamom Cashew Bars

4 dozen bars

Cardamom is a favorite spice among many Scandinavian people. A member of the ginger family, cardamom has a delightful spice-sweet flavor.

Crust (right)
1 1/2 cups packed brown sugar
1/2 cup fat-free cholesterol-free egg
    product or 2 eggs
3 tablespoons all-purpose flour
2 teaspoons vanilla
1/2 teaspoon ground cardamom
1/4 teaspoon salt
1 egg yolk
1 1/2 cups cashews, coarsely crushed
Orange Glaze (right)
Shredded orange peel, if desired

Heat oven to 350°. Prepare Crust. Beat remaining ingredients except cashews, Orange Glaze and orange peel in medium bowl with electric mixer on medium speed about 2 minutes or until well blended. Stir in cashews. Spread over baked crust.

    Bake 19 to 22 minutes or until top is golden brown and set around edges. Cool in pan on wire rack. Prepare Orange Glaze; spread evenly over baked layer. Cut into 2 × 1 1/2-inch bars. Garnish with orange peel.

CRUST

1/2 package (8-ounce size) reduced-fat
    cream cheese (Neufchâtel)
1/2 cup powdered sugar
1/4 cup packed brown sugar
2 teaspoons vanilla
1 egg yolk
1 1/2 cups all-purpose flour

Grease rectangular pan, 13 × 9 × 2 inches. Beat cream cheese and sugars in medium bowl with electric mixer on medium speed until fluffy. Beat in vanilla and egg yolk. Gradually stir in enough flour to make a soft dough. Knead dough on floured surface 1 minute (do not overknead). Press dough evenly in pan. Bake 15 to 20 minutes or until very light brown.

ORANGE GLAZE

3/4 cup powdered sugar
1 tablespoon orange juice

Mix ingredients until smooth and spreadable.

1 BAR: Calories 99 (Calories from Fat 25); Fat 3g (Saturated 1g); Cholesterol 10mg; Sodium 55mg; Carbohydrate 16g (Dietary Fiber 0g); Protein 2g.

Chocolate Apricot Squares

25 squares

Any flavor of jam is delicious in this recipe. To make cutting this dessert easier, simply wet the knife to keep it from sticking.

1 cup all-purpose flour
1/4 cup powdered sugar
1/4 cup margarine, softened
3 egg whites
1/2 cup granulated sugar
1/2 cup apricot jam
3 tablespoons miniature semisweet
    chocolate chips

Heat oven to 350°. Spray square pan, 9 × 9 × 2 inches, with nonstick cooking spray. Mix flour, powdered sugar, margarine and 1 of the egg whites. Press in pan. Bake about 15 minutes or until set.

Increase oven temperature to 400°. Beat remaining 2 egg whites in small bowl with electric mixer on high speed until foamy. Beat in granulated sugar, 1 tablespoon at a time; continue beating until whites are stiff and glossy. Do not underbeat.

Spread jam over baked layer. Sprinkle with chocolate chips. Spread beaten egg whites over jam and chocolate chips. Bake about 10 minutes or until meringue is brown. Cool completely. Cut into 1 1/2-inch squares.

1 SQUARE: Calories 80 (Calories from Fat 20); Fat 2g (Saturated 1g); Cholesterol 0mg; Sodium 30mg; Carbohydrate 14g (Dietary Fiber 0g); Protein 1g.

Orange Trifle

12 servings

1 package (about 16 ounces) white angel
    food cake mix
1 package (1.1 ounces) sugar-free vanilla
    instant pudding and pie filling
Skim milk
1 tablespoon grated orange peel
1 container (4 ounces) frozen whipped
    topping, thawed
6 tablespoons orange juice
1/4 cup sliced almonds

Heat oven to 350°. Prepare cake mix as directed on package except divide batter between 2 ungreased loaf pans, 9 × 5 × 3 inches. Bake until tops are deep golden brown and cracks feel dry, 45 to 50 minutes. Do not underbake. Immediately invert pans; cool cakes completely. Remove cakes from pans; freeze 1 cake for future use. Cut remaining cake into 1-inch cubes.

Prepare pudding and pie filling as directed on package except use skim milk. Fold orange peel and half of the whipped topping into pudding. Place one-third of the cake cubes in 2-quart serving bowl; sprinkle with 2 tablespoons of the orange juice. Spread one-third of the pudding mixture over cake cubes; repeat twice. Spread remaining whipped topping over top. Cover and refrigerate at least 3 hours. Sprinkle with almonds before serving.

1 SERVING: Calories 175 (Calories from Fat 35); Fat 4g (Saturated 1g); Cholesterol 0mg; Sodium 315mg; Carbohydrate 31g (Dietary Fiber 0g); Protein 4g.

Orange Trifle

Mississippi Mud Bars

3 dozen bars

1/3 cup plus 1 tablespoon margarine
    or butter
5 squares (1 ounce each) unsweetened
    chocolate
3/4 cup Bisquick Original or 2/3 cup
    Bisquick Reduced Fat baking mix
3/4 cup plus 2 tablespoons granulated sugar
2 eggs
2 teaspoons vanilla
1 1/2 cups miniature marshmallows
2/3 cup sour cream
1 1/2 cups powdered sugar

Heat oven to 350°. Grease and flour square pan, 9 × 9 × 2 inches. Melt 1/3 cup of the margarine and 2 1/2 squares of the chocolate in 1 1/2-quart saucepan over low heat, stirring frequently; cool. Beat chocolate mixture, baking mix, granulated sugar, eggs and vanilla in medium bowl on low speed 30 seconds, scraping bowl frequently. Beat on medium speed 1 minute. Spread in pan.

Bake 20 to 25 minutes or until toothpick inserted in center comes out clean. Immediately sprinkle with marshmallows. Cover and let stand 5 minutes or until marshmallows soften. Uncover; cool completely.

Melt remaining 2 1/2 squares chocolate and 1 tablespoon margarine; cool slightly. Stir in sour cream and powdered sugar until smooth. Spread over marshmallow layer. Cover and refrigerate at least 2 hours or until firm. Store in refrigerator; bring to room temperature before serving. Cut into 2 × 1-inch bars.

1 BAR: Calories 115 (Calories from Fat 55); Fat 6g (Saturated 3g); Cholesterol 15mg; Sodium 65mg; Carbohydrate 14g (Dietary Fiber 0g); Protein 1g.

Peanut Butter–Marshmallow Treats

3 dozen squares

32 large marshmallows or 3 cups miniature marshmallows
1/4 cup reduced-fat margarine
1/2 teaspoon vanilla
5 cups peanut butter cereal

Spray square pan, $9 \times 9 \times 2$ inches, with non-stick cooking spray. Heat marshmallows and margarine in 3-quart saucepan over low heat, stirring constantly until marshmallows are melted and mixture is smooth; remove from heat. Stir in vanilla. Stir in half of the cereal at a time until evenly coated. Press in pan; cool. Cut into about 1 1/2-inch squares.

1 SERVING: Calories 50 (Calories from Fat 10); Fat 1g (Saturated 0g); Cholesterol 0mg; Sodium 60mg; Carbohydrate 9g (Dietary Fiber 0g); Protein 1g.

Cheesecake Sherbet

8 servings

1 cup sugar
2 cups buttermilk
1 teaspoon grated lemon peel
1/4 cup lemon juice

Mix all ingredients until sugar is dissolved. Pour into 1-quart ice-cream freezer. Freeze according to manufacturer's directions.

1 SERVING: Calories 130 (Calories from Fat 10); Fat 1g (Saturated 1g); Cholesterol 2mg; Sodium 65mg; Carbohydrate 28g (Dietary Fiber 0g); Protein 2g.

Two-Week Menu Plan

DAY 1

Breakfast
Oatmeal *(3/4 c)*
with brown sugar (2 t)
Raisins *(1 T)*
Banana
Skim milk *(1 c)*

Meal Totals	Calories	Fat	Fiber
	350	1	8

Lunch
Pork Pita
Spicy Tortilla Chips *(12)*
Carrot sticks *(1/2 c)*
Skim milk *(1 c)*

Meal Totals	Calories	Fat	Fiber
	460	10	10

Dinner
Fish with Fennel Rice
Green beans *(1/2 c)*
Whole wheat dinner roll
Reduced-fat spread *(2 t)*
Mineral water

Meal Totals	Calories	Fat	Fiber
	655	13	7

Snack
Fat-free frozen yogurt *(1/2 c)*
Chocolate chips *(1 T)*

Meal Totals	Calories	Fat	Fiber
	155	3	0

DAILY TOTALS	CALORIES	FAT	FIBER
	1620	27	25

DAY 2

Breakfast
Morning Parfait
English muffin
Reduced-fat peanut
butter *(2 t)*

Meal Totals	Calories	Fat	Fiber
	350	9	4

Lunch
Vegetable Beef Soup
Hearty Multigrain Bread
Nonfat fruit yogurt *(1 c)*
Orange

Meal Totals	Calories	Fat	Fiber
	670	18	7

Dinner
Italian Chicken Skillet
Green beans *(1/2 c)*
Whole wheat dinner roll
Reduced-fat spread *(2 t)*
Mineral water

Meal Totals	Calories	Fat	Fiber
	650	17	6

Snack
Savory Popcorn *(1 c)*
Apple juice *(3/4 c)*

Meal Totals	Calories	Fat	Fiber
	145	1	0

DAILY TOTALS	CALORIES	FAT	FIBER
	1815	45	17

DAY 3

Breakfast

Honey raisin wheat bread
Reduced-fat peanut
  butter *(2 t)*
Grapes *(1/2 c)*
Skim milk *(1 c)*

Meal Totals	Calories	Fat	Fiber
	330	7	2

Lunch

Garbanzo Bean Sandwich
Fresh carrots, broccoli
  and celery *(1 c)*
Fat-free vegetable dip *(2 T)*
Pear
Skim milk *(1 c)*

Meal Totals	Calories	Fat	Fiber
	595	10	19

Dinner

Spicy Curried Chicken
  with Couscous
Steamed vegetables with
  yogurt sauce
Sparkling cider *(1 c)*
Cheesecake with Strawberry
  Topping

Meal Totals	Calories	Fat	Fiber
	715	12	4

Snack

Pudding pop

Meal Totals	Calories	Fat	Fiber
	95	0	0

DAILY TOTALS	CALORIES	FAT	FIBER
	1735	29	25

DAY 4

Breakfast

Whole grain cereal flakes
Banana
Skim milk *(1 c)*
Orange juice *(3/4 c)*

Meal Totals	Calories	Fat	Fiber
	365	1	6

Lunch

Vegetarian Burger Sandwich
Tomato soup *(1 c)*
Soda crackers *(6)*
Apple
Skim milk *(1 c)*

Meal Totals	Calories	Fat	Fiber
	655	10	9

Dinner

White Bean and Chicken
  Chili
Fluffy Corn Bread
Honey *(2 t)*
Skim milk *(1 c)*
Honey-Lime Fruit Salad

Meal Totals	Calories	Fat	Fiber
	660	11	8

Snack

Baby carrots *(1/2 c)*
Reduced-fat peanut
  butter *(1 T)*

Meal Totals	Calories	Fat	Fiber
	120	6	2

DAILY TOTALS	CALORIES	FAT	FIBER
	1800	28	25

DAY 5

Breakfast

Onion bagel
Reduced-fat cream
  cheese *(2 T)*
Poached egg
Grapefruit *(1/2)*
Skim milk *(1 c)*

Meal Totals	Calories	Fat	Fiber
	375	10	3

Lunch

Lemon Greek Salad
Whole wheat pita *(1/2)*
Hummus *(2 T)*
Fresh berries *(1/2 c)*
Nonfat fruit yogurt *(1 c)*
Cranberry raspberry
  iced tea *(1 c)*

Meal Totals	Calories	Fat	Fiber
	490	11	10

Dinner

Meat Loaf
Baked potato
Reduced-fat spread *(2 t)*
Ginger Glazed Carrots
Skim milk *(1 c)*
Mississippi mud bar

Meal Totals	Calories	Fat	Fiber
	515	17	5

Snack

Graham crackers *(4)*
Melon chunks *(1 c)*
Skim milk *(1 c)*

Meal Totals	Calories	Fat	Fiber
—	250	4	2

DAILY TOTALS	CALORIES	FAT	FIBER
	1630	42	20

DAY 6

Brunch

Southwestern Frittata
Reduced-fat cream
  cheese *(2 T)*
Poached egg
Grapefruit *(1/2)*
Skim milk *(1 c)*

Meal Totals	Calories	Fat	Fiber
	840	31	5

Dinner

Zesty Lime Steak
Chili-Corn Pudding
Tossed salad *(1 c)* and
  fat-free dressing *(2 T)*
Hearty multigrain biscuit
Skim milk *(1 c)*
Brown Sugar Strawberries

Meal Totals	Calories	Fat	Fiber
	680	18	6

Snack

Apple
Whole wheat crackers *(6)*
Reduced-fat cheddar
  cheese *(2 T)*

Meal Totals	Calories	Fat	Fiber
	215	6	6

DAILY TOTALS	CALORIES	FAT	FIBER
	1735	55	17

DAY 7

Breakfast

Oatmeal *(3/4 c)*
  with brown sugar (2 t)
Raisins *(1 T)*
Banana
Skim milk *(1 c)*

Meal Totals	Calories	Fat	Fiber
	350	1	8

Lunch

Roast Beef Pocket Sandwich
Sweet-and-Sour Broccoli
  and Baby Corn
Fresh carrots, broccoli
  and celery *(1 c)*
Fat-free vegetable dip *(2 T)*
Orange
Skim milk *(1 c)*

Meal Totals	Calories	Fat	Fiber
	465	4	10

Dinner

Mixed herb spaghetti
  and clam sauce
Mixed peas and carrots *(1/2 c)*
Dinner roll
Reduced-fat spread *(2 t)*
Gingerbread with Orange
  Sauce
Skim milk *(1 c)*

Meal Totals	Calories	Fat	Fiber
	705	14	6

Snack

Baked pita chips
Salsa *(1/4 c)*
Reduced-fat cheddar
  cheese *(2 T)*

Meal Totals	Calories	Fat	Fiber
	160	4	5

DAILY TOTALS	CALORIES	FAT	FIBER
	1680	23	29

DAY 8

Breakfast

Orange Frost
Buttermilk Toasted Oat
  Scone
Fruit preserves *(2 t)*
Skim milk *(1 c)*

Meal Totals	Calories	Fat	Fiber
	390	6	2

Lunch

Crustless Tuna Quiche
Mixed fresh fruit salad *(1 c)*
Tomatoes, basil, dressing
Breadsticks *(2)*
Nonfat fruit yogurt *(1 c)*
Diet iced tea *(1 c)*

Meal Totals	Calories	Fat	Fiber
	525	11	6

Dinner

Pork Fajitas
Cajun Side Dish
Skim milk *(1 c)*
Poached Raspberry Pears

Meal Totals	Calories	Fat	Fiber
	610	15	16

Snack

Cranberry juice *(3/4 c)*
94% fat-free microwave
  popcorn *(3 c)*

Meal Totals	Calories	Fat	Fiber
	155	2	2

DAILY TOTALS	CALORIES	FAT	FIBER
	1680	34	26

DAY 9

Breakfast

Mocha Whip
Bagel *(1/2)*
Reduced-fat peanut
  butter *(2 t)*
Poached egg
Grapefruit *(1/2)*

Meal Totals	Calories	Fat	Fiber
	385	11	4

Lunch

Baked brown bread *(2 slices)*
Turkey *(2 oz.)*, fat-free
  mayonnaise, tomato, lettuce
Garden potato salad
Skim milk *(1 c)*
Apple

Meal Totals	Calories	Fat	Fiber
	440	4	8

Dinner

Broiled Dijon Burger
Baked potato
Reduced-fat spread *(2 t)*
Ginger glazed carrots
Skim milk *(1 c)*
Mississippi Mud Bar

Meal Totals	Calories	Fat	Fiber
	740	15	7

Snack

Jungle Toss
Fat-free hot chocolate *(3/4 c)*

Meal Totals	Calories	Fat	Fiber
	130	2	0

DAILY TOTALS	CALORIES	FAT	FIBER
	1695	32	19

DAY 10

Breakfast

Baked Herb Omelet
Basil Pepper Biscuits
Orange juice *(3/4 c)*

Meal Totals	Calories	Fat	Fiber
	515	13	5

Lunch

Chicken Gazpacho Salad
Cantaloupe wedge
  (1/4 melon)
Whole wheat pita *(1/2)*
Skim milk *(1 c)*

Meal Totals	Calories	Fat	Fiber
	560	5	4

Dinner

Turkey Pasta with Pesto
Easy Cheesy Crescent
Steamed broccoli *(1/2 c)*
Skim milk *(1 c)*
Almond Apple Crisp

Meal Totals	Calories	Fat	Fiber
	685	21	7

Snack

Sugar-free chocolate
  pudding *(1/2 c)*

Meal Totals	Calories	Fat	Fiber
	70	1	0

DAILY TOTALS	CALORIES	FAT	FIBER
	1830	40	16

DAY 11

Breakfast

Zucchini-Apricot Bread
Reduced-fat cream
 cheese *(2 T)*
Nonfat fruit yogurt *(1 c)*
Apple juice *(3/4 c)*

Meal Totals	Calories	Fat	Fiber
	380	7	0

Lunch

Seaside Crab Rolls
Two-Potato Salad with
 Dill Dressing
Pear
Skim milk *(1 c)*
Frosty pink lemonade pop

Meal Totals	Calories	Fat	Fiber
	545	4	11

Dinner

Thin Crust Create-a-Pizza
Tossed salad *(1 c)*
Skim milk *(1 c)*
Orange trifle

Meal Totals	Calories	Fat	Fiber
	510	15	2

Snack

Reduced-fat peanut
 butter *(1 T)*
Graham crackers *(4)*
Raisins *(1 T)*

Meal Totals	Calories	Fat	Fiber
	255	10	2

DAILY TOTALS	CALORIES	FAT	FIBER
	1690	36	15

DAY 12

Breakfast

Blueberry Corn Muffin
Reduced-fat spread *(2 t)*
Fat-free cottage cheese
 (1/2 c)
Cranberry juice *(3/4 c)*

Meal Totals	Calories	Fat	Fiber
	340	8	2

Lunch

Rainbow Seafood Pasta
Parmesan Pepper Roll
Grapes *(1/2 c)*
Skim milk *(1 c)*

Meal Totals	Calories	Fat	Fiber
	490	6	3

Dinner

Fiesta Taco Casserole
Spicy Tortilla Chips *(12)*
Guacamole *(2 T)*
Salsa *(1/4 c)*
Skim milk *(1 c)*
Maple crust

Meal Totals	Calories	Fat	Fiber
	705	27	9

Snack

Pretzel rods *(1 oz.)*
Orange

Meal Totals	Calories	Fat	Fiber
	155	1	4

DAILY TOTALS	CALORIES	FAT	FIBER
	1690	42	18

DAY 13

Breakfast

Double-Fruit Shake
English muffin
Reduced-fat peanut
   butter *(2 t)*
Nonfat fruit yogurt *(1 c)*

Meal Totals	Calories	Fat	Fiber
	515	9	5

Lunch

Southwest Grilled Chicken
   Salad
Corn muffin
Reduced-fat spread *(2 t)*
Nectarine
Skim milk *(1 c)*

Meal Totals	Calories	Fat	Fiber
	480	13	5

Dinner

Meat and Potato Skillet
Jicama-Spinach Salad and
   Lime-Yogurt Dressing
Peach Bread Pudding
Skim milk *(1 c)*

Meal Totals	Calories	Fat	Fiber
	530	11	7

Snack

Southwest Snack
Cranberry juice spritzer
   (1/2 c juice with seltzer water)

Meal Totals	Calories	Fat	Fiber
	155	2	1

DAILY TOTALS	CALORIES	FAT	FIBER
	1680	35	18

DAY 14

Breakfast

Bran flake cereal *(1 c)*
Banana
Skim milk *(1 c)*
Orange juice *(3/4 c)*

Meal Totals	Calories	Fat	Fiber
	405	1	10

Lunch

Creamy Fish Chowder
Soda crackers *(6)*
No-knead bran roll
Reduced-fat spread *(2 t)*
Cucumber slices *(10)*
Skim milk *(1 c)*

Meal Totals	Calories	Fat	Fiber
	510	11	2

Dinner

Oven-Barbecued Chicken
Sweet-and-Spicy Carrot
   Salad
Macaroni with marinated
   tomatoes
Skim milk *(1 c)*
Chocolate-cherry cobbler

Meal Totals	Calories	Fat	Fiber
	700	20	4

Snack

Fat-free frozen yogurt
   (1/2 c)
Fresh berries

Meal Totals	Calories	Fat	Fiber
	115	0	2

DAILY TOTALS	CALORIES	FAT	FIBER
	1730	32	18

NUTRITION GLOSSARY

Have you been confused by the terms used by nutrition and health experts? Consult this list for explanations of some key words.

Additive: Substance added to food to perform certain functions, such as to add color or flavor, prevent spoilage, add nutritional value or improve texture or consistency.

Carbohydrate: Key human energy source. All simple sugars and complex carbohydrates (starches) fit into this category.

CHD: Coronary heart disease. High blood cholesterol levels and the buildup of fatlike plaques limit the flow of blood to body tissues on the lining of artery walls, which may cause tissue damage (heart attack, stroke) and death. Risk factors include a family history of CHD, smoking, high blood pressure and lack of exercise. Dietary guidelines, exercise and/or drug treatment are usually warranted. Also called atherosclerosis.

Cholesterol: Essential fatlike substance found in animal foods that is needed by the body for hormones to function properly. Our bodies also make cholesterol.

Dietary fiber: Often described as the components of plant foods that are not broken down or absorbed by the human digestive tract. Fiber is a complex carbohydrate based on its chemical structure.

Fat: Provides energy—more than twice the amount supplied by an equal quantity of carbohydrate or protein. Also provides essential nutrients, insulation and protection of body organs.

Food Guide Pyramid: Nutrition educational guide from the U.S. Department of Agriculture and the U.S. Department of Health and Human Services designed to teach people about foods and the recommended number of servings from each food group needed in order to maintain a balanced and healthy diet. It replaces the former Four Basic Food Groups. See diagram on page 20.

HDL: High-density lipoprotein. This type of cholesterol helps to remove cholesterol from body tissues and blood and return it to the liver to be used again. This recycling process has earned it the reputation of "good" cholesterol.

LDL: Low-density lipoprotein. Often tagged the "bad" cholesterol, low-density lipoprotein cholesterol travels through the bloodstream depositing cholesterol on artery walls and making cholesterol available for cell structures, hormones and nerve coverings.

Minerals: Essential elements other than carbon, hydrogen, oxygen and nitrogen, nutritionally necessary in very small amounts. Minerals are inorganic elements, such as calcium and iron, and are found in our foods and water.

Nutrients: Substances necessary for life and to build, repair and maintain body cells. Nutrients include protein, carbohydrates, fat, water, vitamins and minerals.

Protein: Vital for life and provides energy and structural support of body cells and is also important for growth. Made from amino acid building blocks that contain nitrogen.

Saturated fat: Primarily found in animal foods, this type of fat is solid at room temperature. Diets high in saturated fats have been linked to higher blood cholesterol levels; however, not all saturated fats have the same blood cholesterol-raising potential.

Unsaturated fat: Found most commonly in plant foods, this type of fat is usually liquid at room temperature. Unsaturated fats may be monounsaturated or polyunsaturated. A laboratory process called hydrogenation is used to alter the chemical structure of unsaturated fats, making them saturated and more shelf stable.

Vitamins: Essential substances, found in small amounts in many foods, necessary for controlling body processes. Vitamins, unlike minerals, are organic compounds containing carbon. Vitamins include vitamin A, B vitamins (such as thiamine, niacin, riboflavin) and vitamin C, among others.

GRAINS GLOSSARY

Want to eat more grains, but not sure how? Use our handy glossary to help you out.

Amaranth: A drought-resistant grain that once was one of the primary foods of the Aztecs of ancient Mexico. Amaranth seed is very tiny and can be milled into flour or puffed like rice or corn. The flavor of amaranth is sweet and nutlike. It has been called a supergrain because of its superior amino acid profile. Rich in lysine, one of the eight essential amino acids, its protein composition is more complete than other vegetable proteins. The seed also contains unusually high levels of calcium (six to seven times as much as wheat), iron, phosphorus, magnesium and potassium.

Arborio rice: From northern Italy's Piedmont region, arborio is the premium grade of Italian rice. It is a unique short, plump rice that absorbs a great deal of liquid without becoming soggy, making it ideal for dishes that need slow, gentle cooking such as risotto, paella and jambalaya. If unavailable in your area, regular medium-grain white rice can be substituted.

Barley: One of the first grains ever cultivated. Pearl barley is the most commonly available and has the hull, most of the bran and some of the germ removed to shorten cooking time. It contains niacin, thiamine and potassium. One cup of cooked barley provides the same amount of protein as a glass of milk.

Basmati rice: Known for its delicious flavor, nutty aroma and firm consistency, basmati was originally developed in the foothills of the Himalayas in northern India. It is grown in only a few parts of the world because of the special soil required for this unique rice.

Brown rice: Unpolished rice, meaning the outer hull has been removed but the germ and bran layers have not been "polished" off. This gives it a nutlike flavor and chewier texture than white rice. It is also a good source of fiber and thiamine.

Buckwheat kernels: Also called roasted buckwheat kernels or groats, these are the hulled seeds of the buckwheat plant. Roasted groats are often called kasha. Although technically a fruit, buckwheat kernels are used as a grain. Buckwheat contains phosphorus, iron, potassium, vitamin E and B vitamins. It has a pungent flavor that can be overpowering. Buckwheat flour is usually mixed with all-purpose flour for pastas, pancakes, muffins and quick breads.

Converted (parboiled) rice: A rice that has been steamed and pressure-cooked before milling, a process that forces residual nutrients into the kernel's heart, making it a bit higher in vitamin content than regular white rice.

Corn: Sometimes forgotten as a grain because it is usually eaten as a vegetable. Whole kernel corn adds a naturally sweet flavor and a crunchy texture to breads, main dishes and side dishes. Paired with legumes or small amounts of animal protein from dairy products or eggs, corn provides a complete protein. Cornmeal is available either as yellow, white or blue, depending on the type of corn used. Cornmeal is available in degerminated and whole grain forms. As *degerminated* indicates, the germ and bran have been removed. This type is widely available at grocery stores. Stone-ground whole grain cornmeal may be found in co-ops or health food stores. It contains the germ and the bran, which gives it more flavor, texture and fiber. Grits are coarsely ground from hulled kernels of corn by a dry milling process. Hominy is dried corn kernels from which the hull and germ have been removed. Hull removal is either done mechanically or by soaking kernels in slaked lime or lye. Hominy is sold both canned, which is softened like beans, or dried.

Instant (precooked) rice: Rice that is commercially cooked, rinsed and dehydrated before packaging, resulting in a very short cooking time. White, brown and wild rice are all available in this form.

Jasmine: An aromatic long-grain rice originally grown in Thailand. This rice is similar to regular long-grain white rice in appearance but is moister and more tender.

Millet: A small, round yellow seed that resembles whole mustard seed. When cooked, whole millet has a chewy texture and a mild

flavor similar to brown rice. It is a very high-quality protein, is particularly high in minerals, and is thought to be the most digestible of all grains.

Oats: Oats eaten for breakfast as oatmeal are steamed and flattened groats (hulled-out kernels). They are available either as regular (old-fashioned), quick-cooking or instant. Regular and quick-cooking oats are often used interchangeably. If a recipe specifies just one type, do not substitute the other—they have different absorption properties. Oats contribute fiber, thiamine, phosphorus and magnesium to the diet.

Quinoa ("keen-way"): Once the staple food of the Inca Indians in Peru. Quinoa is a small grain with a soft crunch and can be used in any recipe calling for rice. Be sure to rinse it well before using to remove the bitter-tasting, naturally occurring saponin (nature's insect repellent), which forms on the outside of the kernel. Quinoa provides B vitamins, calcium, iron and phosphorous and, unlike other grains, is a complete protein.

Texmati rice: A cross between basmati and regular long-grain white rice that is grown in the United States. Like basmati, it has a nutty flavor and aroma and is available as both white and brown.

Wheat berries: Hulled whole grain wheat kernels that still have the bran and germ. Cooked wheat berries can be used like rice in salads and side dishes. Wheat provides B vitamins, vitamin E and complex carbohydrates.

Wheat bulgur: Whole wheat that has been cooked, dried and then broken into coarse fragments. It's different from cracked wheat because it is precooked. Bulgur supplies phosphorus and potassium and also contains some iron, thiamine and riboflavin.

Wheat flour: Available in several different forms. Quick-mixing flour is instant all-purpose flour, which means it disperses instantly in cold liquids, resulting in smooth gravies, sauces and batters. Cake flour is milled from soft wheat, which has a weaker gluten structure, creating tender cakes with greater volume. All-purpose flour is either milled from hard winter wheat or a blend of hard and soft winter wheat to provide a flour that produces acceptable results over a wide range of baked products. Bread flour is milled from hard winter wheat, hard spring wheat or a combination of the two and provides the gluten structure needed in yeast breads. Quick-mixing, cake, all-purpose and bread flours don't contain the bran or the germ of wheat. Whole wheat flour is ground from the whole wheat kernel, usually from hard spring wheat, and contains the nutrients of whole wheat berries.

Wheat germ: The embryo of the wheat kernel, commonly known as wheat berry. Because it's high in oil, wheat germ is usually toasted to extend its shelf life. It has a nutty flavor and can be sprinkled over cereal or used in baked goods. It is a good source of thiamine, niacin, riboflavin, potassium and zinc.

White rice (regular): Rice that has been milled to remove the hull, germ and most of the bran. It is available in long, medium and short grains. The shorter the grain, the stickier the cooked rice will be. Long-grain is the most common all-purpose rice. Medium-grain works well in puddings because of its creamier characteristics. Short-grain white rice is not widely available.

Wild rice: Actually an aquatic grass native to North America. It is more expensive than other rice because of its limited supply. Stretch it by mixing with other rice or grains. Wild rice contains fiber, B vitamins, iron, phosphorus, magnesium, calcium and zinc.

Metric Conversion Guide

Volume

U.S. Units	Canadian Metric	Australian Metric
1/4 teaspoon	1 mL	1 ml
1/2 teaspoon	2 mL	2 ml
1 teaspoon	5 mL	5 ml
1 tablespoon	15 mL	20 ml
1/4 cup	50 mL	60 ml
1/3 cup	75 mL	80 ml
1/2 cup	125 mL	125 ml
2/3 cup	150 mL	170 ml
3/4 cup	175 mL	190 ml
1 cup	250 mL	250 ml
1 quart	1 liter	1 liter
1 1/2 quarts	1.5 liters	1.5 liters
2 quarts	2 liters	2 liters
2 1/2 quarts	2.5 liters	2.5 liters
3 quarts	3 liters	3 liters
4 quarts	4 liters	4 liters

Weight

U.S. Units	Canadian Metric	Australian Metric
1 ounce	30 grams	30 grams
2 ounces	55 grams	60 grams
3 ounces	85 grams	90 grams
4 ounces (1/4 pound)	115 grams	125 grams
8 ounces (1/2 pound)	225 grams	225 grams
16 ounces (1 pound)	455 grams	500 grams
1 pound	455 grams	1/2 kilogram

Note: The recipes in this cookbook have not been developed or tested using metric measures. When converting recipes to metric, some variations in quality may be noted.

Measurements

Inches	Centimeters
1	2.5
2	5.0
3	7.5
4	10.0
5	12.5
6	15.0
7	17.5
8	20.5
9	23.0
10	25.5
11	28.0
12	30.5
13	33.0
14	35.5
15	38.0

Temperatures

Fahrenheit	Celsius
32°	0°
212°	100°
250°	120°
275°	140°
300°	150°
325°	160°
350°	180°
375°	190°
400°	200°
425°	220°
450°	230°
475°	240°
500°	260°

Helpful Nutrition and Cooking Information

Nutrition Guidelines:

We provide nutrition information for each recipe that includes calories, fat, cholesterol, sodium, carbohydrate, fiber and protein. Individual food choices can be based on this information.

Recommended intake for a daily diet of 2,000 calories as set by the Food and Drug Administration:

Total Fat	Less than 65g
Saturated Fat	Less than 20g
Cholesterol	Less than 300mg
Sodium	Less than 2,400mg
Total Carbohydrate	300g
Dietary Fiber	25g

Criteria Used for Calculating Nutrition Information:

- The first ingredient is used wherever a choice is given (such as 1/3 cup sour cream or plain yogurt).

- The first ingredient amount is used wherever a range is given (such as 2 to 3 teaspoons milk).

- The first serving number is used wherever a range is given (such as 4 to 6 servings).

- "If desired" ingredients such as "two tablespoons brown sugar, if desired" and recipe variations are *not* included.

- Only the amount of a marinade or frying oil that is estimated to be absorbed by the food during preparation or cooking is calculated.

Cooking Terms Glossary:

Cooking has its own vocabulary just like many other creative activities. Here are some basic cooking terms to use as a handy reference.

Beat: Mix ingredients vigorously with spoon, fork, wire whisk, hand beater or electric mixer until smooth and uniform.

Blend: Mix ingredients with spoon, wire whisk or rubber scraper until very smooth and uniform. A blender, hand blender or food processor can be used.

Boil: Heat liquid until bubbles rise continuously and break on the surface and steam is given off. For rolling boil, the bubbles form rapidly.

Chop: Cut into coarse or fine irregular pieces with a knife, food chopper, blender or food processor.

Crisp-tender: Doneness description of vegetables cooked until tender but still retaining some of the crisp texture of the raw food.

Cube: Cut into squares 1/2 inch or larger.

Dice: Cut into squares smaller than 1/2 inch.

Grate: Cut into tiny particles using small rough holes of grater (citrus peel or chocolate).

Grease: Rub the inside surface of a pan with shortening, using pastry brush, piece of waxed paper or paper towel, to prevent food from sticking during baking (as for some casseroles).

Julienne: Cut into thin, matchlike strips, using knife or food processor (vegetables, fruits, meats).

Mix: Combine ingredients in any way that distributes them evenly.

Sauté: Cook foods in hot oil or margarine over medium-high heat with frequent tossing and turning motion.

Shred: Cut into long thin pieces by rubbing food across the holes of a shredder, as for cheese, or by using a knife to slice very thinly, as for cabbage.

Simmer: Cook in liquid just below the boiling point on top of the stove, usually after reducing heat from a boil. Bubbles will rise slowly and break just below the surface.

Stir: Mix ingredients until uniform consistency. Stir once in a while for stirring occasionally, often for stirring frequently and continuously for stirring constantly.

Toss: Tumble ingredients lightly with a lifting motion (such as green salad), usually to coat evenly or mix with another food.

Ingredients Used in Recipe Testing:

- White rice is used wherever cooked rice is listed in the ingredients, unless otherwise indicated.

- Ingredients used for testing represent those that the majority of consumers use in their homes: large eggs, canned ready-to-use chicken broth, and vegetable oil spread containing *not less than 65% fat.*

- Fat-free, low-fat or low-sodium products are not used, unless otherwise indicated.

- Solid vegetable shortening (not butter, margarine, nonstick cooking sprays or vegetable oil spread as they can cause sticking problems) is used to grease pans, unless otherwise indicated.

Equipment Used in Recipe Testing:

We use equipment for testing that the majority of consumers use in their homes. If a specific piece of equipment (such as a wire whisk) is necessary for recipe success, it will be listed in the recipe.

- Cookware and bakeware *without* nonstick coatings are used, unless otherwise indicated.

- No dark colored, black or insulated bakeware is used.

- When a baking *pan* is specified in a recipe, a *metal* pan was used; a baking *dish* or pie *plate* means oven-proof glass was used.

- An electric hand mixer is used for mixing *only when mixer speeds are specified* in the recipe directions. When a mixer speed is not given, a spoon or fork was used.

Index

Page numbers in *italics* refer to photographs.